To Mish and Jay,

Hope you enjoy!

Oman
Emerges

An American Company
in an Ancient Kingdom

All best wishes.

Lois M. Critchfield

Selwa Press

Selwa Press
1101 Portola Street
Vista, California 92084 U.S.A.
www.SelwaPress.com

LCCN: 2010928629
ISBN: 978-0-9701157-8-2
Copyright © 2010 by Lois M. Critchfield

Cataloging-in-Publication Data

Critchfield, Lois M.

Oman emerges : an American company in an ancient kingdom / Lois M. Critchfield. -- Vista, Calif. : Selwa Press, c2010

p. ; cm.

ISBN: 978-0-9701157-8-2
Includes bibliographical references and index.

1. Oman--Economic conditions--20th century. 2. Oman--Politics and government--20th century. 3. Tetra Tech Inc.--History. 4. Critchfield, James H., b. 1917- 2003. 5. Economic development--Oman--History--20th century. 6. Petroleum industry and trade--Oman--History--20th century. I. Title

HC415.35 C75 2010   2010928629
333.9/5353--dc22   1007

Printed in the United States of America
1 2 3 4 5 6 7 8 9 10

To Jim

TABLE OF CONTENTS

PART III
CRITICAL DEVELOPMENTS IN OMAN 1980–1990

Illustrations

ACKNOWLEDGMENTS

In January 1993, James Critchfield, whose American company Tetra Tech International had worked in Oman from 1975 to 1988, wrote to His Majesty Sultan Qaboos bin Said that he was organizing his extensive documentation of the company's years in Oman and hoped to put the story of Tetra Tech into some more permanent form. He told the sultan that it had been a great and unique privilege to participate in the sultanate's development. He believed that his involvement left him with a valuable perspective, supported by a comprehensive record of this period in the sultanate's development. Sultan Qaboos's response, dated March 9, 1993, wished him well and said he was sure the book would be of interest to future generations.

Unfortunately, the book Critchfield intended to write and which he worked on in the ensuing years was not completed before his death in 2003. But his notes and files remain, and they are the foundation upon which this work is based. Ultimately, Jim's papers will be publicly available at the Georgetown University Lauinger Library as the James H. Critchfield Oman Papers, 1968-1991, and will be part of the university's extensive Middle East special collections.

This book focuses on the early development of Oman's petroleum industry and the renaissance of a nation as the sultan's small but increasingly valuable oil base allowed him to transform his country into a modern state. Soon after taking over the nation in 1970, Sultan Qaboos began inviting American petroleum professionals to advise the government on oil production programs. In 1975, he contracted with the very small American engineering firm Tetra Tech International to advise on petroleum oil pricing and reservoir engineering planning. Tetra

Tech soon found itself involved in contracts to develop water resources in the sultanate. The selection of Tetra Tech to manage the development programs in the Musandam Peninsula and the Buraimi Oasis region broadened the presence of Americans in Oman, a territory that had previously been the exclusive purview of British advisors.

This book in no way includes all the details of the early years when Oman was going through these changes. Geologists, economists and those interested in the Middle East will find much in James Critchfield's archival records to keep them busy analyzing those days. Oman is unlike any other Arab nation, and I hope my effort here will be interesting enough to entice future generations to learn more about this amazing country and its leader.

To those who have speculated over the years that Tetra Tech International was a CIA cover organization, I respond with the story that Critchfield, when provoked, would relate about his meeting CIA Director William Casey for the first time in the 1980s at a Washington gathering. When introduced, Casey said, "Oh, yes, Jim Critchfield! You are the man who has proved there is life after CIA." If the CIA were to establish a cover business in the Middle East, it is not likely they would have chosen someone as well known in intelligence circles as Critchfield to run it. In fact, after Critchfield left the Agency in 1974, he had no contact with the CIA until 2000 when its director George Tenet asked him to help out on a presidential interagency working group dealing with the declassification of documents related to Nazi war criminals. Critchfield graciously accepted the task.

In writing this book, I have acted more as a surrogate than the primary author. Much of what is written here is the work of James Critchfield himself, in a form organized and presented by a wife who, after many years of marriage, could second-guess what he was thinking.

I wrote the book sitting in a room surrounded by a hundred boxes of business files containing letters, memos, reports, technical studies, maps and charts. It was somewhat of a lonely experience – as writing often is. But along the way, I had support and encouragement from a number of friends and associates, and I thank them all for their help. My appreciation goes both to former participants in the Oman experience and others who helped me understand it.

On the subject of the early days in Oman, I thank D. Patrick Maley, a pioneer in the effort to get Tetra Tech established in Oman. On the later years, Arthur Rypinski read and critiqued much of the text and helped me stick with the important issues. In August 2006, several former associates attended a mini-reunion of the Tetra Tech International staff at my Outer Banks beach home and we discussed the work at length. Thanks to Kirk and Nga Agon, John and Josee Sasser, John and Rose Bannigan, Robert Zunzer and Lee Miller for bringing the story to life.

Matthew Hopper, PhD, UCLA 2006, organized my files and produced an archival-quality Finding Aid, which will ultimately find a resting place in the Georgetown University Library's Middle East collection. I could not have worked without this. College of William and Mary student Sulaiman Bah's research on modern-day Oman provided material for the final chapter.

I also had the good fortune to capture the interest of other friends and associates in this effort. Dr. James Bill, College of William and Mary professor emeritus and an expert on the region, helped me structure the story. Dr. Robert G. Landen, author of *Oman Since 1856* and a distinguished historian, devoted many helpful hours during the lengthy process of rewriting. David Campagna, PhD geologist, translated complicated technical language into prose we could all understand. Former Exxon executive Ward Wheatall helped me keep the oil story in context of the times.

Lois Critchfield
Williamsburg, Virginia
February 6, 2010

As a CIA retiree, I am required by the Official Secrets Act to submit all manuscripts to its publication review board for approval to publish. On January 31, 2007, the board determined that this book contains no classified information and has no security objection to its publication. As part of this approval, the board requires that the following disclaimer be included with the publication:

This material has been reviewed by the CIA to prevent the disclosure of classified information. All statements of fact, opinion or analysis expressed are those of the author and do not reflect the official positions or views of the CIA or any other U.S. government agency. Nothing in the contents should be construed as asserting or implying U.S. government authentication of information or agency endorsement of the author's views.

PROLOGUE

In early 1985 James Critchfield, president of Tetra Tech International, a company that had been advising the Sultanate of Oman in the development of its natural resources for the previous ten years, requested that General Ali bin Majid Al Ma'amari, head of the Palace Office and a longtime friend, set up a personal meeting with Sultan Qaboos, Oman's leader. Over the years, Critchfield had maintained a very close relationship with Sultan Qaboos and his advisors, but he asked for direct audiences with the sultan only when he felt there were critical issues to discuss.

Tetra Tech International was a respected member of Oman's emerging development sector and Critchfield was valued for his knowledge and esteemed for his character. At least twenty years older than the sultan and his entourage, Critchfield was looked upon as somewhat of a father figure. A genuine WW II American war hero, and a skilled spymaster during the Cold War, in his current life he was a man who knew a lot about the geopolitics of oil. He first met Sultan Qaboos in 1970 when he was the CIA's national intelligence officer for energy, a post created shortly after the first OPEC oil crisis. After years of service he had proven to the sultan and his inner circle that he was worth listening to. However, lately forces at work within the sultanate were lobbying against the cautious and conservative advice that Critchfield had been promoting at the Ministry of Petroleum and elsewhere in the government.

The question for Oman's petroleum industry had long been, "Do we maximize oil production to increase oil revenues today or do we spread oil production out over a longer period of time while exploring for more?" Oil on the world market in 1985 was selling for $28 per barrel, down from a high of $41 per barrel in 1981. The British-dominated Petroleum Development (Oman) production and exploration company, 60% owned by the government of Oman, 34% by Shell, 4% by Total-Compagnie Francaise Petroles, and 2% by Partex, the company of the famed Calouste Gulbenkian, favored and pushed for maximizing production. Tetra Tech International's oil consultants consistently warned the Ministry of Petroleum — to the extreme displeasure of PDO — of the economic consequences of over-production. This was a critical issue for Oman, because, unlike its neighbor Saudi Arabia, Oman's oil reserves are modest, only about 2% of those of the Saudi kingdom.

Tetra Tech International played an active role in those early days of Oman's development. While it was one of many American and British companies that did business there, Tetra Tech was unique in that it sat on the government's side of the table in assessing what was required to get an almost non-functioning economy up and running. The Oman government was boss, and Tetra Tech served at the pleasure of the sultan.

While initially hired as oil consultants, Tetra Tech quickly became involved in the development of water resources and was the key player in the various water management programs, such as the Public Authority for Water Resources. It soon became the on-site manager of the Musandam Development Committee and later ran the Regional Development Committee in the area of Buraimi. At its height, Tetra Tech had over 200 employees scattered throughout the country.

Tetra Tech International's base of operations was in Rosslyn, Virginia, overlooking the Potomac River, the skyline of Georgetown University and the monuments of the nation's capital. Its small staff acted as the support arm of all the projects on the ground in Oman. Over the years, a symbiotic relationship developed between the Omanis and the Tetra Tech employees. It was a friendly relationship that went beyond business. Tetra Tech was known for mentoring young Omanis who came to the United States for advanced technical training as well as for other educational pursuits. The warm hospitality that Omanis are well known for was shown to Tetra Tech staffers living in Oman.

Critchfield was in his Rosslyn office on January 10, 1985 when he got the word via telex that Sultan Qaboos would see him on January 12. He boarded a British Airways flight at Dulles Airport at 6:00 that evening and, stopping in London only for his connection to Muscat, he arrived in Oman close to midnight the following evening. He headed for a few hours of rest at his "home away from home," — the Muscat Intercontinental Hotel. On January 12, he went to the sultan's nearby palace in Seeb for the meeting. It was the end of a busy day for the sultan. He had met with several of his ministers, the PDO/Shell management team, and out-of-town guests Otto von Hapsburg and his daughter. Critchfield was to be the last visitor of the day. By the time he was ushered into the sultan's quarters, it was 7:30 PM. Critchfield did not know at the time that this would be the last meeting he would have with the sultan on issues they had been discussing since they first met more than ten years before.

> Your Majesty, [Critchfield began] I think this audience is probably the most significant I have ever had with you. I realize my role has often been to report to you on the unglazed facts as we understand them. We have no ax to grind, no cause to protect. I am also aware that coming to you from time to time with my views always runs the danger of evoking a negative reaction and criticism from one or more ministers, who may see his interests not being served. Nevertheless, when I perceive that matters are going seriously astray, I feel that I have the responsibility to come to you.

So, as the sun slowly set on the Gulf of Oman, casting a shadow on oil tankers headed from the Strait of Hormuz to deliver their precious cargo to the world market, Critchfield spoke about Oman's economic future. His main concern was that the current plans by PDO and the Ministry of Petroleum for increased oil production were putting the nation at risk. "At the planned rate of production," he said, "Oman's reserves after 20 years will be seriously depleted unless increased exploration is undertaken simultaneously. The facts, however, are showing that new discoveries are lagging behind production." Critchfield pulled from his briefcase an impressive-looking report prepared by one of his Texas-based petroleum reservoir engineers and handed it to the sultan. "Over the next ten years," he continued, "it is critically important that Oman lower production and at the same time increase exploration. Unless more oil is discovered, there will be a rapid run down in oil production by the late 1990s."

Critchfield had advised the Ministry of Petroleum that the price of oil, for the first time in OPEC's history, was not being determined by OPEC, but almost entirely by market forces. It was his belief that oil prices would be in a correcting phase during the next two or three years and could fall below $20. A lowering of oil prices on the world market would directly impact Oman's ambitious development program. His advice was to get prepared by postponing major capital expenditures for one or two years. He was confident that the long-term prospect was for higher oil prices, but a period of some austerity was called for.

He gave the sultan another report his staff had prepared indicating that if oil continued to be produced at the planned rate and development projects currently on the drawing board were carried out on schedule, electricity and water demand in the Greater Capital Area alone would triple by 1990, requiring an infusion of a half-billion dollars per year over the next five years. At the current price of oil, such development spending could not be sustained. Sultan Qaboos was clearly shocked by this assessment and voiced his skepticism about Critchfield's analysis, but as the meeting came to a close he took the reports and said he would carefully study them. It was an unsettling meeting for both men.

In ongoing discussions during that year at the top levels of Oman's government, including the Ministry of Petroleum, Critchfield urged that more attention be given to long-term planning. Despite the disparity in size, the Sultanate of Oman was in roughly the same position as the Soviet Union and the United States in regard to its oil resources. It had a production plateau that would extend well into the 1990s, it held significant but as yet almost untested heavy oil reserves, and there was a need to make major investments in exploration and enhanced oil recovery. With an extended coastline on the western Indian Ocean and the main oil shipping channels passing through Omani waters in the Strait of Hormuz, the sultanate would inevitably have to shape policies for its own development and national security in the next ten, twenty and forty years, taking into account the future role of Gulf oil in the world economy. The threat of a drop in the price of oil was a short-term consideration. Critchfield was certain that oil prices would eventually rise as oil would become an increasingly valuable commodity between 1995 and 2005.

As it turned out, world oil prices dropped by fifty percent in 1986. The price of OPEC oil fell to $10-15 a barrel, and in Oman it hit a bottom of $6.80, eventually recovering to about $14. Panic set in. By mid-1986, some development projects were put on hold and orders were given to all ministries to cut costs. Critchfield should not have been surprised when he was notified that Tetra Tech International would also be taking some deep cuts.

But the crisis of 1986 passed, and today Oman, like its neighbors in the region, enjoys substantial revenues resulting from higher and higher oil prices. This has allowed the nation to modernize at a rapid pace and bring a high standard of living to its citizens. But the nation is still vulnerable to the ups and downs of the world oil market.

The story, as presented here, sets forth in some detail how Tetra Tech International, which entered Oman in 1975 and operated there for almost thirteen years, played an essential role in helping a young nation turn itself into a modern one. Always sitting on the government side of the table, Tetra Tech advisors sometimes found themselves caught in the middle of differences of opinions with PDO, Oman's British-operated oil production company, other foreign consultants seeking business opportunities in Oman, and Omani ministers who did not always agree with the course of events being orchestrated by this American company. Life was never dull, whether it be at the PDO negotiating tables in London and The Hague or dealing with water rights with a local *wali* (governor) of one of Oman's provinces. There were successes and there were disappointments, but ultimately the benefits experienced by both sides were incalculable. It is a story that could probably never be repeated.

PART I

OMAN IN TRANSITION

Five thousand years ago, Oman was known as Magan. The country was famous for its copper exports. In ancient times, too, frankincense produced in what is now Oman's southern governorate of Dhofar fetched a high price from the peoples of surrounding regions who coveted it for their social and religious rituals. Oman forged strong trading links with its northern neighbors via land caravans and with others by sea. In medieval times the Omani city of Sohar became one of the most important seaports in the Islamic world.

Until the mid-nineteenth century, Oman was one of the leading maritime trading powers of the Indian Ocean. By the early twentieth century, however, the country had fallen into decline. It became increasingly isolated and inward looking as its economy remained essentially a pre-modern one. Most Omanis lived only a subsistence existence. Not until the 1960s did this situation begin to change as Oman took its first halting steps to exploit its oil resources.

1

TWO CENTURIES OF FRIENDSHIP

In September 1790 George Washington was still president of the new American republic when Robert Folger sailed into Muscat, then a major Indian Ocean seaport. Captain of the Boston-based *Rambler,* the first American flagged vessel to visit Oman, he was soon followed by a stream of American merchant seamen sailing the waters of these eastern seas, frequent visitors to Muscat, Sohar and other Omani-controlled ports such as Zanzibar.

Oman, situated on the Arabian Peninsula's southeastern corner, has a coastline stretching some 1,200 miles. Today its population totals about 2.5 million, 1.9 million of whom are native Omanis, the rest being expatriates (guest workers). The country is somewhat smaller than California or slightly larger than Great Britain depending on your perspective. It is bordered by the sea, the sands of a great desert to the west, and high mountains on both the northern and southern frontiers." Oman was best described by Robert Landen in his book *Oman Since 1856.* "Of the four territorial compartments surrounding the Persian and Oman gulfs, Oman is the most isolated. With the sea enclosing the country on three sides and with the forbidding sandy wastes of the Rub Al-Khali (Empty Quarter) on the fourth, Oman is, in effect, almost an island. The country's contacts with the rest of the world have been, with few exceptions, via the sea."[1]

Oman's present ruler, Sultan Qaboos bin Said, is the latest sovereign from the long-established Al Bu Said dynasty, which assumed power in the country during the mid-eighteenth century after expelling Persian invaders. Since that time the dynasty has endured frequent internal power struggles as well as threats from outside rivals. Early rulers such as Ahmad

[1] Robert Geran Landen, *Oman Since 1856: Disruptive Modernization in a Traditional Arab Society,* p.29, Princeton University Press, 1967.

bin Said, Sultan bin Ahmad, and Said bin Sultan built a formidable navy, annexed Zanzibar and parts of east Africa, and nurtured maritime commerce along the Indian Ocean's coast from India to Africa. Many Omanis traditionally earned their living from maritime pursuits such as fishing and trade. Legend has it that Sinbad the Sailor set sail for China from Sohar, a city situated on Oman's northern coast, which today is a thriving fishing and agricultural town with an emerging industrial base. Oman was the first Arab state to conclude a "treaty of friendship and commerce" with the United States when Sultan Sayyid Said bin Sultan Al Bu Said, a shrewd and respected ruler, signed such an accord in 1833. The agreement not only served both parties equitably, but also expressed warm hospitality on behalf of the Omanis toward the Americans. After signing the pact, Sayyid Said was received aboard the visiting American warship the *Peacock*, which would carry the treaty from Muscat back to the United States. Two years later a copy of the ratified document was returned to Muscat.

After the establishment of diplomatic relations, a consul represented American interests in Oman. By the mid-nineteenth century, however, these were confined largely to sporadic commercial dealings. In 1840, the Omanis returned the *Peacock*'s visit when the sultan's ship *Sultana* sailed into New York harbor with a cargo of dates, rugs, coffee and gifts for President Martin Van Buren. One of these presents, a magnificent Persian carpet, can currently be seen at the Smithsonian Museum First Ladies exhibit. New Yorkers were fascinated by the distinctive Omani vessel and thronged to see it. This first visit of an Omani vessel was a spectacular event, but it did not portend flourishing commercial ties between the two countries.[2] Although Omani-American relations remained cordial from that time on, it would be 1996 before another Omani ship called into New York harbor. In that year the *Shabab Oman*, following much the same route as did the *Sultana* 156 years earlier, sailed from Muscat to New York. The vessel, a wind-powered sailing ship operated by the Royal Oman Navy, made the voyage to participate in the U.S. "tall ships" naval review commemorating the centennial of the Statue of Liberty.

During the nineteenth century, American ships continued to visit Oman occasionally. In 1860, for example, a distinguished American

---

[2] The Middle East Institute, *The United States and the Sultanate of Oman*, Washington, D.C. 1990.

naval officer, Cornelius Kinchiloe Stribling, visited the port of Muscat when he commanded the East India Squadron.[3] It would come to pass that more than a hundred years later, in 1972, Cornelius Stribling Snodgrass, a grandson of Stribling well known in oil circles, would become petroleum advisor to Sultan Qaboos. As will be related elsewhere in this book, Stribling Snodgrass made a major contribution to the development of Oman's oil industry.

The United States maintained its consulate in Muscat up to 1915. From that date until the 1970s, American interests in Oman were covered by American diplomats posted in Aden, Dhahran or elsewhere in the Middle East. Although the old 1833 agreement was renewed in 1958, the United States did not send any permanent representatives to the sultanate throughout the reign of Sultan Said bin Taimur, the father of the current leader, Sultan Qaboos. During that time, only Britain and, later, India were represented diplomatically in Muscat. Indeed, Britain handled virtually all of Oman's foreign affairs between the early twentieth century and the end of Sultan Said's rule in 1970. During his reign, there was little need for American diplomatic representation since there were few contacts official or otherwise between the two countries.

Omani-American contacts remained unsubstantial in the 1950s, but one colorful American entered the scene at the time. This was Dr. Wendell Phillips, an archaeologist and explorer who had been working in south Arabia. In 1952, he burst into Oman, virtually through its back door, after he and his expedition had to flee southern Yemen when local tribal leaders turned hostile.[4] Sultan Said, who had met Phillips three years earlier, befriended him and invited him and his party to continue their research on the Omani side of the border. This enabled the group to travel extensively throughout Oman.

Among their investigations was a project to find the lost city of Ubar. Adventurers from the previous century, mainly British, had searched in vain for the so-called "Atlantis of the sands." Even before the time of Christ, Ubar, according to legend, was an important trading center that shipped frankincense and other luxuries to the Mediterranean. Located on the edge of the Rub al Khali desert, Ubar was said to have suffered some sort of catastrophe and disappeared around 300 AD. Myth warned that trying to find the city would lead only to madness. Phillips

[3] US Department of Navy, Navy Historical Center.

[4] Wendell Phillips, *Unknown Oman*, David McKay Company, Inc. New York, 1966.

and his companions set out to find Ubar relying upon local guides, who managed only to confuse the explorers and cause them considerable discomfort. In the end, Phillips had to admit defeat after aimless wanderings through the harsh desert. Ubar was eventually found by the American archaeologist Nicholas Clapp in 1990. Clapp utilized images taken by the space shuttle Challenger that revealed desert tracks converging at a point that ultimately proved to be Ubar. Artifacts uncovered at the site included 4,000-year-old crystallized frankincense.[5]

Sultan Said personally supported Phillips in much of this activity. Theirs was a unique and almost brotherly relationship, but Phillips was taken totally by surprise when, in the spring of 1952, the sultan announced to him: "And by the will of God we shall have oil, for I am granting you the oil concession for Dhofar."[6] When his father died in 1931, Sultan Said was only 21 years old and the inheritor of a bankrupt treasury. Ever after he worked aggressively to enhance his persistently limited resources. Although he was able to restore financial stability to his government's budget in the 1930s, he still had to exercise extreme caution afterward, lest it fall out of balance. Sultan Said knew oil would solve this perennial problem. Phillips knew little about the oil business but wasted no time seeking the expertise required. In 1953, he contracted with Cities Service and Richfield Oil Corporation to begin exploration and drill test wells. As it turned out, Phillip's concession produced no bonanza for any of the parties involved.

Phillip's concession was not the first Omani oil concession. In 1925, the Anglo-Persian Oil Company received permission to prospect, but quickly abandoned the search. In 1937, Sultan Said, eager to see oil prospecting started in his county, awarded a 75-year concession to a subsidiary of the Iraq Petroleum Company (IPC) known as Petroleum Development (Oman and Dhofar) Ltd.[7] It had four shareholders, each with an interest of 23.75 percent: Royal Dutch/Shell group, Anglo-Persian Company, Compagnie Francaise des Petroles, and Near East Development Company. The remaining five percent was held by Partex.

[5] Nicholas Clapp, *The Road to Ubar: Finding the Atlantis of the Sands*, Mariner Books, 1999.
[6] *Unknown Oman,* p. 241.
[7] IPC has a fascinating history of its own dating back to the famous "Red Line Agreement" of 1928 in which Calouste Gulbenkian, a wealthy Armenian oilman who became known as "Mr. Five Percent," took a red pencil and on a map of the Middle East drew free hand a line around the former Ottoman Empire. The area within, including Oman, was

After Sultan Said's grant of a concession to Petroleum Development (Oman and Dhofar), he hoped to see oil development activities rapidly initiated. But these expectations were dashed as various complications – especially IPC's preoccupation with expanding its Iraqi fields as well as the massive interruptions accompanying World War II – hindered oil-related development in Oman until the 1950s. Moreover, Petroleum Development (Oman and Dhofar) showed virtually no interest in Dhofar.

Ultimately, Sultan Said prevailed on the company to surrender the Dhofar part of the concession in 1951 and the firm's name was abbreviated to Petroleum Development (Oman) (PDO). Not until 1956 did PDO drill its first exploratory well. This was a dry hole. It was followed by still other failures. One of the ironies of Oman's oil history is that when oil was finally found in 1962, it was only a few hundred yards from where the original well was drilled. They had drilled on the wrong side of the fault.

Shell was the only large company remaining in PDO by the end of the fifties, as most other shareholders had dropped out of the endeavor. Finally in 1962, commercial quantities of oil were found in central Oman at Yibal and at Fahud. Production began in the mid-1960s. From that time on PDO operations were managed by Shell.

But the sultan did not forget Wendell Phillips. In 1965, he bestowed on Phillips yet another concession, this one offshore, and on December 12, 1965, Phillips contracted with the West German oil company Wintershall to participate in his new concession. But again success eluded him.

The later 1960s were difficult years for Oman. Although Sultan Said's government began to receive modest royalties from the newly opened central Oman fields, the sultan discouraged all but the most limited modernization. Except for supporting the buildup of Oman's oil industry, he focused primarily upon strengthening his military capabilities and neglected matters such as education, health care, and socio-economic development. Consequently, most Omanis continued to live a backward, subsistence existence with little or no contact with the outside world. Increasing numbers of Omanis, including members of the elite, refused to accept this situation and left the country seeking

bound by an agreement to be explored by the IPC consortium of companies and not by any of them individually. The agreement remained in force until 1948 when the Americans pulled out to strike a separate deal in Saudi Arabia.

opportunities elsewhere in the Middle East, particularly Saudi Arabia and the Gulf states. Discontent took a violent turn in Dhofar, where a rebellion broke out among the mountain tribes of the province. Propaganda and arms provided by Oman's neighbor, the leftist, Soviet- and Chinese-supported Democratic Republic of South Yemen, encouraged the ever more ominous insurgency that threatened to spill out of Dhofar into Oman's northern provinces. In short, the late 1960s were a time when the rapidly changing world appeared ready to intrude forcefully into the country.

It is somewhat amazing to think that during this time, the world just outside Oman's doors was undergoing significant change. In the late 1960s, both the United States and Great Britain were announcing foreign policy changes that would impact both Asia and the Middle East. The USSR, on the other hand, maintained its expansionist aims through Egypt and Yemen as well as through Iraq and Syria to the Persian/ Arabian Gulf.[8]

These years were a time when the long-muted interest of the United States in Oman began to evolve into a more active one. The primary impetus for this shift was provided by the Soviet Union, which was extending its influence throughout Africa and southwest Asia. For over a decade, the Soviets had been pushing their presence in the Middle East toward the Mediterranean, the Indian Ocean and the Arabian Gulf. They were particularly successful in courting Arab "revolutionary" regimes, notably Egypt, Syria, Iraq and South Yemen, in their drive to undermine established Western interests and "moderate" Arab governments. After the mid-1950s, the Soviets channeled not only economic aid but also massive quantities of armaments to their Middle Eastern clients. In South Yemen, a state directly bordering Oman, they took over the important naval base at Aden after the British gave up their protectorate there in 1967. This move directly threatened the stability of the entire western Indian Ocean region as well as the Arabian Peninsula. The Arab-Israeli war of 1967, however, disrupted the advance of Soviet influence into the Middle East. Large stocks of the arms that had been inserted into the region were destroyed, the Suez Canal was closed, pro-Soviet Arab

---

[8]Although there is no hard and fast rule about how the Gulf is referred to and there is a constant struggle between the Arab littoral states and those who believe the established geographical term Persian Gulf should be honored, in this book this body of water will hereinafter be referred to as the Arabian Gulf.

states were weakened, and moderate nations gained time to adjust to the rapidly evolving situation.

A second impetus to the United States' reassessment of the role it should play in the Middle East was thrust upon it by Great Britain's decision to complete its abandonment of what its government regarded as expensive and outmoded commitments in the Indian Ocean area. Britain's withdrawal from Aden in 1967 was followed in 1968 by an announcement that their military forces would leave the Arabian Gulf by the end of 1971. This came as a shock to the Gulf's Arab rulers, all of whom long had relied on British advice and military support. Moreover, previous British attempts to promote cooperation as well as political and economic unity among the Gulf Arab states had failed. Thus, the consensus was that a "power vacuum" would be created in the Arabian Gulf after the British military withdrew. A consequence of this could be Soviet penetration of the relatively defenseless area, which contained huge and vital energy resources.

Just as Britain was rethinking its role in the region in the late 1960s, so too was the United States. This was an outgrowth of foreign policy reviews that began in anticipation of the eventual end of the Vietnam War. These discussions focused initially on East Asia, but eventually other regions – notably the Middle East – began to be injected into the conversations. As early as 1966, the Department of State's Middle East Interregional Group, a body that incorporated participants from various government agencies, including the CIA and the Department of Defense, came to the conclusion that America's Middle East policy was badly outdated. One suggestion was that the United States support an effort by the Middle East nations to form some type of regional arrangement to counter Soviet activities there, a Middle Eastern version of NATO. Such a policy would also encourage these nations to bear more of the burden and accept a diminution of American and British roles.[9]

Little changed, however, until July 1969 when President Richard Nixon announced a new policy for East Asia. This stated that America would not sacrifice its national security interests in the region or default on its commitments to its friends, but it would expect its allies there to assume more responsibility for ensuring stability in the region and for their own military defense. Soon this "Nixon Doctrine" began to be

[9] James H. Critchfield *Oman Papers, 1968-1991*, Memorandum dated January 28, 1970.

regarded in American governmental spheres as a policy that should be applied to other regions as well. Consequently, serious speculation about possible changes in America's approach toward the Middle East began to occupy various parties in the government as well as within media and academic circles.

A salient worry in all these concerns was how the prospective "power vacuum" in the Gulf region should be treated. The situation in Oman appeared to be especially troublesome, given the growing internal unrest and the external threat facing the sultanate. Other countries, particularly Saudi Arabia, shared this concern about Oman. In 1967, the Saudis tried to address the possibility that Soviet- and Chinese-supported revolutionary influences could spread out of South Yemen into Oman and the Arab Gulf states. This prompted a Saudi attempt to nurture the creation of an independent buffer state in the Hadramaut, which would have interposed a barrier between South Yemen and Oman. Ultimately, this venture failed.

Meanwhile, discussion continued in the United States concerning possible policy alternatives for dealing with the Middle East and with the looming "power vacuum" in the Gulf and in Oman. However, events on the ground overtook these conversations before they resulted in concrete policy decisions. In July 1970, Sultan Said's regime in Oman was overturned. His son, Qaboos bin Said, stepped in and took over in a swift transfer of power. This new reality signaled the beginning of another phase in the American-Omani relationship.

2

SULTAN QABOOS TAKES THE REINS OF POWER

Sultan Said sent his son Qaboos to England in 1958, first for private tutoring and then for three years at the Royal Academy at Sandhurst, where he was initiated into the rigors and discipline of military training. He left Sandhurst in 1962 and spent six months with a British regiment in Germany where he became a lover of classical music, which helped to sustain him during the six years of isolation imposed by his father after his return home.

But before Qaboos returned in 1964, Sultan Said unexpectedly sent his son on a "grand tour" of Europe and the Middle East. He might have arranged this because he himself had made an even "grander tour" in 1938 when he traveled to Japan, Hawaii, San Francisco, across the United States, and on to England before returning to Oman.

While Sultan Said took steps in Qaboos's formative years to see that he was educated and exposed to the modern world, once his son was back in Oman, the sultan rarely saw him and did nothing to prepare him for the job he would one day inherit. Qaboos was virtually a prisoner in his own home, where his time was to be spent studying Islamic law and Omani history and culture. Any efforts by Qaboos to get involved in government affairs led nowhere. It was a period of extreme frustration for the young prince.

A significant friend of Qaboos during this time was Captain James Timothy Whittington Landon, a fellow Sandhurst graduate who was born in Canada and raised in Rhodesia. He had not known Qaboos at Sandhurst but met him soon after his arrival in Oman, where he served as a British Special Air Service (SAS) intelligence officer seconded to Oman from the British Army.[1] The SAS is the equivalent of the American Special Forces; its motto is "Who Dares Wins." The young men's mutual interests turned into a friendship Qaboos sorely needed.

On July 23, 1970, 29-year-old Qaboos bin Said forced his father to abdicate and turn over the reins of government to him. Slightly wounded in the skirmish that took place, Sultan Said was flown to London for medical treatment and remained there in exile. Qaboos's decision to take this drastic measure against his father had been carefully planned, and he was duly recognized by the population as their legitimate ruler. There are several versions in print and by word of mouth of the coup d'etat. The fact is the coup was successful, and I will leave the details to others to report, having no first-hand information to add to history.

Britain officially recognized Sultan Qaboos's government on July 29, 1970. A few days later, the sultan flew from Salalah to Muscat, his first visit there, and was greeted warmly by the people, who would soon realize what it meant to be "liberated." Qaboos bore an uncanny physical resemblance to his father. In official photographs, both stand erect and portray a somewhat formal but pleasant demeanor, with dark eyes gazing out from their portraits as if to welcome you to their presence. It would soon become clear that while the young sultan took after his father in looks, the similarities stopped there.

Sultan Qaboos had a daunting task before him: To lead his country literally out of the dark ages. Living conditions were primitive; there were no radios; curfews were enforced between dusk and dawn; and education and health care were extremely limited. There were virtually no official contacts with other Arab and Muslim countries and no social exchanges with the Western world. Most of the Omani elite had sent their children abroad to be educated, and they remained abroad after their schooling was over. The country's finances were in a critical state. Sultan Qaboos had a vision of a better future, but he needed help if he was to achieve it..

In his first public statement to the people of Muscat and Oman, Qaboos pledged to create a modern government and to abolish all the unnecessary restrictions on their lives and activities. He said he would proceed as quickly as possible to transform their lives into prosperous ones with a bright future. He urged all of them to play their part to reach these goals. By so doing, Oman, he said, would take a respectable

[1] According to Chester Nagle, a friend of Landon and military advisor to Sultan Qaboos in 1975, Landon told him he had not known Qaboos at Sandhurst. Interview in June 2007.

place in the world.[2] His first official decree was to change the name of the country from Muscat and Oman to the Sultanate of Oman, thereby taking the first step toward unifying the country.

When a leader is catapulted to the top as quickly as Sultan Qaboos was, one thing not lacking is advice. The new sultan's immediate problem was whose advice to take. Moreover, there were several levels of governance he had to deal with simultaneously. First, he had to gain the support of family members as well as tribal leaders inside Oman. Then he had to move quickly to induce educated Omanis living overseas to return home to participate in his new government. At the same time, he had to deal immediately with the ongoing war in Dhofar that was being backed by both the Soviets and the Chinese. And, not least, he needed to secure recognition from each of the member nations of the Arab League, from Iran, and from important western powers, particularly the United States.

Especially important were his dealings with Oman's old ally and friend, Great Britain. He would build on the already close Anglo-Omani relationship while at the same time showing everybody from the outset that his was an independent country and that he would be the decision maker on both external and internal challenges. While this was not spelled out in writing, his firmness of attitude from the beginning won him almost instant respect from most of those with whom he dealt. Those who did not like the course he set soon found their advice was no longer sought.

Oman under Sultan Qaboos stressed its independence while aspiring to become a forward, open, and outward-looking nation. But the reality was that a close connection to Britain was a part of Oman's history, as Oman and Britain had maintained good relations since the eighteenth century. The sultan's armed forces were built largely upon British military traditions and standards. In 1970, despite the announced forthcoming withdrawal of the British from the Gulf in 1971, they still essentially controlled Oman's foreign and military affairs.

British advisors remained in Muscat, and British leadership in the Dhofar War was significant. This was an obscure conflict against Communist-supported insurgents fought almost entirely in southern Oman along the border between Dhofar and South Yemen. The exact location of this border had never been agreed on. It was in Dhofar between

---

[2] Ministry of Information, Sultanate of Oman.

the *jebal* (mountain) and the shore of the Indian Ocean that the war was waged for ten years. It started in 1965 when *jebali* dissidents from various Dhofar nomadic tribes, which had issues with the former Sultan Said, initiated attacks on the ruler's troops. The dissidents coalesced under the name of the Dhofar Liberation Front (DLF). Before long, the leftist Democratic Republic of South Yemen regime based in Aden, whose territory bordered Dhofar, seized upon the unrest in Sultan Said's territory to push its own agenda by supporting the DLF.

The Soviets and the Chinese soon began funneling arms and supplies to the *jebalis* via the Aden government, and before long the insurgents began calling themselves the Peoples Front for the Liberation of Oman and the Arabian Gulf (PFLOAG). Later, when it was determined that perhaps this name reflected too ambitious a goal, the group abbreviated its name to the Peoples Front for the Liberation of Oman (PFLO). They were a fierce and undisciplined lot and in many ways their own worst enemy. At the same time, British discipline did not always sit well with the sultan's troops on the other side of the border. Casualties mounted, and progress against the insurgents was painfully slow at best.

However, after a determined Sultan Qaboos replaced his father, the campaign against the PFLO expanded and gained strength. At its peak, there were 10,000 Omani, Baluchi (from Pakistan), Jordanian and Iranian troops under the command of British forces. Brigadier John Akehurst, who commanded the Dhofar Brigade during the last two years of the war, has written a splendid book about this ten-year war.[3] Sultan Qaboos was no doubt pleased with the dedication of Brigadier Akehurst and his brave, gutsy British officers. The team, working with what today would be called "a coalition of nations" under British command, either killed the enemy or persuaded the *jebalis* to transfer their allegiance to the sultan. The fierce pockets of resistance soon withered and disappeared. By the end of 1975, the Dhofar War was over.

At the suggestion of the British in 1970, the sultan invited his uncle Sayyid Tariq bin Taimur, whom he had never met, to return to Oman to serve as prime minister. Almost 50 years of age when he joined Qaboos, Tariq had left Oman in the early 1960s and lived in Abu Dhabi, Turkey and Germany with his second wife, a German linguistics professor, and his numerous children. Tariq for some years had worked unsuccessfully

[3] See John Akehurst, *We Won a War: The Campaign in Oman 1965-1975*, Michael Russell Publishing Ltd., Great Britain, 1982.

with Omani exiles to bring about the overthrow of his half-brother Sultan Said.[4] He was a sophisticated, gregarious man and socially an asset to Qaboos in putting forth Oman's image. But Tariq's administrative style was somewhat haphazard and disorganized, and he never actually got around to setting up a reformed governmental structure.

Despite this, he was helpful in getting projects started in Oman, including schools, hospitals, clinics, port and airport construction, and a new palace for the sultan. But eventually disagreements arose over the rather blatant efforts of Tariq, with support from the local British group, to isolate Sultan Qaboos and run the show himself. Although British influence would continue to play a role in Oman, the groups that had helped Qaboos come to power overplayed their hand in an attempt to maintain a British monopoly of influence in Oman. They tried to keep the young sultan isolated in Salalah, but Sultan Qaboos proved he was to be his own man. He told his uncle in January 1972 that he would become his own prime minister and bestowed on Tariq the title of senior ambassador and advisor on diplomatic affairs. On January 3, 1972, the *London Times* reported the resignation of Sayyid Tariq, who was leaving for health reasons. After that, Tariq spent most of his time in Europe. Nonetheless, the two men remained on good personal terms, and Tariq on more than one occasion played the role of elder statesmen on some of the sultan's trips abroad.

Gradually, Sultan Qaboos began to give a new character to his complex ties with Great Britain. The expatriate British community had to accept the reality that they no longer controlled Oman's domestic and foreign policies. Qaboos continued to accept British primacy in matters of military significance and in current oil operations, but he reached out to neighboring Arab nations and Iran to broaden his military base. And, most significantly, he let it be known that he wanted friendship with the United States as well as increased U.S. presence in Oman, including support for his political and military objectives and his development program.

Because almost no Omanis were trained and experienced enough to provide the sultan the support he needed as he moved out from under British influence, he turned to an array of international advisors. Captain J.T.W. (Timothy) Landon, who after the coup became equerry to the sultan, was the most important figure in orchestrating and supporting

---

[4] CIA/DDI/CRS biographic profile, May 19, 1975.

Sultan Qaboos in these efforts. In England, the title of equerry is given to a personal attendant on some member of the royal family. That is a fair description of Landon's role in Oman, but it does not go far enough. Landon advised the sultan on all military and national security affairs and also on the broader issues of Oman's development. He was the man one went to when a decision needed to be made. Captain Landon remained in this role until 1979 when, by then a brigadier, he was replaced by an Omani. But his role did not end there. Retiring to England, Brigadier Landon remained a trusted advisor and, until his death in 2007, was the only non-Omani who had continued without interruption to serve the sultan.

In 1971, Sultan Qaboos met Ghassan Ibrahim Shaker and Yehia Mohammed Omar, two men who would prove to be significant non-Omani advisors for many years to come. They began by introducing Sultan Qaboos to his fellow Arab leaders and to the Shah of Iran.

Ghassan Shaker, born in 1935 in Saudi Arabia, was the son of Ibrahim Shaker, a long-time financial advisor to the Saudi royal family and an important Jeddah merchant. As a young boy, Shaker spent twelve years at the prestigious Victoria College in Alexandria, Egypt. Among his many friends were King Hussein of the Hashemite Kingdom of Jordan, with whom he maintained a close relationship up to the time of King Hussein's death. Shaker went on to study at Cambridge University, England, and was the first Saudi to graduate from there in 1957. He joined his father's bank in Beirut, the *Banque du Liban et d'outré Mer*, where he learned the banking business and the intricacies of working in the Middle East and Europe. During his formative years, Ghassan traveled in circles that afforded him many opportunities to make close and lasting relationships. His classmates and friends were sophisticated and smart. They were more or less the Arab version of the American Skull and Bones society at Yale.[5]

Ghassan Shaker was a handsome man, tall with dark hair and mustache and an elegant manner. He treated those around him with utmost respect, and, as a consequence, prompted dignitaries much older than he to accept him into their fold. At the time he met Sultan Qaboos, Shaker had close ties with the Saudi Royal Family. These connections

[5] Skull and Bones is an elite Yale University society whose members are and have been among the most powerful figures in America. For example, both former President George Bush and unsuccessful contender for president John Kerry are members.

would prove extremely important for Qaboos, as it was Shaker who arranged Sultan Qaboos's first visit to Saudi Arabia to meet King Faisal and to Jordan to meet King Hussein.

Yehia Omar, born in Libya in 1931, was educated in Egypt from 1941 to 1955, the latter two years at the military academy in Cairo. He was a Berber who started his career as a police officer in Tripoli and attended various training courses in Cairo, the United States and Germany in the late 1950s. As a young police officer, Omar had been sympathetic to the cause of Gamal Abdel Nasser, Ahmad Ben Bella, and others, and therefore had excellent connections with aging revolutionaries in all of the North African Arab countries.

A somewhat stocky man with dark, curly hair and thick, dark-rimmed eyeglasses that lent strength to his face, Omar maintained a straight, somewhat military stance at public functions, though among friends he was always relaxed and smiling. His peers genuinely liked him.

When large-scale oil development began in Libya, Omar left the police, went into business operating a catering service for the field crews of the oil companies and eventually became acquainted with the U.S. Air Force officers at Wheelus Air Force base near Tripoli. He quickly matured as an entrepreneur and enhanced his role as a trader and commercial agent among members of King Idris's palace staff as well as key people at Wheelus.

By early 1969, Omar had established a business office in Rome under the name Transworld Trading Company. When Muammer Qadhafi seized power in September 1969, Omar had already moved permanently to Rome. He did not sever all ties with Libya, however, and continued to do some business in the country. Although Omar had a limited formal education, he was extremely quick witted, understood the ways of finance, and was a shrewd analyst of human nature. His business ethics would not have been a model of American entrepreneurship, but they were perfectly acceptable in the Middle East business world.

Basically a one-man organization, Omar became very wealthy in a short period of time. He had homes in Cairo, Rome, Geneva, London and Washington. In Europe and the Middle East, he traveled in his own private Dassault Falcon executive jet that carried Swiss registration and markings. He was involved in the affairs of the top levels of all the Arab states except for Syria and Iraq. These political connections allowed him to participate successfully in various large commercial projects in the Middle East, while his close connections to the leadership in the North African countries made him invaluable to Sultan Qaboos.

While the world of business occupied them daily, both Ghassan Shaker and Yehia Omar were politically oriented, with excellent connections to the top personalities of the Arab and Western governments, including their intelligence services. They understood the importance of political action in the increasingly volatile Middle East. There was nobody in the Sultanate of Oman who could match this. Soon both men were accredited on the Oman diplomatic lists in London, Paris, Rome and Geneva. They were very active in London in particular, and Qaboos used them to keep a more sophisticated eye on the British than his Omani diplomats were capable of doing.

When James Critchfield, the former chief of the CIA's Near East Division and the de facto energy officer for the CIA, met both Shaker and Omar, he saw in them important windows on the Middle East. Each in his own way was able to interpret events that were very quickly having an impact on the world the United States was dealing with. He spent time with both of them, separately and together. By the time the sultan came onto the world stage, Critchfield realized he was well positioned to help the U.S. government, behind the scenes, to develop a meaningful relationship with Sultan Qaboos and Oman.

Critchfield met Sultan Qaboos in London in the fall of 1971 and again in Germany. Critchfield spoke fluent German, which he'd mastered during his postwar years in Germany. Sultan Qaboos, following his Sandhurst experience, had spent six months in Germany with the 1st Battalion, The Cameronians (The Scottish Rifles), carrying out regimental duties and receiving staff training. Both Critchfield and the sultan liked Germany and its people. Critchfield's military background and his years in Germany served him well in his initial meetings with the young sultan.

Despite their age difference, they had that much in common. But it was Critchfield's extraordinary feel for geopolitics and his experiences in the Middle East that most interested Sultan Qaboos and his advisors. The essence of what Critchfield confided to Sultan Qaboos is as follows:

Your Majesty, earlier in my years in government, oil was not considered a national security problem. But it is a given that you cannot deal with the Middle East for long without coming to realize the importance of oil. As long as oil was under $3 a barrel and there seemed to be a limitless supply of it and the producing governments continued to support western objectives, the United States government did not focus too much attention on the subject of oil as a threat to U.S. national security. The United States produced most of its own oil, and gasoline only cost 25 cents a gallon.

Then in the 1960s, there were rumblings that caused my government to start worrying. The major oil companies, the so-called Seven Sisters, took note of the formation of the Organization of Petroleum Exporting Countries (OPEC), which had been established in Venezuela in 1960 and by 1968 was beginning to show some muscle, particularly in the Middle East and North Africa. There were suggestions that if the producing countries did not get more money for their oil, they were now in a position to expropriate and nationalize the companies. It was the beginning of an era in which Middle East oil was going to be a central issue on the world agenda.

Not only oil, but water was also becoming an issue. The Tigris, Euphrates and Jordan Rivers, for example, flowed through many of the region's nation states and disputes on the use of the water were already being heard in these arid lands. Also, there was concern that despite the "Green Revolution" just getting underway, the world population would be competing for food grains and fertilizers to feed their growing numbers. These were critical issues, and I urged my government to delve into them more deeply than it was.

I also believed that the death of Egypt's President Gamal Abdel Nasser on September 28, 1970, just two months after Your Majesty assumed power, left a major void in the greater Middle East. For almost two decades, no Arab leader had contemplated his future without consciously considering the presence and influence of Nasser. Whether you were for or against him, all Arab leaders in calculating policy measures carefully weighed what the reaction of Nasser would be. The hard realities of Nasser's death were that he left behind a Soviet unified command on Egyptian soil – militarily secure, logistically supportable, and strategically placed astride the main communication line between Asia and Europe. This was Nasser's last and perhaps his greatest service for Moscow. Nasser was, in the Soviet's own words, the principal instrument of Soviet policy in the Middle East. When his vice president, Anwar Sadat, assumed power without challengers, he took over what was essentially a weak regime. The year 1970 in the broader Middle East ended quietly as those in the region contemplated their futures.

The situation was volatile. An Arab-Israeli settlement had reached yet another impasse. The Suez Canal remained closed. Libya was beginning price negotiations with its foreign oil companies threatening them with nationalization, marking the beginning of major change in the relationships between the oil producing nations and the oil companies.

As 1971 moved on, Moscow was clearly beginning to worry about its influence in Egypt. President Sadat was gaining political strength, and he has now begun a purge of pro-Soviets from the Nasser old guard. King Faisal in Riyadh and the Shah in Teheran have taken notice and a pragmatic alliance is developing among the three. My government has quietly supported this.

For the first time in modern history, the relationship among these three leaders has presented an opportunity for such an alliance to become a reality. It might now be possible to build through the Red Sea and Egypt an open and prosperous road of commerce from the Gulf and the Indian Ocean to the Mediterranean and Europe. This was not so when Nasser was in power. Both in Riyadh and Teheran, the feeling is that Egypt, under Sadat, is now prepared to play a constructive role in a regional settlement of this nature. They will be meeting quietly on this in the months ahead.

Moscow's opportunities to expand its influence beyond Suez have not been impressive. Even its support of the radical left People's Democratic Republic of Yemen in Aden – which, in turn, supported the militant Dhofari rebel movement that is threatening your borders in Dhofar – is being influenced by a strong Maoist Chinese wing. That is not good news for the Soviets.

It is my opinion that the Middle East is still potentially the most dangerous international problem of the 1970s. The crisis in the Middle East remains frozen in its current pattern and will likely remain so for some time. The superpowers have left the Middle East stacked in a holding pattern.

As for the oil situation, OPEC is beginning to examine the impact of the drop in the value of the dollar in Europe on the real income of its oil-producing states. When OPEC met in Beirut on September 22, 1971, it decided the time had come for each OPEC member to establish negotiations to participate in concessions within its sovereign territory. In other words, it was time, they thought, to become at least part owners of their own oil resources. While this principle has been unanimously accepted within OPEC, there is wide disagreement on what form participation should take. Libya has already indicated it is going for 51 percent participation. Others are looking at 20 percent.

Following the Beirut meeting, the finance ministers of Iran and Kuwait met in October to examine a possible course of action for the Gulf members of OPEC. I know the Sultanate of Oman is not a member of OPEC or for that matter of the Organization of Arab Petroleum Exporting Countries (OAPEC). But what happens in OPEC is important to your negotiations with Shell Oil. Saudi Arabia's Oil Minister Sheikh Ahmed Zaki Yamani expects Oman to follow OPEC's lead.[6]

On that note the two parted. It was very clear that Oman's relationships with its Arab neighbors needed to be clarified quickly. And the rapidly evolving situation with regard to world oil policy added another important dimension to this.

---

[6] James H. Critchfield, *Oman Papers, 1968-1991*, Aide Memoire, November 1971.

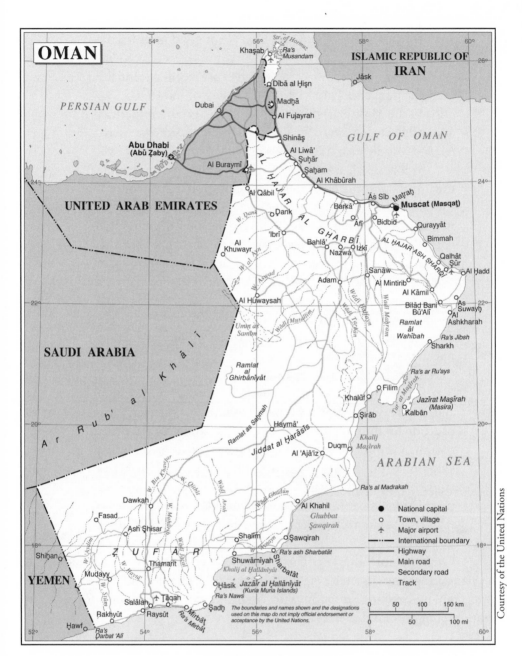

Map of Oman - 2004

3

THE FIRST AMERICAN ADVISORS ARRIVE

On October 6, 1971, Robert B. Anderson, a former deputy secretary of defense and secretary of the treasury in the Eisenhower administration, visited Oman, ostensibly to explore business opportunities. Although Anderson had returned to private business in 1961, he remained an economic advisor to both Presidents Kennedy and Johnson and knew President Nixon. The invitation to meet Sultan Qaboos was arranged by Ghassan Shaker.

On the way to Oman, Anderson stopped in Saudi Arabia. The U.S. State Department, at Anderson's request, had sent a telex to King Faisal informing him that Mr. Anderson would like an audience with him before traveling to Oman. In fact, Anderson had with him a letter from President Nixon to the king supporting Anderson's unofficial trip to Oman. When Anderson met with King Faisal, he got the king's attention when he put before him a map of the world and pointed out that there were five waterways in the world for which the United States would go to war and that one of them was the Strait of Hormuz. He went on to discuss global strategy and geopolitics with the king. At this meeting, King Faisal gave his support to Anderson's planned meeting with Sultan Qaboos.[1] This was a very important step, because Sultan Qaboos had not yet established formal relations with Saudi Arabia.

The very same day, Anderson flew to Dubai, where he was met by Captain Tim Landon and escorted to Oman for the pre-arranged meeting with Sultan Qaboos. There is no official record of this meeting, but the local press reported the next day that Qaboos granted to Anderson the offshore concession previously held by Wendell Phillips.[2] Other reports

[1] James H. Critchfield *Oman Papers, 1968-1991*. From a conversation between James Critchfield and Ghassan Shaker in London in 1993.

of the meeting indicated that Qaboos also asked Anderson to act as an advisor on a wide range of matters, including negotiations related to other oil concessions. Anderson, working out of his New York office, played the role of facilitator for a year or two. But this was his first and last trip to Oman. In May 1973, he sent Sultan Qaboos a formal letter terminating his advisory relationship.[3] Probably the most important role Anderson played was the one in Saudi Arabia prior to the visit to Qaboos.

During this initial phase of development in Oman, there were other Americans who would serve as advisors to Sultan Qaboos. For legal matters, Anderson recommended New York lawyer Thomas W. Hill Jr., whose firm, Spear and Hill, became the legal advisors to the sultanate and in essence wrote their first official decrees. Hill was retained as the sultanate's legal advisor in March 1972. From 1972 to 1975, he played a major role in the negotiation of petroleum concessions and most of the sultanate's financial and legal transactions. His level of activity was such that in 1974 he opened an office in Muscat.

Hill was a veritable whirling dervish. Critchfield characterized him as "a big, bluff New York Irish lawyer who is extremely energetic and apparently effective." Other American advisors in Oman were not so subtle. Hill had been variously characterized as a very difficult person, a megalomaniac, and a know-it-all who wanted to be the sultan. He was, in the opinion of some, too zealous in protecting the interests of Sultan Qaboos and was not shy in letting some Oman government officials know that they had overstepped their authority in signing certain legal documents.

Spear and Hill drafted Royal Decree Number 22/74 dated June 1, 1974, called "The Decree on Contract Signing Procedures," which basically said that no contract would be binding unless signed by His Majesty or by a party specifically authorized to do so in writing by His Majesty.[4] Hill assumed the oversight role in this regard and never hesitated to intervene if he felt the decree was being violated in any way.

---

[2] Phillips was closely involved with the regime of Sultan Said and had been granted concessions by the former ruler. After Qaboos overthrew his father, Phillips lost his influence and ultimately the concessions he once held in Oman.

[3] James H. Critchfield *Oman Papers, 1968-1991*. Memorandum from the files of C. Stribling Snodgrass regarding a telephone conversation between Tom Hill and himself, May 24, 1973.

[4] Ibid., Official Gazette No. 56, Sultanate of Oman.

He managed in the period of less than a year after the decree was issued to alienate not only key Omanis but also most of the sultan's American advisors, who felt he was taking over responsibilities that went beyond his legal mandate.

But, in fact, Sultan Qaboos had given Tom Hill broad powers. When Hill first arrived in Oman, he drafted a terms of agreement letter dated February 18, 1972, listing the firm's duties. Hill wrote that the firm could represent the sultanate in international activities of a business or commercial nature, including negotiating the legal terms of both petroleum and mineral concessions; services in connection to relations with the World Bank, the International Monetary Fund and the U.S. Agency for International Development; appearances before international tribunals of various kinds; and negotiations of certain construction and development agreements. Sultan Qaboos signed the agreement on March 15, 1972.[5]

Another early American advisor was Charles A. Black, whose California company, Mardela Corporation, engaged in marine and freshwater aquatic resource development. Black became the fisheries advisor to the sultanate in 1971. Black was on the corporate board of directors of the Woods Hole Oceanographic Institution, was director of the Oceanic Institute in Hawaii, was a member of the Marine Advisory Committee of the National Marine Fisheries Service and would later become a presidential appointee to the U.S. National Advisory Committee on Oceans and Atmosphere. Mardela's first order of business was to do an extensive survey of the commercial fishery potential in Oman, long known to have rich fishing grounds where Russians, Japanese and Koreans had fished for years.

Mardela set up its office in a leased duplex apartment building in the old town of Muscat just across from the old Muscat mosque. The first office manager that Black sent to Oman to oversee operations had a short stay. After several nights of being awakened by the muezzin's call to prayer at 4:30 AM, he lodged a complaint about the noise. The next thing he knew he was declared persona non grata and asked to leave Oman. Subsequent employees were more carefully briefed.

Mardela began its work with the use of a fisheries research vessel known as the *Darbat*. The American firms Del Monte and Food

5 Ibid., Letter of Agreement dated February 18, 1972, from Thomas W. Hill Jr. to His Majesty Sultan Qaboos bin Said.

Machinery Corporation participated as subcontractors, along with some smaller firms. At the time, no facilities existed for freezing, storing and marketing fish, and all catches were for local consumption. In the beginning, the most important enticement to get local fishermen involved was a gift of a treasured Yamaha outboard. The outboard engines enabled the fishermen to go out farther, stay out longer and increase their catch. It was an example of a simple solution to a complex problem.[6]

A comprehensive report was delivered by Charles Black to Sultan Qaboos on February 1, 1973. It contained the results of a survey that evaluated fish catches, vessels and fishing techniques and also recommended pilot programs for both offshore activity and onshore processing and distribution. The Mardela activity was the first effort to get a fishing industry underway. By the early 1980s, with the help of the United Nations Food and Agriculture Organization, an Oman National Fisheries Company was established, and the Oman fishing industry became a reality.

Of equal importance was the role Charles Black would play in negotiating a median line with Iran on offshore territorial limits in the Hormuz Strait and in representing Oman at the Law of the Sea Conference. On May 22, 1974, Sultan Qaboos met with Charles Black and, in addition to continuing Black's appointment as fisheries advisor, he asked him to initiate negotiations with government officials in Iran concerning the formation of a Joint Fisheries Commission to manage marine resources common to both states.[7] But something happened over the summer. On August 8, 1974, Sultan Qaboos revoked the May 22 instructions stating that all negotiations regarding ocean pollution and conservation of fisheries resources between Oman and Iran would be the responsibility of the Ministry of Foreign Affairs. Black saw the fine hand of Tom Hill in this, but he accepted the revised mandate with good grace. He did subsequently work closely with Deputy Foreign Minister Yousuf bin Alawi bin Abdullah on these matters.

C. Stribling Snodgrass became the petroleum advisor to Sultan Qaboos in February 1972 and remained so until his death in 1974. Snodgrass, a 1922 U.S. Naval Academy graduate, had a distinguished career as a petroleum engineer and during World War II was head of the foreign refining division of the U.S. Petroleum Administration for War.

[6] From interviews with Charles A. Black, September 2004.
[7] From letter of appointment signed by Sultan Qaboos bin Said on May 22, 1974.

He was a vice president of engineering for Bechtel Corporation and subsequently an advisor for multiple governments on the use of their petroleum reserves.[8]

Snodgrass, semi-retired and living on a farm near Leesburg, Virginia, maintained a consulting business in Washington, DC. Through social connections, Jim Critchfield met Snodgrass and was impressed with his background. Snodgrass also held an oil-consulting contract in Jordan, and Critchfield persuaded him to visit Oman after one of his trips to Amman. Snodgrass maintained ties to King Faisal of Saudi Arabia and Petroleum Minister Sheikh Ahmed Zaki Yamani, all of which added to his attractiveness as an individual who would be helpful in giving advice about Oman's future oil program.

After his appointment, Snodgrass set to work immediately. In the ensuing months he made several trips to Oman in which he toured all of the PDO producing fields and initiated a project to obtain data needed for a study of gas utilization and LPG (liquid petroleum gas) recovery. He also began to look into current exploration efforts and negotiations for new concessions.

Snodgrass served Sultan Qaboos during the vital time when the oil exporting nations were negotiating with the major oil companies concerning sharing, ownership and participation, an era that changed the world of energy forever.[9] Although Oman was not a member of OPEC, those were very delicate times. Oman could not ignore what its more affluent neighbors were doing; at the same time, it did not have the leverage enjoyed by the established oil states that possessed large oil reserves. Snodgrass's advice during the period Oman was negotiating with PDO – i.e., Shell Oil Company – was critical.

Another American to appear on the Oman scene was Chester A. Nagle, a former civilian officer in the Department of Defense's international security affairs office. While at the Pentagon, Nagle worked in the office responsible for arms transfers, including the licensing of

[8] The collection of materials relating to Snodgrass's career in the petroleum industry from 1934 to 1974 are available at the University of Wyoming, American History Center, Guide to Mining and Petroleum History.

[9] In 1972, after more than three years of intense negotiations, a participation agreement (meaning partial ownership by the oil-producing states of their own oil resources) was reached with Saudi Arabia and the other Gulf producing nations. The intricacies of these negotiations are reported in detail in Daniel Yergin's authoritative study, *The Prize,* published by Simon and Schuster in 1991.

naval weapons systems. When he left this job, he went with a company called Aeromaritime, a high-tech export business that worked closely with the Pentagon. Critchfield met Nagle in Washington in 1972 and encouraged him to get involved in Oman. He said Oman needed a helping hand in the liaison it was conducting with the Pentagon and the U.S. government to obtain needed military supplies for its ongoing war in Dhofar.

Nagle visited Oman, where he met Tim Landon and, after a period of time, was appointed by Sultan Qaboos as a special military advisor to the Palace Office. He also became an advisor to the Royal Oman Police Force and trained officers in a variety of tasks, including small arms, traffic radar, communications, night vision gear, etc. He visited most of the military installations around the country.[10]

Some books about Oman published in the 1970s seem to conclude that every contact James Critchfield had during those early days marked that individual as a CIA operative. As frequently happens, once this type of information is published, other writers lift the statement out of one book into theirs, with proper attribution of course. Misinformation like this is difficult to correct. The truth is that up until his retirement from the CIA in 1974, Critchfield was in touch with a large number of oilmen regarding oil activities in the Middle East and businessmen with Middle East interests. Some of them were executives of the Seven Sisters, others were independent oilmen, and others were bankers and entrepreneurs. None of them were CIA agents. But they were more than willing to talk with Critchfield about the Middle East. It was good for them and it was good for the country.

To the outsider and particularly to the British, it must have seemed very strange to see Americans in such roles in Oman. And there was no question there were British-inspired internal struggles to neutralize the influence of these Americans. But the fact remains that in those early years, these American advisors played key roles in initiating the development of Oman's basic resources. Pulling the strings were Timothy Landon, Ghassan Shaker and Yehia Omar. They supported the entry of the Americans into the Oman scene. So, too, did Sultan Qaboos bin Said.

In those very early days, no more than a handful of Omanis as well as a few other non-Oman personalities worked with these American

[10] From an interview with Chester Nagle in Washington, DC, on December 8, 2004.

advisors. One of the non-Omanis was John Townsend, who formerly had been associated with the British Whitehead Consulting Group of London. Townsend was a principal advisor on development projects.[11]

Townsend, a native of Sydney, Australia, was working for Whitehead in London when he noticed an ad in *The Economist* in 1968 advertising a position as economic advisor to the government of Oman. Townsend persuaded Whitehead to respond. The result was a contract that brought Townsend to Muscat in April 1969. He left Oman in May 1970 rather disillusioned. He took jobs in Iraq and Abu Dhabi before returning to Oman after Sultan Qaboos took over.

Townsend had a very difficult job, and he did it well. His office was always full of seekers promoting either themselves or one project or another. His reception room was likened to that of a doctor's office full of patients and he was the overworked doctor. He managed to keep a number of balls in the air and had a practical view of what was facing Oman. To one advisor who recommended that Oman form a national oil company, he commented, "We can't even organize the government, much less an oil company."

Townsend skillfully adjusted to the changing circumstances unleashed by the busy new sultan, and he probably was the closest thing to a bridge between the established British influence and the new foreign influences that entered Oman in 1971 and after. He served on the many councils that were put together to get the government operational. After the demise of the short-lived, British-run Interim Advisory Council, the sultan stepped in and by royal decree set up, first, the Supreme Council for Economic Planning and Development, followed by the Supreme Financial Council, the Supreme Petroleum Council, and the Supreme Development Council.

The latter was headed by an Egyptian, Dr. Sharif Loutfi, who had been part of a World Bank survey team that suggested it. Loutfi, a most capable economist, had been recommended for this position by Yehia Omar. Qaboos was the chairman of all of the other councils and, in the early years, acted as his own prime minister, defense minister, foreign minister and finance minister. Landon, Townsend, Shaker and Omar served on these councils in various advisory capacities.

Slowly the sultan began to appoint Omanis of his own choosing to

---

[11] In 1977 John Townsend published a book on his view on Oman's development. See *Oman: The Making of a Modern State*, Croom Helm, London.

significant positions in the government. Without a doubt the key person entering the government at this time was Qais Abd al Munim Al-Zawawi, whom the sultan appointed deputy minister of foreign affairs. Al-Zawawi's father had come to Oman from Saudi Arabia in the 1960s and handled the financial affairs of the former Sultan Said as well as those of Sultan Said's father, Sultan Taimur bin Faisal, who, after abdicating in 1931, lived in Karachi until his death. Qais was born in Karachi and educated in Bombay. When Sultan Qaboos took over, Qais Al-Zawawi, a well-known businessman in Muscat, was running the family's pharmaceutical import business.

His brother, Dr. Omar Abdul Munim Al-Zawawi, who was director of public medical services for the Eastern Province of Saudi Arabia, returned to Oman and entered the business world in partnership with Qais. From that time on, the Al-Zawawi brothers were close advisors to Sultan Qaboos. After his return, Omar Al-Zawawi acquired controlling interest in more than a dozen trading companies and small businesses. He also became a director of the newly created Mina Qaboos Port Authority and the new Seeb International Airport outside of Muscat.

Qaboos also brought into government men from two other prominent business families. One, Muhammed Zubair, a successful and imaginative businessman who had known Qaboos since childhood days in Dhofar, was made minister of industry and commerce in November 1974. In addition to his vast business enterprises, he was chairman of Oman's Chamber of Commerce and served on several bank boards. While minister, he also served on the Development Council and the Supreme Petroleum Council.

Another recruit into the government was Said Ahmed Said Al-Shanfari, also from Dhofar. In 1975 he was appointed minister of agriculture, fisheries, petroleum and minerals. (The ministry was later divided, with the agriculture and fisheries portfolios spun off to a separate office.) The Al-Shanfaris were members of a large and predominant tribe in Dhofar. They were related to Sultan Qaboos's mother and by marriage to Mohammed Zubair. The appointment of Al-Shanfari was essentially a political recognition of the established close association the family had with Sultan Qaboos in Dhofar.

Seeing no future in Oman under the old sultan, the young Said Al-Shanfari had left and eventually ended up in Saudi Arabia. With help from relatives there, he obtained a Saudi passport and went to work for

Aramco at the refinery in Ras Tanura and then on to Dhahran. While there, Aramco paid for him to attend school four hours a day, grooming him for a better position, but Al-Shanfari decided to return to Dhofar. When Sultan Said was ousted, Al-Shanfari was running a contracting business in Salalah. He had virtually no qualifications in petroleum affairs, other than the brief stint with Aramco, but over the years he gained an adequate mastery of oil and gas affairs and became known as a very shrewd and tough negotiator on oil sales.

Prior to the establishment of the petroleum ministry in 1975, all oil matters were handled by Salem Makki, whose title was director of minerals and petroleum. After Al-Shanfari took over oil affairs, Makki went to study for an MBA at Harvard Business School. He returned to Oman in 1976 and was assigned to the foreign ministry's Office of Economic Affairs.

Yousuf bin Alawi bin Abdullah, part of the opposition to the old sultan, had at a very young age joined the Dhofar Liberation Front (DLF), which at the time was associated with the Arab nationalism of Egyptian leader Gamal Abdel Nasser. However, members of the DLF were not really Nasserists; they were Dhofari tribesmen who wanted to overthrow Sultan Said. Bin Alawi left the DLF after the 1967 Arab-Israeli War. When he returned to Oman, he was made part of the new government and would spend his entire career in international affairs.

Another Dhofari who would figure prominently in the sultan's new government was Abdul Hafidh Rajab. He would become the first minister of communications. Rajab was from that group of young, bright Omanis who left Oman under the rule of the sultan's father to go abroad to seek an education. He managed to get his primary and secondary certificates in Kuwait, worked a year for the Getty Oil Company in the Kuwait Neutral Zone and then joined the Arab League unit that was being assembled to fight on behalf of the imamate opposing Sultan Said's rule in interior Oman. His joining was contingent on the knowledge that volunteers with a secondary school certificate would be given a university scholarship upon completion of their tour of duty. However, the only scholarship available when Rajab completed his tour was for study at the University of Kiev in the Soviet Union. Four years later, fluent in Russian, he graduated as an automotive engineer.

There were many other Omani officials beginning important careers in the government, but in the early days, those named above were the key individuals who would be in direct contact with the American advisors.

Without question, the Omani who wielded the most influence in matters related to Oman's development was Qais Al-Zawawi. By extension, his brother Dr. Omar Al-Zawawi, while not officially in the government at the time, became extremely powerful in influencing the sultan. By then, the inner circle of Lt. Colonel Tim Landon, Ghassan Shaker, Yehia Omar, Qais Al-Zawawi and Dr. Omar Al-Zawawi made up a formidable team. It goes without saying that those who could not break into that group deeply resented it. But for the next two years, in the field of foreign affairs, they put Oman on the map. It was an amazing performance.

Critchfield, in the early days of Oman's development, was welcomed by this inner circle. While not a member of the inner body, Critchfield was to become one of the group's closest advisors. The bonds formed among them were lasting. But as with any band of brothers, as time went on there were frictions and disagreements about possible courses of action. Eventually, the inner circle faded in importance, but not before it had set Sultan Qaboos on a course for success.

4

OMAN'S QUEST FOR RECOGNITION

The first official trip Sultan Qaboos made abroad was his visit to King Faisal of Saudi Arabia in December 1971. The visit had been carefully planned by Ghassan Shaker, whose Saudi connections were at the highest levels. King Faisal was persuaded that every effort to achieve a rapprochement with Oman should be made. He had reversed his opposition to supporting Oman's entry into the Arab League and voted for it in September 1971. This gave Oman the jump start it needed to build good relations in the region.

When Qaboos arrived in Riyadh, congeniality reigned and formal relations were established. The many disputes that historically existed between the two countries were extremely complicated and not easily solved, but the two rulers agreed to work on the issues dividing them.[1] The most difficult disagreements involved setting the exact borders dividing Saudi Arabia from Oman and from the United Arab Emirates. Demarcation of the borders in the Rub Al-Khali (Empty Quarter) had never been accomplished by either the British, acting on behalf of the Emirates, the Saudis or the Omanis. It looked as though the two governments might be able to agree on their mutual boundaries once and for all.[2] Almost as important, the Saudis were amenable to providing loans to help bolster the depleted Oman treasury.

Relations between Jordan's King Hussein and Sultan Qaboos were very good. They had met more than once since Qaboos assumed the reins of power. Ghassan Shaker was the principal advisor to Qaboos on his relations not only with Saudi Arabia, but also with Jordan and Iran, and traveled with him on official visits. During the latter period of the Dhofar rebellion (1970-1975), military assistance from King Hussein,

[1] Saudi Arabia had actually abstained from voting on Oman's admission to the United Nations earlier in the month. It was the only Arab member to do so.

[2] Negotiations on the Saudi/Oman border issues were stalemated and it was not until 1990 that the two countries completed a border demarcation agreement.

both in manpower and material, combined with the support provided by the Shah of Iran, tilted the military balance that permitted Oman to ultimately settle the conflict in its favor. Forever grateful, Sultan Qaboos maintained warm relations with both monarchs.

Beginning in November 1972, Sultan Qaboos undertook several important diplomatic trips that created links with the so-called "Arab revolutionary" governments of Egypt, Tunisia, Libya and Algeria. He did some important traveling in other parts of the Arab world. The architect and engineer of this process was the Libyan expatriate Yehia Omar.

As part of his effort to establish ties between Qaboos and the Arab "revolutionary" regimes, Omar believed that these governments, particularly that of Egypt, could use their influence with the South Yemeni leaders in Aden to reduce Soviet influence, neutralize the PFLOAG organization, and achieve a political agreement concerning the Dhofar conflict. Qaboos made his first official visit to Egypt in November 1972 and met with President Anwar Sadat. This was followed by a visit to Libya and President Muammer Qadhafi in December 1972. In August 1973, Qaboos visited Tunisia and met with President and Mrs. Habib Bourguiba.

Omar arranged, through Algerian foreign minister Abdelaziz Bouteflika, to have Sultan Qaboos attend the Fourth Conference of Nonaligned Nations held in Algiers September 5-9, 1973. King Faisal's decision to attend this meeting influenced Qaboos's decision to go there. Sultan Qaboos returned to Algiers on November 28th to attend the Arab Summit. The acceptance of Sultan Qaboos in the Arab world was now complete.

In December 1973, Qaboos traveled to Paris, where he met with President Georges Pompidou. This trip coincided with awarding the French state-owned Elf/ERAP (*Entreprise de Recherches et D'Activites Petrolieres*) group an offshore concession for exploration in the Musandam Peninsula area. This gave the French company concessions on both the Iranian and Omani sides of the Hormuz Strait median line. The negotiations with Elf/ERAP had started back in March 1973 when representatives of the French company met with John Townsend in Muscat to apply for the concession off the Musandam Peninsula. Townsend in turn sent them to Tom Hill and Stribling Snodgrass to work out the necessary legal and technical language. Then, Shell

International Petroleum entered the bidding. Negotiations with both Elf and Shell continued throughout the spring of 1973, when Sultan Qaboos asked Robert B. Anderson in New York to broaden the search and invite other companies to bid. Anderson turned this entire process over to Snodgrass and Hill. The sultan indicated he wanted to invite Japanese companies into the bidding, possibly because, in the early 1970s, Japan was a major importer of Omani oil and was paying top prices. There was no significant response from the Japanese concerning the sultan's offer. In the end, the Elf/ERAP group won out and on December 4, 1973, obtained rights to explore an area covering some 2700 square miles.[3]

Sultan Qaboos made his first official trip to Iran in March 1974, although he had visited in October 1971 to attend the 2,500[th] anniversary celebrations of the founding of the Persian Empire by Cyrus the Great. That elaborate affair was held near Persepolis, where the Shah built a magnificent tent city to house his illustrious guests. It was reported to be the largest gathering of monarchs and heads of state in recent memory. Guests included Britain's Prince Philip and Princess Anne, Hollywood celebrities such as Elizabeth Taylor, and even a CIA Middle East station chief and his wife, who later commented to friends that everything served there except the caviar was catered by Maxims of Paris. It was a grand affair. The Shah and Empress Farah were widely criticized for this lavish spending – mainly by those who were not invited to the party.

Shortly after this trip, the sultan instructed his advisors to develop a plan for fixing the boundaries between Oman and Iran to be finalized by a median line treaty, which would once and for all establish the coordinates in the Strait of Hormuz. Both sides were also drafting a mutual assistance treaty. Sultan Qaboos firmly believed that Iran's friendship and support were essential in maintaining security in the Gulf.

Charles Black, advisor on the Oman side, and Ezzedine Kazemi, head of the Iranian Foreign Ministry legal section, met frequently over the next two years to iron out details of an agreement between Oman and Iran on the Hormuz Strait. The final meetings took place in August 1973 at the Geneva Intercontinental Hotel. The Oman team was headed by Sayyid Tariq bin Taimur, the sultan's uncle, and included Oman's ambassador to the UN, Ahmed Makki, and its ambassador to the United

[3] James H. Critchfield, *Oman Papers, 1968-1991*. From the correspondence files of C. Stribling Snodgrass, June 1973.

States, Sayyed Faisal bin Ali Al-Said. The Iranian delegation was led by Ezzedine Kazemi, Mr. Dabiri, first secretary of the Iranian Embassy in Switzerland, and a representative of the National Iranian Oil Company. The agreement was formally initialed at this time.

In March 1974, after Qaboos met for several days in Iran with the Shah and members of his government, a joint communiqué emphasized the two leaders' desire to cooperate fully to maintain stability and security in the region, to insure freedom of navigation and passage through the Hormuz Strait, to exploit marine and sea-bed resources in the neighboring seas and to prevent pollution in the waters bordering their countries. They charged their governments with taking the necessary joint actions for the materialization of these objectives.[4]

It was on this trip that Qais Al-Zawawi, the newly appointed minister of state for foreign affairs, emerged as an important figure. He was the first Omani official other than the sultan to take charge of key matters of state. By July, the median line negotiations were completed, and on July 25, 1974, the "Agreement Concerning Delimitation of the Continental Shelf Between Iran and Oman" was signed in Teheran; on May 28, 1975, it was ratified in Muscat. Qais Al-Zawawi signed on behalf of Oman.[5]

In October 1974, Qaboos went to the Rabat summit conference attended by the leaders of twenty Arab states. In addition to Shaker and Omar, Qais Al-Zawawi and Sayyid Tariq, the sultan's uncle, were part of the Omani delegation. By this time, Qaboos was beginning to be well established in his relations not only with the Arab world, but also with Teheran, London and Paris. His relations with the British were good, despite the well-publicized British withdrawal from the Persian Gulf region in 1971.

The Omanis seemed entirely confident that the British economy drive would not affect any part of the current British presence in Oman. This was the case because they had gone the extra mile to link everything that would seem advantageous to the British in Oman (oil, business contracts, arms sales, jobs for advisors and mercenaries, civil aviation, banking) with a British guarantee to preserve the status quo in its military presence.

[4] Pars News Agency, Teheran, March 7, 1974.
[5] Joseph A. Kechichian, *Oman and The World: The Emergence of an Independent Foreign Policy*, Santa Monica, CA: Rand, 1995

When outside of Oman, the sultan and his advisors were clearly more at home in London than any other place. It was the vacation location of preference for Sultan Qaboos. Yehia Omar had purchased a home in London's exclusive Wilton Crescent area. Ghassan Shaker maintained a residence at the Dorchester Hotel. Lt. Colonel Tim Landon was in London frequently. Soon, Dr. Omar Al-Zawawi could be found at a suite in the Hyde Park Hotel in Knightsbridge. In fact, many of the meetings of substance concerning oil and financial affairs took place in London. Dr. Al-Zawawi had been brought into a quasi-official role backstopping Yehia Omar on the Supreme Petroleum and Natural Gas Council. At that time, the members of the council were Sultan Qaboos, who was the chairman, Yehia Omar, vice chairman, John Townsend, Ghassan Shaker, Qais Al-Zawawi, Dr. Omar Al-Zawawi, Lt. Colonel Tim Landon, Salem Makki, and Tom Hill, the executive secretary.

Relations with the United States were good, but the sultan had not yet visited Washington. He had indicated his wish to establish ties in early 1972, when he sent Ghassan Shaker to meet with U.S. government officials. At that time, Critchfield made sure the State Department had the background on Shaker and his official role as a key advisor to Qaboos. It was to be a very key meeting. Shaker met with Assistant Secretary for Near Eastern Affairs Rodger Davies, who listened with care and seemed pleased to receive an invitation to visit Oman. Davies told Shaker that the United States was sympathetic to the efforts of the sultan to frustrate the insurgency in Dhofar and advised Oman to turn to Saudi Arabia, Jordan and Iran primarily for assistance in defeating the PFLOAG-backed rebels.[6] The sultan took that advice. From the beginning, he followed a dual policy of forging ties with Saudi Arabia, Jordan and Iran – in his view under the aegis of the United States – while keeping his ties to Great Britain in order.

By December 1974, Sultan Qaboos and all of his advisors were in London preparing for his January 9-10 visit to Washington. Jim Critchfield, now retired from the CIA and working to get his fledgling company, Tetra Tech International, off the ground, spent a few days in London during the second week of December and met separately with Shaker, Omar and Landon. He helped them compile a list of Americans

---

[6] Rodger Davies, a distinguished diplomat, went on to be the U.S. Ambassador to Cyprus and on August 19, 1974, was killed by a sniper's bullet during a demonstration at the U.S. Embassy in Nicosia.

who could play a role in Oman or who might be helpful to the sultan's regime. The sultan's equerry, Tim Landon, was in Wellington Hospital recovering from a kidney operation, but he was well enough to participate in all planning sessions. Tom Hill, legal advisor to the sultan, arrived to attend meetings of the "supreme councils" scheduled for December 16-18. The sultan chaired these meetings and, if he had to miss any sessions, no decisions were made without his approval.

Sultan Qaboos also attended to diplomatic duties while in London. He met with Queen Elizabeth II during the week of December 9 and later with a number of lesser British officials. On December 19, he flew to Paris to meet President Giscard d'Estaing. The sultan's advisors believed that Qaboos was becoming tougher, more independent in his judgments and more capable of handling the government.

The efforts of the past two years had put Qaboos firmly into the mainstream of Arab politics. He enjoyed ties to all the North African Arab states, had identified Oman with the King Faisal/Anwar Sadat axis and had adopted a firmly independent but friendly posture toward the small Arab states of the lower Gulf. He was also enthusiastic about the support he was getting from King Hussein of Jordan. Nevertheless, his relationship with the Saudis had not evolved significantly since its beginning in 1971. Moreover, the Saudis were not making any meaningful contribution to the Dhofar War effort, which was just one part of the poor relations between the two. On the other side of the Gulf, the Shah of Iran was being extremely helpful. Iran's response was more than Qaboos expected. Qaboos felt that the Shah's recent visits to the Arab world, including Cairo, and his tilt toward the Arabs and away from Israel would dampen any criticism about his receiving Iranian military aid. It was against this background that Sultan Qaboos went to Washington.

In the United States, there was both diplomatic and business support for this visit. Earlier in the year, Critchfield had arranged for David Rockefeller, Chase Manhattan's president, to visit Oman. Following that trip, Rockefeller told Secretary of State Henry Kissinger that he personally considered Oman and Sultan Qaboos to be important to the United States and urged Kissinger to invite Qaboos for an official visit. That was one more vote for bringing Sultan Qaboos and President Gerald Ford together.

Not yet feeling at ease with the U.S. government, the sultan decided he wanted a quick turnaround visit of two days, with no visits to New

York or elsewhere. He would travel in his own VC-10, which was part of the recent British package of arms and other sales to Oman. The sultan's official party included Minister of State for Foreign Affairs Qais Al-Zawawi, advisors Ghassan Shaker and Yehia Omar, Sayyid Tariq bin Taimur, Lt. Col. Landon, and economic advisor John Townsend. The sultan and his entourage were put up at the Blair House and given first-class treatment.

According to Critchfield's contacts, Sultan Qaboos came to the United States with no serious problems. He was interested mainly in meeting personally with President Ford and other U.S. government officials. His attitude toward the United States was positive and friendly. He was pleased with the way things had developed since he came to power in 1970 and credited the U.S. government with having played a positive though somewhat indirect and restrained role.

From the beginning, Qaboos had wanted to involve the United States in developing a limited Oman naval presence along his own coast and in the Strait of Hormuz. He also assumed that sooner or later the United States would want military aircraft landing privileges on Oman territory, at least as a contingency arrangement, and that his current relationship with Iran would in the long run facilitate some kind of a military tie with the United States. Qaboos was prepared to give the United States some kind of landing rights at Masirah Island and hoped to link this with a supply of TOW missiles, which he had requested but had not yet received, and a limited naval training arrangement.[7] The British presence on Masirah was packaged with the British military role in Dhofar, but the sultan maintained that the British had no exclusivity in their use of Masirah provided others introduced there were compatible. Therefore he was willing and did offer to the United States the use of Masirah Island for limited purposes.

Without any formal agreements, the Omanis indicated they would like to take the first modest steps to establish a naval training facility that would be used for an in-country training program, including American training of a few Omani cadets. They also hoped at some time in the future they would receive the TOW missiles from the United

---

[7] Masirah is Oman's largest island and was the location of the last British Royal Air Force airfield east of Suez. The RAF had been using Masirah as a staging area since the 1930s. According to GlobalSecurity.org, Masirah was named by Alexander the Great's famous admiral Nearchos around 320 AD. The Royal Air Force of Oman is now based there.

States. The sultan's party was distinctly positive about the short visit. Before taking their leave, however, the Omanis insisted on exercising their sovereign role by being the party that would initially inform the British on any issues they had discussed that would require British coordination.

Shortly after the sultan's visit to Washington, Chester Nagle, the sultan's new military advisor, began to arrange for Omanis to get enough education in Oman to have the English and academic skills to qualify for entrance to the U.S. Naval Academy at Annapolis. Nagle drafted a proposal, identified instructors and a location for the school and completed a syllabus outline. Sultan Qaboos signed off on the project. But that was as far as it got. It faded away when the British stepped in and offered to accept Omani naval officers at Dartmouth, the British naval academy. The language and academic standards for this special two-year course were waived. This was a small but valuable lesson for the sultan's military advisor.

5

THE OIL INHERITANCE

Sultan Qaboos could not have been under any illusions when he addressed his people on July 27, 1970, promising them a prosperous life with a bright future. Oman was not a wealthy oil nation. While it had discovered oil in commercial quantities in 1962, it had only been earning revenues from oil exports for three years.

In 1970, Oman's oil production was 300,000 barrels per day (bpd), and annual oil revenues were $129 million. By contrast, its neighbor Saudi Arabia was producing 3.8 million bpd. Also, 1970 was the year that a new balance of economic power between the international oil companies and OPEC was evolving that would gradually alter the structure of the world energy industry. Negotiations that started on the issue of price alone had by 1970 broadened to include "participation," i.e. the question of ownership.[1] Sultan Qaboos had to not only deal with how best to maximize income but also face the question of whether he would, as his neighbors clearly would soon be doing, become part or even sole owner of his oil production base. Even though Oman was not a member of OPEC, it was expected to follow the organization's lead, a stance that would not necessarily be in the best interests of Oman.

In 1970, Petroleum Development Oman (PDO), a limited liability company principally owned by Shell, continued to manage Oman's oil industry. A British expatriate, Philip Aldous, who was secretary of financial affairs in Qaboos's father's regime, represented the Omani government in its dealings with the British- and Dutch-run PDO. He had no backup staff of petroleum economists or engineers to assist him in this job.

On May 6, 1972, shortly after becoming oil advisor, Stribling Snodgrass held a lengthy meeting with Sultan Qaboos about Oman's oil situation. He discussed the participation negotiations underway in the Middle East and outlined what he felt would be in Oman's best interests as it pursued negotiations with PDO. He discussed the need for an independent study of Oman's oil and gas reserves. He emphasized the importance of a comprehensive geologic survey of Oman, not only for oil and gas, but also for minerals and water. He suggested that the U.S. Geologic Survey (USGS), which had worked with the Arabian American Oil Company and the Saudis in producing geologic maps of the Arabian Peninsula, might do the same in Oman.

From the very beginning of his reign, Sultan Qaboos emphasized the importance of educating Omanis and inserting them into key positions in the government. He said that he felt that one of Snodgrass's primary tasks as oil advisor would be to create a competent and effective oil agency, employing Omanis wherever possible, to deal with all aspects of petroleum and mineral policy in Oman.

When Philip Aldous left his position as secretary of financial affairs in 1973, he was not replaced, and Qaboos instead appointed Salem Makki, an Omani, to the newly created position of Director of Petroleum and Mineral Resources. Snodgrass and his associates did what they could to help Makki centralize in his office all records, data, and background information as well as to develop training programs for Omani citizens to work in the petroleum industry. Salem Makki would be the first Omani to visit the United States to see a wide variety of oil facilities. He would spend time with American companies and learn more about international business. The ultimate aim was to develop a national oil policy that primarily served Oman's interests. During the coming year, Snodgrass worked with Makki, Tom Hill, the sultan's legal advisor, and John Townsend, the head of development, to forge ahead on all these issues. The sultan found in "Strib" Snodgrass what he had hoped Robert B. Anderson might have become following his trip to Oman the preceding October. Snodgrass was a man of substance.

Snodgrass was ably assisted in these efforts by a young petroleum economist and Arabic speaker, D. Patrick Maley. Maley has described himself as the fourth generation of a Pennsylvania/Texas oil family so unsuccessful that he had to work for a living. Actually, he became involved in the oil industry not because of his family, but through his interest and study of economics, international politics and Middle East studies, first at Brown University and later at Johns Hopkins University's Paul Nitze School of Advanced International Studies. After that he attended the American University of Cairo. Today Mr. Maley is a London-based management consultant.

It was not long before Maley developed a good working relationship with John Townsend. And when Salem Makki was in the United States, Maley filled in for him at his petroleum and minerals office in Muscat. When Snodgrass was not in Oman, Maley generally served as his eyes and ears.

He, like so many foreign businessmen seeking opportunities in this emerging nation, lived in the Al Falaj Hotel, one of the Omani capital's very few places to stay. The Al Falaj was never dull. Occasionally Maley would note in one of his telexes to Snodgrass that the generator, which supplied power to the Al Falaj Hotel's air conditioning, seemed to be under repair more often than not and that the thermometer was going through the roof. Snodgrass's comment in return was that it was hot in Washington too – and also wet.[2] In further tweaking, Snodgrass in a telex discussing the grand tour being arranged for Makki around U.S. oil facilities, signed off by writing "keep cool". Maley responded saying that a week-long generator failure at the Al Falaj and temperatures passing 100 degrees Fahrenheit made Snodgrass's admonition impossible; he added, as the saying goes, "blood, sweat and tears." But it was all in good humor. Snodgrass respected Maley's work and on more than one occasion took his advice on matters related to the ongoing participation talks and oil-related negotiations with foreign companies.

Participation Negotiations

Snodgrass was well aware that Oman would be expected to follow the lead of the major Gulf producers, particularly Saudi Arabia, once participation negotiations were undertaken. He discussed this with Sultan Qaboos during an audience on May 6, 1972. He pointed out the vast differences between Saudi Arabia's mammoth reserves, which were developed at minimal cost, and Oman's limited but high-cost reserves.

He thought Oman's interests would best be served by an alternative formula, albeit one in keeping with the spirit of the agreements being negotiated by his Arab neighbors with their concessionaire companies.

[2] Average temperatures in Muscat in June and July ranged from 100 to 120 degrees Fahrenheit.

The sultan requested that Snodgrass follow up on these concerns in his negotiations with PDO's managing director Rudi Jaeckli. Jaeckli told Snodgrass in a meeting two days later that PDO was prepared to offer Oman a deal along the lines of the Saudi/Aramco pattern. That was not what Snodgrass wanted to hear, but since neither Saudi Arabia nor anyone else had concluded a participation agreement, there seemed to be time to work things out.

The inevitable happened during the last days of 1972. Saudi Arabia and the other major Gulf producers reached a "General Agreement" with the international oil companies for an initial 25 percent ownership of their oil resources, rising to 51 percent over a period of time. The oil companies, with little other recourse, signed the agreement on December 21 as an alternative to the more drastic possibility of outright nationalization. While many details remained to be settled, this action marked the beginning of a new world "oil" order.

To prepare for Oman's negotiations with PDO, Snodgrass worked out a timetable to determine the advisability of participating in the PDO concessions. First, he obtained a copy of the General Agreement that had been concluded by Saudi Arabia and the Gulf states. Then he asked PDO to submit figures on the "updated book value" of its assets.[3] The British firm of Deloitte & Company was commissioned to do an audit of the PDO books to be completed by March 31, 1973.

Meanwhile, in January 1973, Snodgrass commissioned the Texas firm of DeGolyer and MacNaughton (D&M) to carry out an independent study of Oman's oil and gas reserves. Established in the 1930s by Everette DeGolyer, one of the most eminent geologists of his time, D&M was a leader among the world's petroleum engineering consulting firms. As pointed out by Daniel Yergin in *The Prize*, the firm met the need for independent appraisals of the value of petroleum reserves, sums which provided the basis for financing by banks and other investors.[4]

Snodgrass had known Everette DeGolyer from World War II days, when DeGolyer was the assistant deputy administrator for the Petroleum

[3] This was a basic issue between the Arab governments and the oil companies. They needed to place a value on the worth of an oil company in any given country. It would be the formula by which the sales price of the 25 percent ownership would be calculated. "Updated book value" would include inflation and other factors. See Daniel Yergin, *The Prize*, Simon and Schuster, New York, 1991, p. 584.

[4] Ibid., p. 392.

Administration for War. More important, Snodgrass had been one of a delegation of three who accompanied DeGolyer in 1943 on his mission to the Middle East to examine oil fields in the region. DeGolyer came back from the trip stunned and enthusiastic about the enormity of the region's oil reserves and communicated the importance of Middle East oil to the U.S. government.

While these professional studies of Oman's oil potential were being undertaken, Snodgrass and his associates, John Townsend and Tom Hill, were studying budget and fiscal matters, including available methods for financing the purchase of Oman's oil industry. It was becoming clear to these men that Sultan Qaboos was planning to finance any necessary buyout of foreign companies with foreign sources rather than using Oman's oil revenues. In a letter to John Townsend dated January 30, 1973, the sultan wrote, "We are already in contact with Saudi Arabia on this subject."[5]

Snodgrass advised Sultan Qaboos to keep in mind the following objectives when deciding whether or not to participate in the PDO concessions: (1) to ensure that the revenue coming to the sultanate would be at least as high per barrel of oil as any obtained under the other Gulf states' participation agreements; (2) to provide an immediate and positive cash flow to Oman; (3) to assure that the sultanate could not be accused by the oil companies of leapfrogging[6] or by its Arab neighbors of caving in to the oil companies; (4) to recognize the limitations of Omani manpower and material resources; (5) to link the oil sector to the national economy in such a way as to closely relate it to Oman's overall development requirements; and (6) to foster the growth of industries to eventually replace petroleum, which must be viewed as a dwindling resource.

The team's schedule called for the completion of this work by the end of July, and if the sultan wished to go ahead with participation negotiations, talks with PDO could begin by the end of August. This was a tall order. Sultan Qaboos could not have helped but be impressed with the efforts of his advisors in providing him with the most independent advice upon which he could make an informed decision.

[5] James H. Critchfield, *Oman Papers, 1968-1991*. From the files of C. Stribling Snodgrass.
[6] In all the years of negotiations between the international oil companies and the oil producers, the accusation of "leapfrogging" – i.e., competing with each other to raise prices – was the most explosive.

On March 5, 1973, at the sultan's palace at Seeb (outside of Muscat), Snodgrass, in a private audience, gave Sultan Qaboos a status report on their work. Based on the terms of the General Agreement, preliminary estimates showed that there could be a positive cash flow for Oman over the period 1973-76 if the updated book value was no more than $192 million, making a 25 percent interest worth $48 million.

A week later, PDO managing director Rudi Jaeckli informed Salem Makki that the updated book value, according to their calculations, was $359 million, of which 25 percent would be $90 million, almost double the ceiling used in the Snodgrass analysis. That certainly gave everyone pause. However, negotiations had not yet started; these were simply preliminary discussions.

On his way back to Washington, Snodgrass stopped in Riyadh. He had an audience with King Faisal on March 7 and a meeting with Petroleum Minister Ahmed Zaki Yamani on March 8. Snodgrass was exploring with the Saudi king the merits of pipelining oil from Saudi Arabia's Shaibah field through Oman to a loading port at Mina al-Fahal on the Gulf of Oman, thus bypassing the Hormuz Strait.[7] On the matter of participation, Snodgrass reported that Zaki Yamani took for granted that Oman would follow the lines of the General Agreement.

Deloitte & Company's final report to Sultan Qaboos, dated May 31, 1973, specifically addressed the question of the book value of PDO assets. It prefaced its study with the comment that other Gulf states were still negotiating the implementation of the General Agreement and it was assumed that any agreement signed by the sultan would be on terms as favorable to the sultanate as those granted elsewhere.

As of January 1, 1973, Deloitte & Company calculated that the book value of PDO was $350 million, of which 25 percent was $87 million.[8] That was still way above the Snodgrass estimate of a favorable price for participation. After obtaining the report and discussing it with the team as well as with the sultan, Tom Hill, in a letter to Snodgrass dated June 11, said he was going to meet with

---

[7] This innovative idea was conceived by Snodgrass and embraced by Ghassan Shaker; many years were spent on the proposed project, which was given the name Keyline. This will be dealt with in more detail later in this book.

[8] James H. Critchfield, *Oman Papers, 1968-1991*. Deloitte & Co, *Report on the Calculation of the Consideration for the Acquisition of an Initial Participation Interest Prepared in Accordance with Clause 5 of a Draft General Agreement*. May 31, 1975.

Mr. Milne of Deloitte & Co. in London the following week about possible adjustments in depreciation costs of some assets.

Everyone on the team, Hill, Snodgrass, Townsend, Makki and Maley, agreed that to use this estimate of the updated book value of the PDO properties would be a gross over-valuation of their worth. It would be a lose-lose situation for Oman. Hill thought the team should come up with something other than the formula of the General Agreement. Shell was well aware that other companies were also experiencing difficulties in negotiating their participation agreements. The Oman team would go back to the drawing board. The D&M report on Oman's petroleum reserves was due by June, and it would be an important document in planning for the future.

Patrick Maley hand delivered an advance copy of the D&M effort to Muscat in May. It was a blockbuster report indicating Oman was in trouble. Geologic conditions – specifically, impermeable layers in some of the fields – revealed that recoverable oil and natural gas reserves would be far less than previously predicted, and this meant greater declines in production than previously forecast.

Salem Makki received the D&M final report on June 1, 1973. It gave estimates of the remaining reserves of crude oil and natural gas in the four producing fields in Oman. The report noted that all the information that went into the analysis came entirely from PDO; independent field examinations of the producing oil fields had not been made, implying that might be a practical next step. The report concluded that production in these fields had peaked in October 1969 at 371,245 bpd and had declined rather steadily to 280,506 bpd by December 1972. Further decline was to be expected. Estimated total reserves were 558 million barrels.[9] The report went into some detail about how available technical methods could be used to enhance oil recovery in these fields. That would be the only way to add to reserves.

Almost before the ink was dry on the D&M report, PDO was disputing the results. The two differed not only on reserve estimates but on the efficiency of water injection in the recovery process and the geologic nature of the producing fields. As Snodgrass pointed out to his colleagues, these differences only illustrated the scientific imponderables

[9] Ibid., *Report on the Oil and Gas Reserves of the Al Huwaisah, Fahud, Natih and Yibal Fields, Sultanate of Oman as of January 1, 1973,* DeGolyer and MacNaughton, Dallas, Texas, dated June 1, 1973.

of oil exploration and production. During most of July and August, meetings were held in Oman and The Hague to go over the figures. On August 22, 1973, D&M submitted a revised estimate of total reserves based on new information obtained from PDO. According to the new estimate, as of January 1, 1973, there were 1,160 million barrels, about double the original estimate.[10] This estimate was still below the PDO estimate of total reserves of 1,382 million barrels.

Salem Makki and Snodgrass asked D&M to do some additional work for the ministry regarding cash flow projections on the four fields currently in production. They were still struggling with the cost of participation and in reality saw no way the sultanate could finance an acquisition out of current revenues. Instead, it would have to finance a buyout.

The next thing Snodgrass knew, Tom Hill was on his way to Dallas unbeknownst to any of the other team members. As stated earlier, Tom Hill was prone to giving very broad interpretations to his duties as legal advisor to Sultan Qaboos. Without clearing his actions with either Snodgrass or Salem Makki, Hill flew to Dallas on July 19 and met with D&M's senior vice president J. W. Watson. Watson gave Hill a copy of their draft report on income projections, which was broken down into five case scenarios. On the spot, Hill cited three of the cases as unworkable and asked the company to concentrate on only two of them. Later that day, Watson wrote a letter to Snodgrass stating that he intended to present all five cases so that Snodgrass and Makki could review them.

When Hill phoned Snodgrass the next day to tell him he had been to Dallas, Snodgrass broke in with these words, "Tom, you told me some time back regarding Charles Black, 'I don't tell Charles about catfish, and he is not telling me about legislation.'" Hill was referring to his opposition to Black's involvement in the Iran/Oman median line negotiations. Snodgrass continued, "This applies equally to our relationship. You keep out of my business and I will keep out of yours. I am fed up with you horsing around, and just why you are doing it I certainly don't know. What you should know is I am fed up and this is all I have to say just now. Goodbye."[11] It is not known whether Hill was chastened by this.

---

[10] Ibid., letter from D&M to Snodgrass containing the revisions and commentary. D&M asked that the previous report be destroyed so as to not confuse the issue. A file copy of this report can be found in the Critchfield Papers.

While tempers began to resemble the summer heat, the group awaited the final report from D&M. It also reviewed plans for participation negotiations with PDO. John Townsend said Sultan Qaboos told him during his latest audience that there was no hurry to arrive at a final solution. Qaboos was unwilling to rush into an agreement that could be overtaken by events when an arrangement more favorable to the sultanate could possibly be obtained by waiting. Qaboos was preparing for a summer vacation and wanted only to deal with the most important matters of state.

The DeGolyer and MacNaughton report, containing all five case studies, was delivered to Snodgrass in Washington in late July. Interestingly, it showed that "nonparticipation" would result in less revenue to the sultanate than either a 25 percent or 51 percent participation. But because of the high costs connected with a buyout, as currently reflected in the PDO updated book value, using revenues to finance it would be too costly. Also, because of the high rate of production decline as outlined in its previous analysis and the possibility of additional future production costs, D&M believed that an alternative solution for Oman would be to obtain its revenue solely from royalty and taxes.[12] That being said, over the summer the advisors began to recognize that some sort of renegotiation of the present concession agreement with PDO was called for. They continued to feel that the General Agreement was not the proper formula for Oman. Indeed, the other Gulf producers, as well as Iran, Iraq and other OPEC producers, were not following the Saudi formula but were instead developing plans that suited their specific circumstances.

Snodgrass asked D&M to recalculate its five cases assuming that participation would be financed by a non-interest bearing loan rather than revenues from oil production. The final version of D&M's report, sent to Salem Makki on August 31, 1973, did not include the earlier comments against participation. In fact, there was no recommendation in the report; the final figures, however, leaned toward 51 percent participation.[13]

Yet another meeting to discuss participation was scheduled with Sultan Qaboos for September 19, 1973. Tom Hill and Strib Snodgrass

[11] Ibid., Snodgrass memorandum dated July 20, 1973.
[12] Ibid. The analysis was contained in a letter sent to Snodgrass on July 16, 1973.
[13] Ibid.

flew to Muscat on September 16; John Townsend, Salem Makki, and a new participant in the team, Yusuf Nimatallah, were already there. Nimatallah, a Saudi citizen, had been in Oman since June. A well-educated and intelligent young man of 36 – though somewhat arrogant, according to Snodgrass – he was sent to Oman by top-level Saudi officials to help evaluate development projects and coordinate certain aspects of Saudi-Oman cooperation. He worked out of the Oman General Development Organization. Patrick Maley, who had come to know Nimatallah well since his arrival in Oman, had the impression that those who made policy in Saudi Arabia were in favor of providing financing if it were shown to be in the best interests of Oman.

The group of advisors prepared a formal letter to Sultan Qaboos on September 10, 1973, recommending that Oman adopt the principle of participation. The letter, addressed to "His Majesty Sultan Qaboos bin Said, The Palace, Muscat," read in part:

> Re: Participation by the Sultanate of Oman in the Agreement, as amended, dated March 7, 1967, between the Sultanate of Oman and the Petroleum Development Oman Ltd. . . .
>
> . . . At the direction of Your Majesty, the undersigned have considered the economic advisability of the Sultan of Oman electing to adopt the policy of participation with respect to the above agreement as generally expressed in the so-called General Agreement between certain of the Arab Gulf states and the oil companies operating in such countries. It is our recommendation the Sultan of Oman adopt the policy of participation subject to the comments, which follow.
>
> In reaching the above conclusion the undersigned have reviewed those participation agreements already concluded as well as those currently being negotiated by the Arab Gulf countries. In addition to detailed economic studies by various of the undersigned, reference has been made to various geological, engineering and economic reports rendered by, among others, DeGolyer and MacNaughton, petroleum engineers of Dallas, Texas and Deloitte and Company, chartered accountants of London. At Your Majesty's direction, inquiry had been made of the brother Arab states with respect to the

availability of funds for a term of between four and ten years without interest for the purpose of financing the purchase by the sultanate of its participation interest. The response has been favorable. The recommendation made above is based upon the above analysis and is subject to conclusion of the financing arrangements to which reference has been made as well as the conclusion of negotiations with Petroleum Development Oman Ltd., which may modify certain of the provisions of the so-called General Agreement.

The undersigned respectfully suggest that, if Your Majesty adopts the recommendation herein, the following program be approved:

1) Simultaneously

a) take immediate steps to finalize the above described financial arrangements.

b) notify PDO of Your Majesty's intention to adopt the principle of participation.

c) consider and make recommendations of the organization and infrastructure problems inherent in participation.

2) Schedule and conduct definitive discussions with PDO which discussions will include reference to the unusual cost and other factors applicable to the properties subject to the above agreement.

3) Report to Your Majesty on the outcome of the above discussions.

4) Implement Your Majesty's decisions.

The undersigned respectfully submit the foregoing for Your Majesty's approval.

Director of Petroleum and Minerals Salem Makki
Petroleum Advisor to the Government Stribling Snodgrass
Economic Advisor to the Government John Townsend
Economic Advisor to the General Development
Organization Yusuf Nimatallah
Legal Advisor to the Government Tom Hill[14]

In Snodgrass's notes of the meeting with Sultan Qaboos, he said

[14] Ibid., from the files of C. Stribling Snodgrass.

that Yusuf Nimatallah, Salem Makki and probably Ahmed Makki (Salem's brother, who was the Omani ambassador to the UN) would go to Riyadh as soon as possible to negotiate an $80 million loan from the Saudis. The sultan would also deliver a message to PDO regarding his decision on participation, proposing that discussions begin in early November in London. The sultan also ordered Tom Hill to draw up a plan to establish an Omani national oil company. Snodgrass's final comment was that as far as he could tell, the sultan had already made up his mind on all these points before their meeting.[15] There is no hard evidence to support this, but one supposes that the sultan's advisor on oil and gas matters, Yehia Omar, and his other advisors in London had weighed in on all of this.

After a gathering of concerned parties in London that included representatives of the Oman government, PDO, Shell Petroleum Company, Ltd., and the two minor owners Campagnie Francaise des Petroles and Partex (Oman) Corporation, a Memorandum of Understanding was issued on November 9, 1973, affirming the government's intention to participate in the oil concessions and the crude oil production and exploration operation of the PDO effective January 1, 1974. On that day, Oman would become a part owner of its own oil business.

Elsewhere in the Arab world, several developments were significantly altering the playing field. The policies of Egypt's Anwar Sadat and Saudi Arabia's King Faisal had become the mainstream of Arab politics, replacing the revolutionary socialism of Gamal Abdel Nasser. The Arabs, through systematic cultivation of the nonaligned nations, dramatically expanded their influence in the Third World. They reached an accommodation with Europe and Japan, with France leading Europe in a new pro-Arab policy. France, with at least tacit approval from the other European nations, offered European arms to the Arabs as an alternative to Soviet arms. Soviet power in the Middle East had begun to wane.

By 1970, the United States had acquiesced and tolerated French Mirage aircraft going to Libya for Egyptian end use and, a year or so later, for Libyan leader Muammer Qadhafi buying U.S.-licensed arms from Italy. By the spring of 1973, the Arabs felt sufficiently confident of this apparent shift in Western attitudes to engineer Arab League military maneuvers in Egypt, which principally used European-

[15] Ibid., handwritten aide memoire from the files of C. Stribling Snodgrass.

manufactured military aircraft. When Europe and the U.S. did not react, the Saudis upped the ante by sending C130s to Egypt during the maneuvers. The U.S. did no more than register mild disapproval. Bolstered by this attitude, King Faisal and President Sadat went to Paris in the early summer of 1973 and ordered more French military aircraft, this time openly as a Saudi purchase for Egyptian Air Force end use. For the first time, King Faisal had achieved recognition as a leader in the Arab world and a power in the Third World.

There were two major events that shook the Middle East at this time. First, Anwar Sadat launched the Yom Kippur War against Israel on October 6, 1973. Second, on October 16, 1973, Saudi petroleum minister Ahmed Zaki Yamani, speaking for the Arab Gulf states and Iran, raised the price of oil by 70 percent to $5.11 a barrel. Oman had no role in either of these happenings, and while the October war hardly impacted Oman, the action by Yamani and friends would prove to be a great financial windfall.

The Yom Kippur War's connection to the world of oil was not military, but rather political and economic. It stimulated an Arab oil embargo. On October 17, 1973, the Arab members of OPEC announced that as a result of the Yom Kipper War, they would no longer ship oil to nations that supported Israel, targeting in particular the United States and the Netherlands They also announced a five percent cut in oil production, with additional cuts to come as required.

By a coincidence of history, three years of OPEC negotiations with the oil companies were at the same time reaching a critical stage. The Yom Kippur War had not followed the pattern of the 1967 war, which had produced a quick Israeli victory. It was taking longer. Now the United States was faced with a major and much-publicized re-supply operation to Israel. Only a day or so after Yamani's historic announcement of the oil price rise, the United States publicly announced a multi-billion–dollar arms package for Israel. The oil embargo was probably the minimum action that King Faisal could have taken at the time without losing the position he and Anwar Sadat had carved out among the Arab and Third World nations.

Of course, everyone over a certain age in the United States remembers the 1973 "energy crisis" and the long lines at gas stations. For every informed observer of this surprising turn of events, there was a theory on what caused it. American tempers were raging. The blame game was in high gear. James Critchfield had his own view of the energy crisis of 1973. He considered the Arab oil embargo to be a half-hearted affair from the outset. The execution of it was turned over entirely to the international oil companies, who pursued a pragmatic and effective burden-sharing plan.

Post-embargo studies revealed that the actual oil shortage in the United States was by no means as severe as judged by the public queuing up at gas stations; gasoline stockpiling in the United States actually increased in the six months after the Arab oil embargo decision. The alarms sounded the country into a much needed total national effort to prepare itself for the real energy crisis that lay ahead. The exaggerated treatment of the embargo psychologically added to the atmosphere in which the combined forces of inflation and recession were already making serious inroads on the Western economies and placed further strain on U.S. relations with the Arabs and the Third World, where an alliance was clearly forming.[16]

This was the world Oman found itself in as it became part owner of PDO, initially acquiring 25 percent participation, a figure that would increase to 60 percent by the end of 1974. What did this mean for Oman? With the ownership question behind them, Omanis could look forward to riches beyond their wildest imaginations. In a year's time, oil revenues would more than quadruple to over $800 million and, not long after that, to over $1 billion.

In three short years, Sultan Qaboos could make good his promise to his people "to transform your life into a prosperous one with a bright future."[17] It was like winning the lottery without buying a ticket.

Oil Concessions

A serious reality of the oil business is that oil exploration needs to be going on all the time. Fields currently under production have their limits. New fields have to be discovered, or else one day you find yourself out of business. Another reality for Oman was that exploration was not a government operation. Private enterprise has to come in with sufficient

[16] Ibid. *The US International Energy Policies and the Middle East – May 1975*, by James H. Critchfield, President, Tetra Tech International, Rosslyn, Virginia.

[17] Oman Ministry of Information, Statement by His Majesty Sultan Qaboos bin Said al Said, July 27, 1970.

funds to invest, and companies are not willing to do this without specific ground rules. In short, this was a fiercely competitive business on both sides of the bargaining table.

Negotiations for awarding concessions to foreign oil companies were held concurrently with the planning for participation. On May 11, 1972, Sultan Qaboos sent a letter to the director of USGS. He noted the comprehensive program undertaken in Saudi Arabia, and said that the sultanate of Oman urgently required coverage of Oman, particularly in relation to water, oil and mineral resources. He hoped that USGS expert Dr. Glen Brown could visit Oman and consult on this matter. Dr. Brown had been intimately concerned with the geology of the Arabian Peninsula since 1943 when he was posted to Saudi Arabia as a respected water geologist. He was the perfect man for the job. He visited Oman in June 1972 and met with the sultan.

During the summer, USGS worked on a program proposal to study the mineral, oil and water resources incorporating satellite imagery. The proposal went to John Townsend, who responded that the Oman government had quite recently had an attractive no-cost proposal to do the same work from another government, as well as low-cost offers from commercial firms. So the USGS proposal was turned down. USGS went back with a revised cost estimate and, in May 1973, a proposal to send a two-man USGS team was accepted. Satellite imagery would be used to illustrate the team's report.

Two USGS geologists went to Oman in November 1973 and carried out a most successful survey. They established good working relations with PDO. In fact, Rudi Jaeckli wrote to Snodgrass that the exercise was a very happy one, and that Robert Coleman was one of the most gifted field geologists he had ever met Although Jaeckli was in favor of keeping the USGS activity going, the government was not willing at that time to commit more funds.

In early 1973, USGS, at no cost to the Oman government, produced a map of petroleum concessions and oil fields of Oman and adjacent countries. This map proved very useful in dealing with international oil companies interested in acquiring new concessions. The first new concession in Oman was awarded on February 4, 1973, to a consortium led by the Sun Oil Company. This embraced an offshore area near Masirah Island that had previously been granted to and subsequently withdrawn from Wendell Phillips. The second concession was offshore of the

Musandam Peninsula, just across the Strait of Hormuz from Iran, and was awarded to the French Elf/ERAP group, which also held the concession on the Iranian side of the Strait.[18] The major difference between the Shell and Elf bid was the $1.5 million signature bonus that the French included; a Shell offer of $500,000 for the concession had been rejected out of hand.

However, PDO, Shell's operating company, remained the major concessionaire in Oman. The PDO concession totaled 50,000 square miles in north and central Oman.[19] Its concession was originally an income tax-royalty agreement, which was first granted by Sultan Said bin Taimur in 1937 and renewed by him on March 7, 1967. Under this agreement, the company was obliged to pay a royalty of 12.5 percent of the posted price plus 50 percent of the net profit after deducting operating expenses. The posted price is the official, as opposed to the market, price. Royalties are always computed using the posted price.

On June 18, 1969, PDO signed a supplemental agreement with the former sultan, adding the territory of the southern province of Dhofar to its concession. Several companies had actively explored for oil in Dhofar, beginning with Cities Service in 1953.

In the 1960s, John Mecom, who had acquired Cities Service, made another effort in conjunction with Pure Oil and Continental. That acreage was relinquished in 1969 after several years of unsuccessful exploration. In 1970, PDO acquired the exploration rights for all of Dhofar, but by the end of 1973, PDO reduced its Dhofar concessions to one area containing the heavy oil fields of Marmul and Amal. The area was about 25 miles from the coast at an elevation of 1,000 feet. Pipeline transportation to the coast was feasible and would be inexpensive. Proven reserves were large, but suitable production techniques had not been explored, nor was there a market for heavy oil at that time.

From 1967 through 1972, PDO exploration efforts had drilled 958 wells, of which 589 were dry and 369 were producing oil. On December 4, 1973, Sultan Qaboos and Rudi Jaeckli, representing PDO, renewed the 1967 agreement and listed in detail the areas on the mainland and offshore held by PDO for exploration and exploitation, as well as those relinquished back to the government and available for interested companies.

[18] Ibid., from the files of C. Stribling Snodgrass.
[19] Ibid. Ministry of Petroleum and Minerals, *Summary of Petroleum Exploration and Producing Agreements,* January 1, 1982.

Oil companies did not clamor at Oman's door for concession rights. The smaller companies were not interested in paying signature bonuses. Others were interested in the areas that had already been awarded. It may well be that the sultan missed an opportunity to attract the smaller companies, or perhaps it is better said that the sultan's advisors missed the opportunity.

The president of one small petroleum company from Dallas, Texas, who wanted a concession in Oman, described his frustration at not being able to compete with the giants. He first approached the Oman government in August 1973 in a letter to Salem Makki expressing an interest in securing a concession. In October, he wrote to Snodgrass, amplifying on his interest. He said he thought the sultan should get some acreage back from Shell to encourage other companies to come in, thereby creating competition, lowering drilling costs and consequently finding a lot of new oil. In his words,

> The world desperately needs oil and it is not a question of the reserves being there, but lack of enlightened leadership in the governments that do not know how to entice companies to come in. You are in a position to create more reserves for the world if the sultan can be convinced that competition is another key factor. But if Oman insists on bonuses they will only get a few companies to go along.
>
> I am really talking about the American independent oil producer, who discovered more oil and gas than did the major companies in America and they are still discovering seventy percent of the oil and gas being found today. These are the people we must entice to go overseas. The only way you can do this is to create a climate of confidence, trustworthiness and fair play. The real problem is these underdeveloped countries let greed get in the way of sound judgment. Many of these countries are quite short sighted and may I say penny wise and pound foolish. By seeking these large bonuses, they are simply driving away 95 percent of the oil companies. It is obvious, as the British found out in the North Sea, it is better to have twenty companies looking for oil than to charge a $2 million bonus and have two companies. I feel quite certain that if the British had asked for a bonus on every tract, there would not

be one oil field out there in the water today. It would seem to me that if you could get 10-20 million acres released (Shell had the country long enough) and split them up in say 50,000 to 200,000 acre tracts, and try and get several dozen companies to come in, that it would not be unreasonable to have over a million barrels per day within ten years. Competition is the key to the success in finding oil in quantities. I would much rather work where there are other companies, than by myself.[20]

As it turned out, between 1975 and 1982, several large oil companies were awarded onshore concessions; the signature bonuses got larger as the years went on. For example, in 1981 a Japanese group paid a signature bonus of $7 million for an onshore concession.[21]

Financial Crisis

In 1974, oil revenues for the sultanate of Oman went from about $200 million to well over $800 million. OPEC's hard-line stance by the end of 1974 brought the oil price to over $10 per barrel. In Oman, the windfall set in motion a massive increase in spending. Most of the new money appeared to go into military expenditures, but it went elsewhere as well – eventually creating a financial crisis of some proportions.

When the sultan returned to Oman from his visit to European capitals and the United States in January 1975, he was greeted with the news that Oman had an immediate financial crisis involving a current deficit of more than $200 million. Not good news. The British Bank of the Middle East (BBME), Oman's principal banker, calculated that government borrowings, which were being serviced not only by BBME but by other banks and governments, had escalated significantly in the last six months of 1974. While much of this deficit did not have to be

---

[20] The president of this small company, who will remain unnamed, bid on three tracts in June 1974, but no contract resulted. Correspondence from the files of C. Stribling Snodgrass.

[21] Ministry of Petroleum and Minerals, *Summary of Petroleum Exploration and Producing Agreements*, January 1, 1982.

[22] John Townsend, *Oman: The Making of the Modern State*, London: Croom Helm Ltd., 1977, p. 148.

repaid immediately, BBME held a short-term note of $100 million due in 1975. Other banks had similar short-term notes.

This should not have come as a surprise. Back in the summer of 1974, John Townsend warned Sultan Qaboos he must begin to curtail spending.[22] At the time, Qaboos issued a decree ordering that no further capital projects would be undertaken before January 1976, with the exception of those already in process. Unfortunately, this decree was essentially ignored. Oman and its oil-rich neighbors were engaged in a spending frenzy, and. this rush to spend "petrodollars" was beginning to destabilize world commerce.

It is not difficult to explain what happened. When oil revenues more than quadrupled in 1974, Sultan Qaboos, anxious to see a successful outcome to the Dhofar War, committed almost half his revenue to military expenditures. The remaining funds were chipped away by one development project after another, many of which were not put up for open bid. Most of the projects were for building the infrastructure Oman so badly needed. The cash drawdown that created this crisis occurred between November 1974 and January 1975. It totaled $377 million.

Advisors to Sultan Qaboos leaped into action. Morgan Grenfell and Company. Ltd., Hambros Bank Ltd. and BBME, all of whom had made loans to Oman, were asked to send a team to examine the financial situation. On February 3, 1975, the Supreme Financial Council gave Morgan Grenfell a broad mandate to lead this effort. The team studied budgets, institutional organization, financial controls, major current contracts and cash shortfalls. They met with most of the top officials of government, the expatriate advisors, officials of PDO and Shell, and the British-run defense department. The dynamics of this team's work took an interesting turn. Morgan Grenfell had, through Tom Hill, been in touch with Chase Manhattan Bank and had shared with Chase its recommendations for coping with the crisis prior to presenting it to Sultan Qaboos. Clearly they were looking for alternative sources of lending.

The Morgan Grenfell report, even after all these years, stands out as a major contribution to putting into perspective what was going on in Oman. It was a wake-up call, not only for the sultan but for all of his advisors. While the report warned that immediate action was needed to alleviate the cash crisis, the short-term problems were mostly solved before the final report was issued. BBME made loan advances to cover Oman's cash shortfalls, and Saudi Arabia came forward with a $100 million grant, $100 million in project loans and a $50 million write-off of a previous Omani debt That went a long way in solving Sultan Qaboos's crisis.

What was important about the Morgan Grenfell report was the frankness with which it portrayed the way the nation was going about its business. The report showed that the economy of the sultanate was intrinsically sound and viable, but that the institutional government structure did not have enough trained personnel to cope with the rapid growth in the economy resulting from the substantial increases in revenues. Government gold and foreign exchange reserves were down 42 percent from those held in 1971. The report estimated that current government reserves could cover only one month's imports; the norm was six months. Because of increased spending in 1974 and early 1975, borrowings had increased dramatically: from $32 million at the beginning of 1974, to $274 million in December. Since most loans were short or medium term in nature, they precipitated this crisis.[23]

The report noted that there were no official budgets or forecasts for 1976 onward, implying the lack of any long-term planning. A thorough study of the 1975 budget concluded that if no cuts in military or development expenditures were made, the 1975 deficit could exceed $600 million.

Noting that almost half of the budget was going into military expenditures, the report explicitly pointed out that this had major economic consequences. Funds and manpower were being diverted from projects that would produce an economic return. It was hoped that as the military situation in Dhofar improved, major cuts in military spending could be made. The report recommended, however, that the government immediately cancel the British Aircraft Corporation (BAC) contracts for Jaguar fighter aircraft and Rapier air defense missiles. Over $20 million had already been committed to this project, which was projected to cost $768 million over a nine-year period. Morgan Grenfell pointed out that there was no clause limiting the level of escalation of this figure, so it could grow considerably higher over time. This was as far as Morgan Grenfell could go in influencing the sultan to reconsider

[23] Ibid. The figures cited here and in the subsequent paragraphs were taken from the Morgan Grenfell Report dated March 11, 1975, sent to Spear and Hill by Morgan Grenfell Ltd., London. All figures have been changed from Omani riyals to US dollars at the rate of OR 0.345 to $1.

his high-cost air defense program. Realistically, he could afford to disregard the cost, because both King Hussein of Jordan and the Shah of Iran were making contributions in this area at no cost.

The report offered considerable detail on development projects, although the Morgan Grenfell team had not gained access to all contractual information. Working with what they had, the team saw a need to severely curtail development expenditures and improve fiscal accounting.

The report recommended that all projects, as they were reviewed, be categorized as *Essential, Desirable* or *Non-Essential.* It pointed out specific projects where major cost overruns existed, such as the first desalination plant, which went over budget by $140 million, and the Intercontinental Hotel, which went over by more than $14 million. Another issue involving government spending was road construction. While it was recognized that developing a road system was an integral part of Oman's modernization, contracts frequently were awarded without obtaining competitive offers or when the availability of necessary financing was uncertain. Cost overruns were still occurring even as this report was being drafted. (It is true that overruns are not unique to Oman. For example, any American can point to the "Big Dig" in Boston that took 13 years to complete and cost $10 billion more than its original estimate of $4 billion.)

In its final section, the Morgan Grenfell report recommended that the Supreme Financial Council be expanded to include more members who were resident in Oman and a thorough review of all development contracts. Other recommendations included retention of a leading firm of consulting engineers to provide advice; review of all defense expenditures, particularly those related to the air defense system; appointment of a leading firm of international accountants as permanent advisors to the government; and notification of all government ministers regarding the country's serious financial problems and the need for them to be personally responsible and accountable.

When the report and these recommendations were put before Sultan Qaboos on March 17, 1975, he wasted no time in responding. Attending the meeting in Salalah were Deputy Chairman of the Supreme Finance Council Qais Al-Zawawi, Equerry Col. Timothy Landon, Secretary-General of the National Development Council Sharif Loutfi, Leon Spolianski, a representative of Spear and Hill, Morgan Grenfell team leaders Christopher Reeves and David Douglas-Home, Hambros Bank Ltd. officer Rupert Travis, and British Bank of the Middle East officer Gordon Calver.

Sultan Qaboos reviewed the report and agreed that there should a reduction in the development program in 1975, *but* that no contracts would be cancelled until all had been reviewed. He stated that no new contracts would be awarded in 1975 and 1976, *except* possibly those related to natural gas and mining. There would be no defense budget cuts for 1975, *but* it was conceivable for 1976. He noted, however, that as successful military advances were made, monies could be transferred to civilian pacification projects. He did not want to eliminate the air defense program provided by BAC, *but* he would consider revising the related infrastructure projects and obtaining new credit terms. He *disagreed* with the recommendation that the Supreme Development Council retain a consulting engineering firm, stating that they could retain the engineers they thought necessary whenever they needed professional advice. (It is interesting to note that the sultan was doing just that with Tetra Tech Inc.) After some discussion, he did see merit in retaining a firm of international accountants, although his initial instinct had been to hire individual accountants on an as-needed basis.

The BBME member advised Sultan Qaboos that the bank would be prepared to roll over part of its advance that was coming due in April. The Morgan Grenfell team leader Mr. Reeves discussed the realities of the current market and advised that $200 million was probably the maximum that could be raised at this time. Sultan Qaboos thanked the bankers and stated he was fully aware of the steps the government would have to take to reduce the amount of outside financing.

There was nothing more the Morgan Grenfell team could do in Oman. It had laid out its case. It had used some carrot-and-stick tactics. But the sultan always had the option of going to other sources for financing in the United States and Europe; he didn't have to go British. While Sultan Qaboos may have been sobered by Morgan Grenfell's findings, it was clear he was not going to stop in his tracks. He would continue the war in Dhofar, which was very close to being won, and he would move on, perhaps more carefully, with Oman's modernization.

This whole episode points out an interesting dichotomy in the manner in which Sultan Qaboos ran his country. While the Morgan

Grenfell team was poring over contracts and statistics in Oman and meeting all officials willing to be interviewed, it is clear that Qaboos was working over the problem independently. He was consulting with his trusted inner circle and in the end came to his own conclusion on how to get out of the financial box he was in. It would be done his way.

There were other forces at play here that the sultan clearly recognized. Back in February, Sultan Qaboos and Qais Al-Zawawi learned that the British Ambassador to Oman, Mr. D. F. Hawley, had invited some local British expatriates to his farewell gathering – Hawley was completing his tour of duty in Oman – at the British Embassy in Muscat. Present were PDO manager Rudi Jaeckli, Brigadier Semple, the key figure in military purchases by the sultanate, John Townsend and the BBME head in Oman. Reports trickled back about their critical remarks directed primarily at the Omanis; specifically, that the sultan and his ministers were not up to the tasks ahead of them. Next in line for British criticism were the foreign Arab advisors. And beyond these were the other foreign influences – American, German, French, Iranian and Jordanian – that were diluting the British position.

Ambassador Hawley recommended to this group that the task of the Morgan Grenfell team be upgraded from conducting a fact-finding mission to undertaking a more basic examination of Oman's credit and the degree of control exercised by the British banks, particularly BBME, which had historically exercised considerable influence over Oman's finances.

This was a wonderfully classic British end run that did not work. Some of the sultan's advisors saw this as a move by the British to recover influence over the affairs of the sultanate that they had lost during the past few years. They even suggested that the current British moves represented an effort to precipitate a crisis. The sultan's advisors took the position that he should not be pressured into an arrangement that would give the three British banks the opportunity to reestablish British domination of the sultan's budget and expenditures. At a minimum, they wanted him to introduce official banking relationships with American, German, French or Arab banks. They felt that over time the Oman government would gradually improve its performance in budgeting and programming. In that respect the current crisis could have the beneficial effect of stimulating reform.

The British were, for obvious reasons, giving very high priority to anything that reinforced the British position in the oil-rich Middle East.

Oman was the last almost exclusively British stronghold in the Arabian Gulf since its withdrawal from the region in 1971. The move by Sultan Qaboos to introduce other influences into Oman had been deeply resented and resisted by the British.

British and American relationships in the Middle East had always existed in a state of both cooperation and competition, U.S. presence over the years had never measured up to that of the British. Except for Saudi Arabia, the British had been the predominant presence in the region. The truth is that Americans and Britons usually followed a path that is rather similar to that of siblings. They scrap and fight to attain an advantage, but when they are both threatened, they walk arm in arm. The situation in Oman was one of scrap and fight. It was never open warfare, but a very subtle competition they both engaged in, each hoping to win the advantage over the other. But as history has repeatedly shown, when the going gets tough, the British and Americans are blood brothers. Witness Iraq after 9/11/2001.

All the Omani insiders began to recognize that as revenues and expenditures increased, the need for a system of checks and balances was apparent. What would emerge was a kind of "Office of Management and Budget" approach in which decisions of any magnitude would be approved by the appropriate minister, the financial official controlling the budget and, finally, the sultan himself as the principal executive of the nation.

John Townsend's position as economic advisor to Sultan Qaboos came to an end during the summer of 1975. Some have said that he was a victim of the changes that came from the financial crisis and the subsequent examination by Morgan Grenfell. But Townsend's departure was more a matter of timing. Sultan Qaboos saw this as an opportunity to spread the responsibilities of government more broadly, and he transferred many of the central functions of management and planning to the various Omani ministries. Not too long after that, Said Al-Shanfari from Dhofar became minister of the newly created Ministry of Agriculture, Fisheries, Petroleum and Minerals. Future planning for developing Oman's natural resources would now be in his hands.

PART II
OMAN'S CRITICAL DEVELOPMENT BEGINS

Sultan Qaboos took over a country with little infrastructure. And it was a large piece of real estate, over 190,000 square miles. All of it needed attention. The country was divided into three separate and diverse governorates, Muscat, Dhofar and Musandam and five regions, Batinah, Dhahirah, Dakhliyah, Sharqiyah and Wusta. And within these regions were the wilayats or districts, many of them run by local tribal leaders, who although loyal to the sultan also wielded power at the grass roots level.

By 1975 when Tetra Tech International, Inc. arrived in Oman, there were already many development projects underway. The challenges for Tetra Tech would be to advise the government on the development of its oil, gas and water resources and on the development of two remote areas, the Musandam, which commanded the Hormuz Strait, and Dhahirah, where the historic Buraimi Oasis was located.

6

LAUNCHING TETRA TECH

James Critchfield retired from the Central Intelligence Agency in 1974 and was considering what to do with the rest of his life. After a temporary sojourn with the State Department, he went into the private sector and hung out his shingle as a consultant.[1]

One of his early contacts in Washington was Nicholas Boratynski, president of Tetra Tech Inc., an engineering firm based in Pasadena, California. Tetra Tech was the brainchild of Boratynski, a Russian émigré who at age 18, with his two sisters, was sent by the family out of Russia to safety in the West. Boratynksi did not speak English when he arrived in America, but he had earned an engineering degree from a Moscow university. When he entered college in California he found that mathematics was a universal language. He soon learned English, made new friends and, in 1966, after spending some time working for big corporations, formed his own company, Tetra Tech, which specialized in the application of advanced technology to problems involving water, oil and gas, and energy generation.

Bt the time Critchfield met Boratynski, Tetra Tech had been doing substantial business with the United States government – for the Department of the Navy, the Department of the Interior, the Federal Energy Administration and other agencies. Tetra Tech had an office in Rosslyn, Virginia, called Systems Group, which was located just across the Potomac River from Washington. Systems Group dealt mainly with the U.S. Navy and the Pentagon. In consultation with the Office of Naval Petroleum and Oil Shale Reserves, it developed the engineering plan for evaluating the Navy's oil reserves in Alaska.

---

[1] State Department contracted with Critchfield to prepare analytical reports on OPEC oil pricing and related matters on oil company/OPEC matters. The one-year contract, dated November 11, 1974, was for $7,000. When he became a full-time employee of

In addition to being well represented in Washington, Tetra Tech had an office in Houston that focused upon reservoir engineering and oil and gas exploration. Its Pasadena, California, headquarters employed over 200 engineers with specialties in water resources, ocean and coastal management. It also maintained academic ties with the University of California and other institutions doing advanced research in the development of water resources.

On one of his frequent trips to Washington, Boratynksi visited Critchfield, who had rented a small office downtown and operated from it with the help of a part-time secretary. Boratynski told him, "Jim, you are wasting your money. I have space at my office in Rosslyn. I will make it and a secretary available to you at no charge and we can discuss getting Tetra Tech involved in your part of the world." Critchfield accepted, of course.

Meanwhile, Stribling Snodgrass, who had served the sultan so well, died quite unexpectedly in July 1974 from a heart attack. He was 73 years old. Critchfield was fully aware of the contribution Snodgrass had made in Oman, and when Snodgrass's wife, Frances, offered him Strib's files, he accepted them. When Tetra Tech became involved in Oman, these files became an important source of information. An added bonus was that Snodgrass's talented assistant, Patrick Maley, became a Tetra Tech consultant.

By October 1974, Critchfield had formulated a business plan that, in his opinion, would work in Oman. Because of his ties to Sultan Qaboos's inner circle, he thought there was a reasonably good chance of obtaining a contract there. He warned Boratynski, however, that much of the type of engineering work that Tetra Tech did was too sophisticated for Oman to absorb at the outset, since the country was not very advanced in developing its water, oceanic, mineral and agricultural resources. The reality, he told Boratynski, was that Oman was remote, difficult to get to and not the easiest place in which to do business. Be that as it may, Oman had problems that Tetra Tech was well qualified to address.

Tetra Tech Inc. in June 1975, he ended his State Department contract, which was accepted by Assistant Secretary of State for Economic Affairs Tom Enders. Enders expressed his appreciation for Critchfield's work, which he said had been most useful in the development of US international energy policy. Taken from State Department correspondence dated November 11, 1974, and June 23, 1975.

Tetra Tech put together a briefing of the company's capabilities, pointing to areas where it could be helpful by playing an independent consulting role to the Oman government in its initial stages of development. Critchfield recommended a "soft sell," believing that such a strategy might lead to a broader relationship later. Boratynksi bought this approach, and the Tetra Tech group in Rosslyn produced a briefing book for Boratynski and Critchfield to present initially to Tom Hill's firm Spear and Hill in New York and then to the Supreme Petroleum and Natural Gas Council in London.

The briefing book was in fact quite sophisticated in its approach.[2] After outlining what Tetra Tech did in the fields of oil and gas, water and energy generation, it pointed out what it could do in Oman when the sultanate's oil was gone. In particular, it concentrated on the urgent need for a program to prevent the current waste of associated gas as well as a program for the optimum use of non-associated gas. At the time, Oman's natural gas industry had yet to be created. It was losing valuable potential income because of the flaring of natural gas associated with the production of oil.

Strib Snodgrass had briefed the sultan back in November 1972 that Oman was experiencing substantial losses by not utilizing this byproduct gas for field operations. Instead, PDO was flaring gas and then producing non-associated gas to support its needs in the field. A year and a half later, Snodgrass presented a formal report on gas conservation to Sultan Qaboos, noting that each day's delay translated into a daily loss of $50,000.[3]

In a more perfect world, Critchfield thought, Sultan Qaboos would have acted on the advice of Snodgrass and brought in a large firm, such as the Houston-based Williams Brothers construction company, to build a gas industry and keep everyone else out of the action, including the Supreme Petroleum Council. But instead, he ended up getting fragmented advice on the question of gas development. Spear and Hill had come under criticism for having bungled the gas project, producing one company after another, plus a bewildering array of consultants,

---

[2] James H. Critchfield, *Oman Papers, 1968-1991*, Tetra Tech Briefing Book for the Sultanate of Oman, 1975 .

[3] Ibid. Correspondence dated January 28, 1974, from Stribling Snodgrass to His Majesty Sultan Qaboos. Oman's natural gas situation will be covered in more detail in a separate chapter.

without having accomplished anything other than create a stack of unpaid bills.

The original contract retaining Tetra Tech in a general consulting capacity was signed on November 18, 1974. The Supreme Petroleum Council would pay Tetra Tech $50,000 per year plus expenses to monitor the development of oil and gas resources and provide advice relevant to the use of Oman's natural gas.

In December 1974, Critchfield went to London to meet with the key members of the council. He met separately with Yehia Omar, Ghassan Shaker, Tom Hill and Tim Landon, all of whom found the contract acceptable; it then went to Qais Al-Zawawi, who signed it in his capacity as deputy chairman of the Supreme Financial Council. As a first task, Critchfield was asked to prepare an analysis of the world oil market by February 1, 1975.

Critchfield learned while he was in London that Sultan Qaboos had actually made the decision to retain Tetra Tech well before they met in New York. He respected Critchfield's advice and thought that Tetra Tech might be the answer to a broader spectrum of development activities in Oman. And it turned out to be so.

As Critchfield spent more time observing Hill at close range, he learned to handle their relationship very carefully. He had come to realize that the peripatetic lawyer was involved in just about every aspect of Oman's development activities, and not always productively. Hill had taken over Snodgrass's role as oil and gas advisor. He had been trying to elbow Snodgrass out before his death, but Snodgrass had been too dignified to fight the issue and, with more than 40 years under his belt as a successful, highly competent oilman, he was not about to get embroiled in such conflicts.

Interestingly, it was not the oil and gas business that brought the first Tetra Tech team to Oman. It was water. During Sultan Qaboos's January 1975 Washington visit, Dr. Omar Al-Zawawi and Yehia Omar spent time at Tetra Tech's Rosslyn office being briefed on the company's water resource management capabilities. Shortly after that, Tetra Tech was invited to send a team to Oman to make recommendations regarding water resources countrywide and to survey Oman's coastal and port engineering problems, particularly in the Musandam Peninsula.

Dr. Omar Al-Zawawi took charge of the visit and offered to assist the team in any way possible. He ran interference in assembling and making available existing data and studies. Other firms had done water resource surveys, but Oman's water problems were far from being solved. On February 20, Al-Zawawi's office in Muscat notified Tetra Tech that an air freight shipment of documents would arrive at Washington Dulles International Airport on February 21.

Furthermore, Al-Zawawi recommended that important Tetra Tech messages be directed to his brother Qais Al-Zawawi. In his capacity as deputy chairman of the Development Council Qais would ensure that actions did not fall between ministerial stools.

The Tetra Tech mission was divided into two stages. A survey team, made up of three highly qualified specialists and one non-technical member, went out in March to do an overview. They were given 60 days to submit a preliminary report to the Development Council on the state of water resources and on ports and harbors. The team members were Dr. Bernard Le Mehaute, Tetra Tech vice president in charge of engineering and a hydraulic and coastal engineer, Dr. Choule Sonu, a specialist in coastal environmental engineering and harbor design, Dr. John Tsern, the head of Tetra Tech's water resources department, and Patrick Maley, who was in charge of getting the team where it needed to go – no easy task. It was agreed that Tetra Tech would be paid $70,000 plus travel and expenses for this specific project.

The Tetra Tech team was directed to learn as much as possible in the time they were there. Once on the ground, they met with ministry officials responsible for infrastructure, petroleum, agriculture and fisheries. Oddly, Minister of Communications Abdel Hafidh Salim Rajab, who was in charge of water resources development, did not make himself available for interviews. Rajab would eventually be given a copy of the team's report. The team did not make an issue of this snub.

After initial interviews in Muscat, the group traveled from north to south. They made on-site inspections of well drilling and inland water development, looked at harbors and oil pollution problems and examined work currently being done by other foreign companies. In that regard, the team was completely aboveboard in fielding any questions as to why they were there. Their survey, they said, had been requested by the Development Council, which saw a need for coordination and follow-up on work already done. In fact, Tetra Tech was there to determine whether there was a role it could play in advising the Oman government in these important areas.

While the water team was making its rounds, Critchfield began to work on an oil and gas proposal that would eventually establish a critical role for Tetra Tech in Oman. He sought the help of Sam Patterson, head of Tetra Tech's Houston office, a seasoned petroleum engineer and a take-charge kind of guy. They immediately began a talent search for an oilman to be assigned directly to the petroleum ministry; Said Al-Shanfari had just taken over that post as minister.

Kenneth E. Bodine, a petroleum engineer and a lawyer, filled this bill. He had degrees from the Colorado School of Mines and the University of Denver. Bodine had already had an extensive career in the Middle East, serving as vice president of Continental/Marathon/Shell operations in Libya, general manager for Amoco in Indonesia and deputy general manager of Phillips/Ashland/Signal Oil in Kuwait. Bodine, his wife Patricia and their three children had just returned to Denver from Libya and were in the process of getting settled when Critchfield and Patterson contacted him. Seasoned in the ways of the Middle East, Ken and Pat were enthusiastic about this new and exciting possibility. Bodine and Sam Patterson went to Oman to look things over.

While Critchfield continued drafting the proposed oil and gas contract and negotiating the details with Minister Al-Shanfari in London, Patterson and Bodine were meeting ministry officials in Muscat and trying to figure out how to get Tetra Tech up and running with a minimum of wasted time and motion. As in the case of the water team, Dr. Omar Al-Zawawi smoothed the way and offered the services of his business staff to help in any way they could. Things like housing, transportation and communications were major obstacles to deal with in a nation still so new that the amenities were in short supply and highly sought after.

By June 1975, it all came together. Nicholas Boratynski established Tetra Tech International (TTI) Inc. to handle all foreign operations, and James Critchfield was appointed its president.[4] The government of the Sultanate of Oman entered into a three-year agreement with TTI to provide full advisory and engineering services to the Ministry of Agriculture, Fisheries, Petroleum and Minerals with respect to Oman's oil, gas and mineral resources. For an annual fee of $924,500, TTI would

[4] Oman was not the only prospective client TTI was seeking. Critchfield introduced Tetra Tech specialists to contacts in Jordan, Iran, Saudi Arabia and Egypt, and efforts were under way to sell TTI services there.

provide a resident advisor to function within the ministry; the vice president of Tetra Tech's Exploration and Geotechnology, Houston, would monitor on a continuing basis Oman oil, gas and mineral developments and provide advice on the utilization of these resources; and the TTI president would give special attention to the world crude oil and products markets and to other developments that might influence the oil and gas interests of Oman. Other specialists would be made available by Tetra Tech for permanent or temporary assignment in Oman to perform tasks identified by the minister. This would include at least two professional engineers resident in Oman and assigned to the ministry full-time.

During the months leading up to the contract signing, Critchfield consulted and coordinated all the details, not only with Al-Shanfari, but more importantly with Colonel Timothy Landon, Qais Al-Zawawi, Yehia Omar, Ghassan Shaker and Dr. Omar Al-Zawawi; these were the existing members of the Supreme Petroleum and Natural Gas Council. Their agreement and backing were prerequisites to obtaining the sultan's final approval.

By this time, the Tetra Tech water team had completed its survey report. Drs. Tsern and LeMehaute met with Dr. Omar Al-Zawawi at the Beirut airport on April 8 and briefed him on their findings. Their briefing went beyond what would be included in the official report, which would be submitted after their return to the United States. Dr. Tsern told Al-Zawawi that, while they saw progress being made to solve Oman's water problems, the cost of this progress had been extraordinarily high. Private enterprises seeking contracts were taking advantage of government officials, who lacked the technical capability to supervise the contractors. These companies tended to promote their own interests and were realizing extremely high profits.

One example was the Swedish company VIAK's design of floodway and sewerage work, which was extremely costly and uneconomical. The cost in Oman averaged $100,000; the same work in the United States would be $5,000-10,000. Dr. Al-Zawawi was chagrined to hear this, as he was the one who brought VIAK to Oman to create the master plan and design of the Greater Capital Area.

Another example was Sir Alexander Gibb & Partners, which still had a year to go on its contract but had already spent all its funds. It would need another $10 million to complete the fieldwork and engineering analysis outlined in the contract. Tsern felt that Alexander Gibb had not carried out a thorough examination of the groundwater recharge system. He noted that since the present water supply depended solely on groundwater sources, it was essential that the storage capacity in the aquifers and their respective recharge systems be identified in an orderly manner. He also pointed out that there were no rain gauges in the area around the Wadi Samail watershed, which was a main recharge source for the present water supply wells serving the Greater Capital Area.

Tsern added that he was aware that the British dominated all sectors of the economy in Oman. As for the water survey, they had blocked his team's investigation and showed total non-cooperation. Dr. Al-Zawawi was very much surprised to hear this. Among other reactions, he felt it was a lack of respect for his brother Qais, who had ordered the survey.

In early May, the official report was delivered to Dr. Al-Zawawi, who sat on it for about six weeks. The reason, apparently, was that further ministerial changes were about to take place, which would have a direct impact on some of the report's recommendations. The only other official who saw the report immediately was Colonel Landon.

The Tetra Tech team's official report covered all water matters, including water supply, wastewater reclamation and agricultural irrigation. On the positive side, the team took note of efforts to obtain technical assistance from the United Nations FAO to establish a water resources center. Although there were already five foreign consulting firms active in Oman – Sir Alexander Gibb & Partners (British), VIAK Consulting Engineers (Swedish), Pencol Ltd. (British), Renardet-Sauti-ICOE (French-Italian) and Sir William Halcrow & Partners (British) – the team felt additional work was needed. The government, they believed, should have a better system for data monitoring, improved techniques for water resources analysis and further technical training of Omanis.

They pointed out there was no long-term water policy or detailed water development program. The report recommended that the government proceed with establishment of the water resources center to coordinate and review the work currently underway by foreign consultants, continue the hydrological monitoring program begun by them and basically get organized. The report also stated that the priorities should include but not be limited to an overall assessment of short- and long-term requirements, an examination of the capacity of water desalination plants, a drilling program for hydro-geologic investigation, and the reclamation of wastewater effluent. The Ministry of Communications, which was responsible for water resources development, needed a technical advisor to coordinate these numerous activities – implying, of course, that Tetra Tech International would be pleased to assume that role.

On the oil front during the summer of 1975, TTI went into high gear to get operations up and running. Kenneth Bodine, with only a day to prepare, left Denver on June 7th for Oman. Once there, Minister Al-Shanfari had him back on a plane the next day; they went first to Europe then Canada and then the United States – San Francisco, Houston and finally Washington DC. Bodine found time during this whirlwind visit to spend a weekend in Denver to assure Pat that they had a future in Oman. Bruce Edmonds, a British-born petroleum engineer who had been in Houston for 26 years, was picked by Sam Patterson to join the team.

Bruce J. G. Edmonds had attended the Royal Military Academy at Sandhurst AND the Infantry School in Mhow, India, and served as a British Army officer from 1943 to 1947. He was discharged with the rank of captain. He received a degree in petroleum engineering from Texas A&M University and worked with various Texas oil companies as a petroleum engineer. He became a specialist in all aspects of drilling, production and reservoir engineering. Married with four grown children, Edmonds and his wife Kathy were anxious to experience living abroad and were ideally suited for the job Tetra Tech had to offer.

Bodine and Edmonds were the first two TTI men to be permanently resident in Oman. In addition to their assignments as advisors to the Minister of Petroleum, Bodine was also to be the senior TTI representative in Oman, and Edmonds would be his deputy. But there was still no office in Muscat.

The non-petroleum projects that Tetra Tech was discussing with the Oman government, such as development in the Musandam Peninsula and water resources planning, required a generalist to set up an office to handle all non-petroleum matters and to act as a coordinator between Oman and TTI in Rosslyn. That man was Kirk Agon.

Agon had recently returned from Vietnam and was exploring job opportunities. Before the fall of Saigon, he met and later married Nga

Tran and became the stepfather to her two small children, Chau and Ngoc. They would start a new life in the United States, or so they thought. They arrived in Washington and began the process of looking for jobs. Agon met Critchfield, who asked him to think about an assignment in Oman. Soon both Agon and his wife were on their way to Muscat. They would be there for the next nine years. The children were college age before they got to know their adopted country.

Fortuitously, Charles Black's fisheries operation, Mardela Corporation, was vacating a two-story office apartment complex in Muscat and offered it to TTI. Called the Nasib apartments, after the owner who lived above the quarters, it would provide TTI with an office, a telex and minimal living quarters. Charles Black also facilitated the reassignment of Mardela's telephone and telex facilities to TTI.

As the summer ended, Critchfield outlined for Kirk Agon what his priorities should be in the coming weeks. They were wide ranging and not necessarily connected. Agon's Muscat office would be the nerve center for all projects, those already underway and those to come. On petroleum matters, he would provide support to Ken Bodine and Bruce Edmonds in the ministry and facilitate Houston's efforts to keep Bodine current on oil pricing data. He would also assist in getting on top of all the oil concession agreements. These were important priorities. But no less important were the tasks of preparing for a TTI role in water resources development and in the Musdandam/Hormuz area.

Critchfield's priorities for himself were more complex. He knew that he served at the pleasure of Sultan Qaboos and Qaboos's closest advisors, a group of men who respected him because of his experience, dating back to the days of World War II and his years involved with the Middle East during the period of Soviet expansionism.

Critchfield also understood that the changes brought about by OPEC and the emergence of the oil producers as the key players in the Middle East had changed the playing field. Although Oman did not have the huge oil reserves its neighbors had and thus was not a major force in the oil arena, it nevertheless was an important player in the geopolitics of the area. The Hormuz Strait, with Oman on one side, Iran on the other, and its borders with Saudi Arabia, the UAE, and Yemen, provided Oman with many reasons to be involved whether or not it wanted to be.

Whatever assistance TTI would provide in the years to come would focus on strengthening the nation to deal with its future. Therefore, Critchfield identified that the mission of his company would be to:

1) Assist in the building of Oman's oil industry: maximize revenues through obtaining fair prices, improve production methods, accelerate exploration and introduce reservoir engineering technology.
2) Develop a foundation for water resources management in Oman.
3) Originate a development program for the Musandam Peninsula that would serve as a blueprint for other regions in Oman.

Critchfield knew that his friendship with the inner circle would only last as long as his company's performance remained high. The commitment he made to them in 1975 carried with it the burden to produce results. It started with the introduction of Bodine and Edmonds into the petroleum ministry and Agon in a central TTI office in Muscat. Eventually, TTI would have up to 200 personnel on the ground working on these development challenges.

7

TTI TAKES UP RESIDENCE AT THE MINISTRY OF AGRICULTURE, FISHERIES, PETROLEUM AND MINERALS

When Minister Said Al-Shanfari took over the petroleum ministry, he found that, like it or not, he was going to have a relationship with Tetra Tech International. He may have found that curious, but he warmed up to the idea when he discovered that technical expertise was badly lacking in the ministry. TTI would play a big role in helping him to get organized. The TTI contract provided for petroleum engineering advisors to work in the ministry alongside the Omani officials. Additionally, the contract called for institutional services to be provided by Tetra Tech, Houston, particularly in the fields of geology and geophysics, to backstop the ministry in its dealings with PDO.

Said Al-Shanfari had a lot on his plate. Since early June 1975, he had been almost totally preoccupied with petroleum matters. And although he was increasingly turning to TTI and Jim Critchfield for assistance, he made it clear to Critchfield, whom he saw several times in London and Washington, and to Ken Bodine in Muscat, that his style was to play things close to the chest. He wanted all dealings with foreign companies, including TTI, under his control, and he wanted to be the one to release information within the Oman government on negotiations with third parties.

In this context, Critchfield's close ties with the inner circle could be both an advantage and a disadvantage. In the final analysis, though, Critchfield thought multiple ties – Bodine with the minister and he with the sultan's closest advisors – were both essential and workable, as long as they did not get tangled up in each other's shoestrings. It remained Critchfield's view that Oman would benefit most from an institutional role, which would permit all elements of TTI to be tested in their abilities to contribute something that was really needed by Oman and accepted by Omanis as useful and valuable.

As a first step, Al-Shanfari told Critchfield that he was satisfied with Bodine's role in the ministry. Sam Patterson had made several visits to Oman over the summer and had begun work in Houston to support the minister. Patterson had also accompanied Al-Shanfari to meetings in London and The Hague with Royal Dutch Shell. Al-Shanfari inherited this way of doing business when he took over petroleum affairs. In the long run, Critchfield was not sure Al-Shanfari would maintain the modus operandi and keep the Houston office and Patterson in the picture. It would be his call. Keeping Houston directly involved would run up the bill, and Critchfield was accountable to the Omanis for the value of this support. If this institutional concept was not demonstrably effective, he felt it would not last more than a year or so. But the relationship was still in a formative stage, and TTI was only one quarter into its oil and gas contract.

The TTI Rosslyn office was involved almost daily in a variety of Oman affairs. This was partly due to the fact that TTI was running a two-track relationship: Bodine with the minister, and Critchfield with other elements and personalities in the Oman government. Critchfield had had several meetings over the summer with Qais Al-Zawawi, Dr. Omar Al-Zawawi, Yehia Omar, Ghassan Shaker and Tim Landon, some in London and some in Washington. As a matter of fact, he lamented that in some respects communications on these two tracks were better than internal communications between TTI and Tetra Tech in Pasadena, whose corporate procedures had inevitably slowed things down.

Much of the interchange between Bodine and Critchfield was in preparation for the role TTI would play in the pricing negotiations with PDO scheduled for October 1975 in London. As a result of the participation agreement with PDO, which was implemented on January 1, 1974, Oman was now 60 percent owner of its oil production operations.[1] In actual practice, until January 1, 1975, Oman, with the agreement of PDO, generally adhered to OPEC pricing, thus alleviating a need for price negotiations between PDO and the government. After that, Oman split with the OPEC system, and by April 1975 it had dropped its price through the OPEC floor, an action which provided cheaper oil to PDO shareholders (mainly Shell) for its 40 percent share,

---

[1] Per the Letter of Agreement dated July 12, 1974, retroactive to January 1974. From James H. Critchfield, *Oman Papers, 1968-1991*

as well as a favorable price for Oman's equity oil, 50 percent of which also went to Shell.[2] These moves created circumstances in which Shell found it useful to increase production and lift every barrel of buyback oil available. Oman production in 1975 rose by 17 percent to 350,000 bpd, while most OPEC production declined.

Critchfield was very concerned that Oman would rush into a precipitous restructuring of PDO. PDO had sent the Omanis two papers dated September 16 and 18, 1975, proposing the establishment of a jointly owned (60/40) commercial company registered in the Sultanate of Oman. If Oman agreed to the proposals for restructuring drawn up by PDO, the deal would be cast in concrete and could only be changed by the unanimous consent of the membership.

Accepting this would put Oman politically out in front in a way that could be very damaging. Critchfield felt that Oman was already vulnerable for having departed from the OPEC pricing structure and for having rapidly expanded production while everyone else was cutting back. While he was sympathetic to Oman's decision to raise production and sell cheap, he knew that handing over a gold-plated deal to the foreign companies in PDO would be a mistake. The Oman side should bargain for time to give the matter full study.

Up to this time, all technical analysis had been done by PDO. PDO was not happy that the new ministry wanted to get into the technical side of petroleum planning, and it was increasingly upset by the presence of TTI advisors sitting on the side of the government. PDO manager Rudi Jaeckli and the Royal Dutch Shell team in London went to great lengths to obstruct the flow of data to the ministry. Jaeckli complained that the government's desire to make independent judgments was a vote of no confidence in him and in Shell. It would take many months for this conflict to be resolved.

The Keyline Proposal

In October 1975, Critchfield wrote to Ghassan Shaker informing him that he was reopening with the Omanis the old subject of bringing Rub al Khali oil and gas out through Oman. Shaker had been instrumental in trying to get Saudi support for a South Arabian Pipeline Authority, dubbed the Keyline project, when Stribling Snodgrass had conceived of the

[2] Ibid. *Oman's Current Development Problems.* September 23, 1975.

idea. Critchfield wanted Shaker's support to renew Saudi interest in the project.

The proposal was to create a free zone through which Saudi oil and gas would be moved from the Shaibah field in the eastern region of the Rub al Khali east or south to an Arabian Sea free port in Oman operated by the joint venture to be known as the South Arabian Pipeline Authority (SAPA). From an Oman point of view, if the Saudis would commit to bringing out its Shaibah oil through Dhofar, Oman could then develop an industrial corridor through Dhofar that would benefit the people of Oman, Saudi Arabia and South Yemen as well. A common economic stake in this would produce stability through interdependence.

The Shaibah field alone was capable of producing 500,000 bpd. Other areas of the Rub al Khali had not yet been fully explored. A free zone corridor would have to be given a treaty status comparable to the Suez Canal Zone guaranteeing Saudi Arabia a long-term equity. A free zone could be large enough to include a petrochemical plant, transportation and other industries based on long-term cooperation between Oman and Saudi Arabia. SAPA could attract major foreign investors and the best in technology. A pipeline and port authority along these lines could be a most promising income-earning asset available to the sultanate as it looked to a future of declining oil production. Access to Rub al Khali associated gas would provide new dimensions for the planned development of gas-based industries in the free zone corridor.

For Saudi Arabia, a major oil outlet that would be independent of both the Strait of Hormuz and the Bab el Mandeb on the Red Sea would be strategically attractive.[3] But the conventional wisdom in Saudi Arabia and Aramco was that it would never again put any of its oil out through a pipeline that crossed the territory of another country. There had been numerous pipeline disruptions over the years, such as Tapline, the 1,000-mile pipeline to the Mediterranean coast that was shut down in the mid-1970s at the onset of the Lebanese civil war. However, the political circumstances and potential advantages in the case of Oman were different from that of Tapline – or at least those in support of the Keyline project felt that to be so. The economic potential, in their view, outweighed the risk. No small consideration was that a pipeline through

---

[3] Even today, most of Saudi light crude oil is exported from the Arabian Gulf via the huge Abqaiq processing facility. The primary export terminals are at Ras Tanura and Ras al Ju'aymah on the Gulf and Yanbu on the Red Sea.

Oman was an obvious way of reducing the growing shipping congestion at Arabian Gulf ports.

At a meeting between King Khalid bin Abdul Aziz and Sultan Qaboos in 1977 with their foreign ministers present, the two agreed to survey a pipeline route from Saudi Arabia through Oman, with Tetra Tech International doing the work. The survey was completed in June 1979 and presented to the Saudi and Omani foreign ministries. The work was never covered by a contract, and no invoice was submitted. TTI considered it a goodwill and marketing effort with an eye on the longer-term possibility of a more extensive Saudi-Omani pipeline contract.[4]

Exploitation of Natural Gas

Seven years after the first barrel of oil was produced in Oman, there was still no viable program to utilize associated gas. It was routinely flared and given up to the skies. While everyone recognized the need to harness this resource and also to develop a program for non-associated gas, no one in the industry or the government had yet made it happen. Simply put, there was no natural gas industry in Oman. The Oman treasury was losing valuable income from this sector. When Stribling Snodgrass was advising Oman, he recognized the potential of natural gas and had tried unsuccessfully to get a program going.

Shell's technical staff in The Hague did a feasibility study in July 1973. At the time, it concluded that the economics of using Oman gas were generally negative in light of pre-October 1973 prices. The study did not include any supporting data, and those in Oman dealing with oil and gas were not impressed with it. When he saw the report, Snodgrass asked his friend and colleague George Gibson to prepare a preliminary feasibility study with the same terms of reference given to Shell. Gibson, an American petroleum engineer, had been working on projects with Strib Snodgrass for many years He had expertise in gas utilization projects and had done similar work in Assam, Burma, Indonesia, Iran, Pakistan and Saudi Arabia.

No sooner had Gibson agreed to go to Oman than Snodgrass found himself in an unwanted tug-of-war between Salem Makki and John

[4] Tetra Tech International, *Saudi Arabia – Oman Pipeline Study*, June 1979. The report was updated in September 1981 when Japan showed interest in supporting a pipeline system. See Tetra Tech International, *South Arabia Strategic Pipeline System*, September 1981.

Townsend. It seemed that the British firm of Sir Alexander Gibb had also put in a proposal to do a gas study. Makki wanted Gibson, and Townsend decided there was sufficient work for both parties. In the end, Gibson was hired to study the viability of using non-associated gas as the energy source for a proposed electric power generation project and a cement project, while Sir Gibb & Partners would take a look at other possible long-term uses of non-associated gas.

Gibson spent most of December 1973 in Oman, and his report of January 25, 1974, was delivered to Sultan Qaboos with a covering letter from Snodgrass. The report noted that Oman natural gas was a perfect fuel for stationary heat and power installations and contained a ready-made molecular skeleton for the manufacture of fertilizer. Moreover, it contained liquids which, when extracted, were versatile and portable fuels that were in great demand internationally and could also be utilized in domestic heating and cooking or as motor fuel within Oman. Gibson estimated that ultimate proved reserves of non-associated gas in excess of oil field requirements were sufficient to supply 100 million cubic feet per day for almost forty years. There was also a substantial volume of associated gas produced with oil that could be used for oil field purposes as well as for LPG and natural gasoline. The report contained relevant cost, pricing and return on investment figures.

Based on the generally favorable conclusions of Gibson's study, the Oman government made the decision to negotiate an agreement with PDO to obtain the gas reserves it was not utilizing for field purposes for use in an LPG project and an export-oriented ammonia/urea plant.[5]

George Gibson also studied the idea of Oman building its first oil refinery. He suggested a simple refinery designed to supply the Oman market with diesel oil plus asphalt, jet fuel and kerosene. He noted that in 1973 Iraq had brought two such refineries to the Kirkuk area to supply these products at a cost of $3.3 million.[6] Gibson added, however, that if Arabian crude were made available through completion of the Keyline project, a large refinery might be profitable and attractive to Arab investors.

In reviewing the gas situation in early 1975, PDO estimated it would cost $30-35 million to develop the infrastructure to use this gas (about

[5] Summary of the report of George Gibson to Stribling Snodgrass dated January 25, 1974.
[6] "Skid Crude Units Solve Iraqi Problem," *The Oil and Gas Journal*, December 21, 1973, pp.146-47.

150 million cubic feet a day, or the equivalent of 25,000 bpd of oil). PDO suggested that the end use of this gas could take several forms: propane, butane and natural gas liquids (NGL), bulk export of liquid petroleum gas (LPG), bottled LPG for local consumption, and/or use as feedstock for ammonia or urea export. There was nothing new here. Snodgrass and Maley had been pushing for action on all these possibilities up to the time of Snodgrass's death.

After completing this study, PDO officials stated they had no interest in direct investment and proposed that outside investors be encouraged to buy into a joint venture. If such financing failed, it recommended turning to Arab banks for low-interest loans of perhaps 12-15 years, which it estimated could be paid back in five to six years.

The government policy to proceed with gas utilization projects had been spelled out and was definitive; but keeping the pressure on to turn this policy into action remained a challenge. Critchfield felt it was important for TTI to take the initiative to advise the government on the next steps regarding gas. During the summer of 1975, he assigned Patrick Maley the task of preparing a plan with definitive recommendations to be presented to Minister Al-Shanfari before year's end.

Maley's final product, which ultimately went to the government as a TTI report, was divided into four subjects: non-associated gas, associated gas, the need for a refinery, and product demand for local consumption. First and foremost was the recommendation to obtain financing for a 20" pipeline to deliver non-associated gas from Yibal to population centers, interior Oman and the Oman coast. This would allow for the substitution of low-cost gas for export-earning crude oil, thereby saving foreign exchange and increasing government take. It would also provide the basis for development of a mineral industry in Oman to produce non-oil income. As to the utilization of associated natural gas, controversy centered on whether development should emphasize export or domestic use. TTI's recommendation was that this should be a government project designed to conserve resources and improve the lives of the Omani people. Saudi Arabia's LPG export project already under way would make it difficult for marginal LPG export schemes, such as Oman's, to succeed, at least in the short term.

In early 1976, Critchfield made yet another approach to the government, pointing out that over the past three years, Oman had invested in excess of $60 million on materials and services in anticipation of a gas utilization project. It was losing $3-5 million a month in revenues from natural gas liquids, and $1-7 million a month in lost revenues from sales of natural gas.

Representatives of many respected international companies had visited Oman in those three years to study the problem, but no progress had been made toward the construction of facilities necessary to implement a gas program. It was Critchfield's view that Oman was drifting into serious financial troubles. Infrastructure development in Muscat and in Dhofar was outrunning income-producing economic activities. He felt that rapid and intelligent development of a program to use associated and non-associated gas offered the single most promising economic action the government could undertake.

The side effects of a good gas program could be a major cure for some of the economic ailments that were developing. In order to accomplish this, however, Oman needed a substantial injection of outside capital, which was proving difficult to come by. Shell had been clear that it would not provide it and had reacted negatively to a proposal to transmit LPG through its existing crude oil line.

The dilemma was that the main facilities of the new gas infrastructure were physically within the PDO area and were highly integrated with the existing PDO operation. As long as Shell controlled the PDO operation, new capital would be hard to find. Critchfield suggested that one way in which the pipeline issue could be solved was for the Oman government to take it over. It already owned 60 percent of PDO. The government could easily make the case for the pipeline's being already completely depreciated or amortized, in which case it would cost little or nothing. Any cost could be recovered by a transit fee.

The question of who would build the separate 20" gas pipeline had still not been settled. Tetra Tech's advice was to call on PDO's service contractor, TOCO, to install the line. TOCO was the local Williams Brothers company that did most of the pipeline and related work for PDO. Williams Brothers, headquartered in Houston, Texas, was the world's leading pipeline engineering and construction company. It was the logical candidate for the work, since its personnel and equipment were already there. All these factors would impact the ongoing talks between the government and PDO on the restructuring of their relationship. Not an easy task. And in the meantime, the gas continued to be flared.

Minister Al-Shanfari's Non-Petroleum Portfolio

Copper Project

Exploration of Oman's mineral resources also came under Al-Shanfari's ministerial umbrella. This activity had a momentum of its own. Since 1973, Prospection Ltd. of Toronto, Canada, headed by Charles Huston and financed by Douglas Marshall Exploration from Houston, Texas, had been carrying out exploration efforts in Oman, particularly in the area of Sohar on the Batinah coast. The Oman government acquired 51 percent of the venture on January 1, 1974. Copper mining dated back to the Bronze Age, and Oman was thought by some archaeologists to be the lost Magan, which around 1,800 BC was the principal exporter of copper to Sumeria, the flourishing kingdom on the Tigris and Euphrates Rivers.[7]

Marshall/Prospection's efforts had resulted in a feasibility study proposing the production and marketing of 11 million tons of copper ore for export. The study called for $76 million of investment over a three-year period, with a payout over five years and an additional $60 million profit during the next five years – or roughly a 2:1 return in a ten-year period. Exploration had produced indications of very large copper deposits of fairly good quality. TTI was asked to look into this, although Critchfield had the impression that Prospection Ltd. had a lock on Oman copper and would be the company to produce it, with or without TTI's advice.

Agriculture and Fisheries

It had been assumed that, at some point, Sultan Qaboos would split agriculture and fisheries activities away from the Ministry of Petroleum and Minerals. Just the sheer weight of the problems related to these activities made it too much for one man to oversee. But that did not happen. What did happen was that programs related to agriculture and fisheries drifted.

In the case of fisheries, the minister allowed the government's contract with Mardela Corporation and Charles Black to expire. By September 1975, when Black and the minister were back at the

[7]Saudi Aramco World, Volume 34, Number 3, May/June 1983, *Oman: The Lost Land*

drawing board negotiating a new agreement, both appeared interested in some arrangement by which TTI might in fact procure technicians to work as advisors in the ministry, much like Bodine and Edmonds. Critchfield and Black discussed the possibility of Black's becoming a TTI consultant. This fit with Al-Shanfari's desire to have fewer outside consultants and more resident experts within the ministry.

At the same time, Al-Shanfari decided to terminate the government's contract with Food Machinery Corporation (FMC), and as a result he was left without a manager for the Dhofar-based dairy herd of 400-600 Holsteins, a modern dairy provided by FMC, including thousands of paper milk cartons that carried the label "Dhofar Delight." During his visit to Washington the previous July, TTI had arranged for Al-Shanfari to visit a very well run dairy of the same size in Maryland that was operated by the Mormon Church. It was an eye opening experience, and Al-Shanfari attempted, without success, to hire the dairy's manager on the spot. Since then, Al-Shanfari kept after TTI to find a manager for the Dhofar operation. Even though Critchfield did not want to get into the dairy business, he began a talent search. In the meantime, Arabco, the New Zealand fishing and agriculture trading company, submitted a proposal to operate the project using the New Zealand Dairy Board and the Allied Farms of New Zealand for an annual fee of $200,000.

As an alternative to the New Zealand proposal, TTI offered the services of an experienced Pennsylvania dairy farmer who had just turned over his successful business to his son. Joseph W. Ferris accepted the assignment on the contingency that he travel there initially without his family to spend a few weeks becoming familiar with the operation and its potential. The cost would be $1,500 per month salary plus travel, housing and paid vacation. That was more in line with Minister Al-Shanfari's price range.

It was getting close to the end of the first year for Jim Critchfield's initial modest contract with the Oman government and the end of the second quarter of Tetra Tech International's first major contract with the Ministry of Petroleum and Minerals. What started out as a request to provide analyses of oil prices in the world market had evolved into projects related to petroleum developments, exploitation of minerals and water resources, ports and harbors, and even advice on dairy herds. TTI was moving ahead on all these fronts. But the area in which little progress was being made was in utilization of Oman's gas resources. This would continue to be a formidable challenge for both TTI and the Oman government.

8

1975 – YEAR-END EVENTS

In early October 1975, Sultan Qaboos appointed Dr. Omar Al-Zawawi to follow the pricing and organization talks with Shell Oil Company as his personal advisor. Al-Zawawi had been a member of the Supreme Petroleum Council since late in 1974 and had spent many hours since then studying the oil industry as well as Oman's relations with Shell. He would, on the sultan's behalf, be a backstop to Yehia Omar. Omar had told the sultan more than once that eventually he would like to become less involved, and by this point he was spending less and less time in Oman. Tim Landon seized the opportunity to urge the sultan to bring in Al- Zawawi.

Critchfield wondered how Al-Shanfari would react to this, given his desire to run everything out of his office in the ministry. With Al-Shanfari turning to Bodine and Dr. Omar turning to Critchfield for advisory services, communications on this double track could be a problem. Initially, Al-Shanfari had shown little interest in TTI's becoming involved in the financial side of oil. But as he approached the November pricing meeting in London and discovered how little he knew about negotiating prices with Shell, he began to ask Ken Bodine for data.

To support this effort, TTI prepared a background study for the Oman government on OPEC pricing and how it saw Oman setting its own oil price against this background.[1] On January 1, 1974, the worldwide price for a barrel of Arabian light marker crude was $10.12. (Based on that number, each OPEC oil-producing country then adjusted its own price according to production costs, freight differentials and quality premiums.) Oman adhered to this method of OPEC pricing until April 1, 1975. After that, it no longer added costs related to its

[1] James H. Critchfield, *Oman Papers, 1968-1991*, "Pricing Oman Crude – October 1975."

freight and quality premiums; as a result, its average government take was $9.69. Oman was underpricing its oil. In mid-1975, the average price at which Oman crude was being sold was lower than the official price of Arabian light, regardless of the fact that Oman crude had both a quality and a transportation advantage. It was Critchfield's view that Oman should use the OPEC formula where possible.

In fact, Oman was pursuing both production and pricing policies that put it well outside the policies that OPEC's member nations were at least paying lip service to. Probably more serious in the long term was that Oman was expanding its production by underpricing. Critchfield argued that some of the oil currently being produced and sold at below-market prices could profitably be left in the ground to be sold a few years later in an oil market that would remain strong and support higher prices.

Oman had increased its production in 1975 to 385,861 bpd. This decision increased the loss of flared gas and set the stage for a faster rundown of future production. Most exporters in OPEC were also producing at capacity, but Saudi Arabia was supporting a policy of prorationing, i.e., limiting oil production based on market demand. Oman rejected this idea. Oman also continued giving incentives to its buyers (Shell, CFP, Partex and independent client C. Itoh), making Oman's oil at that time in history the best buy in the world. Critchfield estimated that by departing from the OPEC pricing system earlier in the year, the loss to Oman during 1975 was well over $100 million.

TTI Brings in a Top Gun

Critchfield felt it was critical that TTI put in a good performance in support of the Oman side. He never took for granted the security of TTI's position in Oman. He knew without consistent top performance, it would not survive. To help him on this, he brought in Thomas C. Barger, the retired chairman of the board and chief executive officer of the Arabian American Oil Company (Aramco). He reminded Barger that he was one of the reasons Tetra Tech was in Oman. Previously, Barger had been asked to replace Strib Snodgrass; he declined the offer, but suggested that a little outfit called Tetra Tech might fill the bill.

Barger was one of the best known and most respected oilmen in the industry. His career began as a young geologist in 1938 when Standard

Oil of California sent him to Saudi Arabia to help explore for oil. Aramco grew from zero oil production to 10 billion barrels of oil produced at the time of Barger's retirement 31 years later. It was the first company to produce over 1 billion barrels of oil in any one year. It has been written that Tom Barger was "the most intelligent, resourceful, imaginative, judicious, energetic and honest executive east of Rockefeller Center."[2] Like Jim Critchfield, Tom Barger had been raised and educated in North Dakota. They spoke the same language.

Critchfield persuaded Barger, then resident in La Jolla, California, to become a TTI consultant on Oman's oil and gas problems. Critchfield remarked at the time that "Oman is not just a client. Unless one guards against it, Oman could become a way of life." The Omanis felt very lucky to have a man such as Barger on their side. For the next few years, Barger, fascinated with the special Oman situation and with the country itself, spent many hours reviewing Oman oil issues. He visited there and met with Sultan Qaboos. Barger also introduced a former financial vice president of Aramco, Donald McLeod, who also became a Tetra Tech consultant. McLeod's main role would be to recommend a program for evaluating the financial aspects of PDO and maintaining a tight financial monitoring of the organization.

Oman Changes Its Price Negotiation Strategy

Critchfield pressed Qais Al-Zawawi, Tim Landon and others on the need for a two-sided negotiating table, one side of which would unquestionably be loyal to the government. The government side had to develop competence and bring to the table a fair and equitable position on crude pricing. They needed to focus on production costs and capital investments. From that time on, TTI, represented by Ken Bodine, Bruce Edmonds or Sam Patterson, sat on the government's side of the table during negotiating sessions, while Critchfield worked behind the scenes on oil pricing.

For the two months leading up to the meetings with Shell, Critchfield spent every other weekend in London working with Dr. Al-Zawawi. The final preparatory meetings were held on October 18-19. He and Al-Zawawi examined the Shell restructuring proposal piece by

---

[2] *Tom Barger, Man or Myth*, Saudi Aramco World, Sept/Oct 1969, Volume 20, Number 5.

piece. What Shell proposed would convert PDO from a profit-making British corporation into a non-profit limited liability Oman company. It would also freeze the Shell role and position at the status quo until such time as the sultanate and the foreign companies agreed unanimously to terminate the arrangement. [3]

Oman already owned 60 percent of PDO and its assets in Oman. This equity position was broadly defined and left much room for negotiation and adjustment as circumstances changed. Critchfield speculated, because he did not know, that Shell and the other foreign oil company owners were intending to take advantage of Oman while it was recovering from a cash flow and financial crisis.

It looked as if they wanted to consolidate and freeze the Shell role in the current advantageous position before Oman opted to follow the lead of the other producing countries that were negotiating new relationships with the foreign oil companies. This would create a framework and an arrangement that would forestall any moves by the Oman government to dilute the operational control of Shell. By converting the current British corporation into an Oman limited liability company, Shell would also receive certain tax benefits.

Shell still exercised virtually 100 percent control over management of PDO. In effect, the PDO facilities were an enclave in Oman, just as when major oil companies first went into countries to develop and produce oil. The Shell proposal did not address how Oman would eventually play a greater role in management. The proposed board was to have one director each from the Oman government and the three foreign shareholders, creating a ratio of three to one. The managing director of the new company, the Shell manager, would sit on the board but would have broad authority to run the company.

The proposal stated that the rights, privileges and standards of the present Shell expatriate staff and the character of the facilities of the current PDO operation would become frozen as of "transfer day." This also applied to pay and benefits. These provisions would appear to insulate the Shell operation forever from adjustments due to changing circumstances within the sultanate, which could lead to interminable disputes.

In the final analysis, Critchfield asked, "What is the advantage to the sultanate in negotiating any agreement along these lines at this time?"

[3] James H. Critchfield, *Oman Papers, 1968-1991*, PDO draft proposal dated September 18, 1975, and TTI analysis dated October 16, 1975.

His advice was for the sultanate to take its time to identify and study the arrangements that were evolving in the prolonged negotiations of the other oil exporting nations and to decline to negotiate any agreement at the upcoming meeting.

As it turned out, PDO and the Oman government agreed to set aside the issue of ownership; but negotiations on oil pricing continued. At the insistence of Minister Al-Shanfari, these talks were now to be held in Muscat rather than in London and The Hague. The first were scheduled for October 21.

The pricing meetings with Shell got under way as scheduled on October 21. Bodine, in describing the atmosphere of those opening meetings, reported to Critchfield in Rosslyn that "the sunshine and smiles on opening day evaporated immediately to dark clouds and pained expressions" as the minister delivered his position on prices to Shell. He emphasized that Oman's 34 degrees API (light, low sulfur content) crude was being lifted by PDO companies at a bargain price. What followed were four days of sometimes twice-a-day sessions, day and evening, with Shell insisting on a rock-bottom, 54¢ margin on each barrel lifted. The government, using TTI's recommendation, wanted a 22¢ margin. In the four days of negotiations, Shell would not budge, insisting that 32¢ of the 54¢ per barrel covered exploration and other capital costs. The remaining 22¢, Shell claimed, was the minimum reward or profit it would accept for its expertise and $88 million investment in Oman.

Throughout the four days, Bodine noted that Dr. Al-Zawawi performed admirably in support of the government's position; he had clearly done his homework. The two sides searched for common ground, but in the end Shell called an intermission and its leader, Tim Goral, returned to London for regrouping.[4] Minister Al-Shanfari deferred discussions on the PDO corporate structure and all other matters pending a resolution on prices.[5]

The Shell pricing meetings resumed on November 15, but they soon ended in a stalemate on acquisition costs and buyback prices. Shell agreed to seek approval from its board of Oman's buyback price if the

[4]In a separate negotiation with the Japanese company C. Itoh, which had earlier struck a deal at an excessively low price, C. Itoh agreed to pay 10¢ more per barrel, still a very favorable price. This face-saving measure was congenially described as resulting from "honest judgments about where the market was headed."

[5] James H. Critchfield, *Oman Papers, 1968-1991*, Memorandum from Bodine to TTI Rosslyn, October 22, 1975.

Oman government would agree to freeze this price until June 1976. Shell also wanted an accelerated depreciation schedule, which would lower its acquisition cost and thus increase the margin. The company claimed it was negotiating in Iran to operate on a fee basis with no investment and could not be seen as taking less in Oman. During these meetings and later, Shell went on record that it would put no new capital into Oman that it could not recover in the current year.

On November 23, Critchfield, Sam Patterson and Ken Bodine met in London and put together a formal position for the Oman side to use in the next pricing negotiation session. Bodine presented the paper to Al-Shanfari in Muscat, and Critchfield gave it to Dr. Al-Zawawi in London. The situation was reaching a critical point.

Further meetings would not be held until after Oman's National Day celebrations in Muscat scheduled for November 23, which marked the first five years of Sultan Qaboos's reign. It was a happy occasion for the country. One of those not celebrating, however, was Tom Hill. He seemed to have been operating with blinders on during the recent year. Time after time, he took actions that infuriated Omani ministers. His legal services were no longer being used by Minister Al-Shanfari, his most lucrative client, but Hill was not going to give up without a fight. He sent Sultan Qaboos a lengthy report on what he had done for Oman all those years. It ranged from the drafting of extensive legislation and contract reviews to involvement in almost the entire spectrum of Oman's resource base.[6] But in the end he lost. Spear and Hill went out of business on December 31, 1975, and Hill faded from the scene.

While Critchfield saw this coming, there were some issues about Hill's departure that disturbed him. He worried that companies brought into Oman via Spear and Hill would be under a cloud until revalidated. United States accounting firm Arthur Anderson was cited as an example. Arthur Anderson, which enjoyed a solid reputation in the accounting world, was brought in by Spear and Hill after the recommendation in the Morgan Grenfell report that Oman hire a leading firm of international accountants. Critchfield thought that was sound advice.

He expressed concern to Al-Shanfari that, with the absence of Hill, Ken Bodine would be burdened with additional legal tasks for the ministry. Bodine did not think that would be the case, pointing out that since his arrival in Oman, most of the ministry's legal work was

[6] Ibid., Tom Hill letter to Sultan Qaboos.

Anwar Sadat shakes hands with Sultan Qaboos,
as Ghassan Shaker looks on – 1972

Sultan Qaboos meets Georges Pompidou – 1973

At the Arab League Summit Conference in Rabat, seated directly behind
Sultan Qaboos are (*l-r*) Qais Al Zawawi and Sayyid Tariq bin Taimur – 1974

Sultan Qaboos with Habib Borguiba,
Tunisia – 1973

Sultan Qaboos with Empress Farah and the Shah of Iran – 1971

The Shah greets Sultan Qaboos, Teheran – 1974

Yehia Omar and Sayyid Tariq bin Taimur – 1971

Left to right: Yehia Omar, Sayyid Tariq bin Taimur, Ghassan Shaker, and Captain Tim Landon, National Day, Muscat – 1971

Ghassan Shaker, James Critchfield, Sultan Qaboos and Yehia Omar
at Blair House, Washington D. C. – 1975

Ghassan Shaker, Sultan Qaboos and Ahmed Makki in Libya – 1972

Minister Said Al Shanfari and Tom Barger
beneath an ancient baobab tree in Dhofar – 1977

Tom Barger and Minister Said Al Shanfari – 1977

Sultan Qaboos and Minister Said Al Shanfari at the Royal Place, Salalah – 1977

Yuosuf bin Alawi, in the checkered jacket,
takes lunch in the desert – 1979

James Critchfield inspects a rural waterworks in Buraimi – 1977

Sultan Qaboos decorates James Critchfield with
the Order of the Star of Oman – 1988

already being done by an Omani lawyer, Hamoud Al-Harithi, along with a series of Sudanese lawyers.

In the meantime, TTI's position in Oman was growing, as were Omani demands for advice. Tom Barger was fully committed to assist. Charles Black had continued to cooperate. The Bodine/Edmonds team was functioning. Maley continued in his role, and Agon was getting the field office up and running.

Back in Washington, Critchfield accepted a re-appointment to the Chief of Naval Operation's Executive Panel, a group he had worked with since Admiral Elmo Zumwalt had organized it in 1973. Zumwalt had brought together experts from various academic, business and government backgrounds to advise him on U.S. naval policy issues.[7] Critchfield chaired a sub-panel on energy related issues. This connection with the U.S. Navy would prove extremely useful in indirectly putting forward Sultan Qaboos's thoughts on Indian Ocean naval presence and his interest in developing closer ties.

The first week of December 1975, Critchfield put Oman and Tetra Tech International on hold. On December 4, he married, and he and his wife Lois went off to Jamaica for a week, well actually six days, because his Arab friends called and said "your honeymoon is over; we need you." They were all happy about the marriage and had been most generous with wedding gifts, but important matters required Critchfield's attention. In a December 12 letter to Nick Boratynski canceling a planned meeting in Washington, Jim said, "The six days in Jamaica was the best vacation I have had in years."[8]

When Critchfield arrived in London, he met first with Tim Landon, whom the sultan had recently promoted to brigadier, and then with Yehia Omar. He learned from them that the first attempt at "hard" negotiations with Shell had fallen apart. Tetra Tech's campaign to strengthen the government's position in price negotiations produced somewhat of a political crisis among the many players on all sides of the table. From all reports, Dr. Al-Zawawi had been courteous and correct in all dealings with the Shell officials, but it was clear he pressed them hard to give Oman a better financial break. No one would budge. Shell mounted a rather impressive effort to disrupt this

---

[7] The CNO Executive Panel exists to this day. Critchfield served on it until 1988, under seven CNO's.

[8] The author forgives her husband for not mentioning her!

emerging effort by the Omanis to negotiate on oil-related matters. The talks were put on hold. In the midst of this, Dr. Omar collapsed from physical exhaustion and went to a clinic in Sweden to recuperate.

As a matter of fact, neither Al-Zawawi nor Al-Shanfari was present at the final oil pricing meeting, which took place later in Muscat. Dr. Yusuf Nimatallah, by then a deputy to Al-Shanfari, concluded the negotiations on behalf of the Oman government.[9] The new average acquisition cost of $11.17 was 22¢ short of what the government was asking and less than the current OPEC price. Most of the oil moving in the market at the time was at or close to the OPEC price. That was the end of "Round One."

Critchfield later told Tom Barger that Dr. Omar, who was obviously bright and had been effective in representing his country's interests, had been, as Sherlock Holmes's Dr. Watson would have put it, "done in." Critchfield and Barger both felt that the final deal that was struck without Dr. Al-Zawawi's presence was not fair to Oman.

In Critchfield's view, the British emerged stronger and the sultan weaker. Also the issue of TTI institutional support was clearly at stake. Members of the inner circle felt that the sultan was distressed and shaken by the force of the British reaction to the Omani efforts to take a tougher position on pricing. The current mood was not to press the issue further at that time. Tim Landon tried unsuccessfully to encourage the sultan to strengthen the Omani side of the table. That would have to come another day. The sultan could not be budged.

Minister Al-Shanfari, on the other hand, had steadily, at his own pace and in his own style, grasped the essentials of the oil business in Oman and stayed on a moderate course that was not likely to upset the British or the sultan. His position with the sultan was strong, and Critchfield had to conclude that Sultan Qaboos approved of Al-Shanfari's style of conducting business. TTI would acknowledge this by conducting its affairs in a low-key manner, giving Al-Shanfari all the advice and assistance he needed, but otherwise remaining disengaged from the politics that were whirling about the sultan.

---

[9] Since his arrival in Oman in 1973, Nimatallah had worked himself into an extremely important set of positions – principal petroleum economic advisor, member of the financial council, and chief executive officer for and deputy governor of the Central Bank. From a letter by Patrick Maley to Critchfield, April 11, 1975.

TTI had to figure out how to support the government's interests without producing turbulence that could jeopardize its position. This course of action was frustrating. Critchfield felt that TTI was probably not doing more than 25 percent of what it would be capable of if it had better access to PDO data and if the Oman government would assert the role that should go with a 60 percent equity in its oil business. But Al-Shanfari was the oil minister and Critchfield found him to be an honest, well-motivated and shrewd individual. Critchfield realized that this was probably a turning point in Oman's way of doing business, with the sultan relying less on his foreign advisors.

By the end of the year, the Supreme Petroleum Council had ceased to exist. Ghassan Shaker and Yehia Omar separately met with the sultan and gave him their views that the council had outlived its usefulness. They both, however, would remain personal advisors to Sultan Qaboos on a number of other matters. Dr. Omar Al-Zawawi also withdrew from his role as oil negotiator with Shell.

This all took place just a few days before Christmas. Dr. Al-Zawawi phoned Critchfield and invited the newlyweds for a visit. Lois had joined Jim in London, and Al-Zawawi would be spending Christmas week resting at the Greens Hotel, a Swedish inn north of Stockholm, in Tallberg. Mrs. Al-Zawawi and his three children, Waleed, Areej and Reem, were with him. It was a festive time with horse-drawn sleighs, sledding and the joy of children. The short daylight hours were spent outdoors exploring the winter wonderland. Indoors, the children ruled the day with their pleas to play games. They generally commanded the attention of all.

On Christmas Eve, Dr. Zawawi was called from his villa to the main hotel to take a call from Oman. He was gone for a long time. At last everyone heard sleigh bells and, upon looking outside, saw Santa Claus sitting in a horse-drawn sleigh with presents all around him. The children were so excited they forgot all about their missing father. Santa was passing out the gifts when Areej pulled off his glove, exposing his dark hand and big wristwatch. "You are my daddy," she squealed with delight and gave him a big hug. If anything ailed anyone at that point, they were cured. It was a grand vacation.

Back in London and the real world, Critchfield continued his many conversations with members of the inner circle. What emerged from their talks was a consensus on what should be guiding decision-making in Oman. First of all, they agreed they would not let the outcome of the Shell negotiations deter them. They knew Shell had a good thing in Oman and would fight to preserve its control and independence from any effective government oversight. Still, they recognized that Oman was producing and marketing its crude oil at a maximum rate but without a maximum return. Oman's foreign currency revenues were derived almost entirely from crude oil sales, and this would continue to be the central reality for the next decade.

One major problem was that Oman's oil policy focused only on the short term. The petroleum ministry was more and more becoming the focal point of oil and gas policy, but it was hard pressed to cope with even the immediate decisions. With fairness to both parties, Oman had not yet developed data on any of the possible arrangements that it might seek with Shell and other foreign companies. Critchfield urged that until all options were studied, the government should not entertain any serious negotiations with Shell on future relations. Nevertheless, it was generally accepted that at the current level of operations, crude production from existing fields would decline quite rapidly in the next three to seven years. This led to a feeling of some urgency to speed up exploration efforts and get on with developing alternate revenue producing activities.

Everyone understood that if Oman was to develop a mid- and long-term oil policy, it must have a better forecast of its reserves. They needed an estimate of how much capital investment was required for exploration, development and production of oil and gas resources. World market conditions needed to be studied. There also was a need for a realistic appraisal of foreign companies that could play a role in Oman's development. None of this had been done. Over the mid- and long-term, Oman could develop a diversified and growth economy, but an inventory of its resources was far from complete.

Sultan Qaboos relied on the Development Council, the Financial Council, his personal advisors and the foreign consultants he deemed qualified to create planning policies. While leaving short-term decisions to the ministries, Critchfield, in his role as advisor, encouraged the sultan to keep under his command all long-term planning. Proposals on oil pricing and production policies, options for obtaining foreign capital investments, and development plans for oil, gas, copper and other minerals were issues far too important to de-centralize.

A separate but equally important factor was that Oman had unresolved border conflicts with Saudi Arabia and the UAE. These affected various possibilities for joint economic cooperation and, if not resolved, could have far-reaching influence on Oman's development plans. That was true as well with the unfinished Dhofar war, but its resolution in the near future looked very promising.

9

SETTLING INTO OMAN

TTI did not engage in commercial business of any kind in Oman. For the entire time it was there, it sat on the government's side of the table supporting it in all matters. Some observers found it difficult to believe that TTI would not accept separate contracts for services, but they soon learned that TTI had only one client: the Sultanate of Oman.

Al-Shanfari accepted TTI's role with the Palace Office and Sultan Qaboos. He may have thought of it as an oversight role, but, in fact, the original relationship of TTI was with the Palace Office. As TTI president, Jim Critchfield was expected to report directly to the sultan and his advisors on all aspects of TTI's work in Oman. Critchfield was on a first-name basis with all the members of the inner circle. In their view, TTI was Critchfield. He was the one they turned to for advice and planning. This went back to the days before Tetra Tech. He commanded their respect and in return he made sure that whatever happened, Oman's best interests were served. He was somewhat of a father figure to them. He had been a highly decorated combat officer in World War II and had gone on to have a distinguished career in intelligence. He understood the geopolitics of the volatile Middle East and articulated in a very skillful way how the Sultanate of Oman could come of age within the broader boundaries of the region. His kind and gentle manner belied the fact that he was tough to the core.

In the early stages of TTI's presence in Oman, the three most important people Critchfield dealt with were the sultan's equerry, Brigadier Tim Landon; Dr. Omar Al-Zawawi; and Qais Al-Zawawi. He kept Brigadier Landon in the picture at all times and, when needed, had him run interference. For example, on such basic issues as getting permission to open an office in Muscat, Landon played the role of facilitator. Critchfield briefed Landon extensively on matters related to oil pricing, restructuring of PDO, natural gas and related financial matters. When things appeared to get off track, he knew he could discuss them with Tim. Tim Landon played the role of chief of staff perfectly and made certain Sultan Qaboos was kept informed.

Dr. Omar Al-Zawawi and Critchfield had come through the oil pricing debacle together. Their wounds had healed and both continued to advise the sultan on oil strategy and tactics. Dr. Omar was extremely helpful as TTI established itself in Muscat. He more than once made his staff available for mundane tasks, and always with good grace and friendliness.

Qais Al-Zawawi, in his role of deputy chairman of the Supreme Finance Council, was the key man in getting TTI involved in other major activities, such as the water resources contract and development in the Musandam Peninsula. Without Qais, TTI would not have grown. All this put great responsibility on Jim Critchfield's shoulders. He knew Tetra Tech would not survive in Oman without top performance, but this was not an easy task in a country that was still in the early stages of modernization and in which he had only two oilmen – Ken Bodine and Bruce Edmonds – on the ground; Kirk Agon about to get established; Patrick Maley running between Arlington and Muscat on numerous projects; and Sam Patterson working out of Houston. There was only one way to approach the work, and that was day by day.

Critchfield's first visit to Oman in May 1976 was at the specific request of Minister Said Al-Shanfari. Up to this time, he had met with Brigadier Landon, the Al-Zawawis, Al-Shanfari and other Omanis, including Sultan Qaboos, in either London or Washington. The first year of the Tetra Tech oil and gas contract would be completed in July, and a water resources contract was under negotiation. TTI's office in Muscat was functioning. Critchfield's visit there was overdue. He flew to Muscat on May 7 and was there for ten days.

He stayed with Dr. Omar Al-Zawawi, who arranged most of the informal meetings he held with Omani ministers and other officials. Accompanied by Minister Al-Shanfari, Critchfield had an official audience with Sultan Qaboos on May 9. During the ninety minute meeting they reviewed all oil, gas and mineral activities. Later in the week, Critchfield had a private, informal meeting with the sultan at which Brigadier Landon and Dr. Al-Zawawi were present. This conversation ranged widely over Oman's development program, longer-range planning for use of resources, relations with Oman's neighbors, special problems related to the Hormuz Strait and the Musandam Peninsula, and the need for new foreign investment in Oman's development programs.

Accompanied by Kirk Agon and sometimes Omar Al-Zawawi, Critchfield visited sites all over Oman using government helicopters or light aircraft. He also spent time at the ministry and was able to observe Bodine and Edmonds in action. He took note of the fact that the ministry was staffed with a mixture of Omanis, Sudanese, Pakistanis, Zanzibaris, Saudis and Egyptians. Not one of them was a qualified petroleum engineer, geologist or geophysicist.

From the government perspective, the oil issues facing it were numerous and varied. Oil prices had not yet been firmly established. Until that was done, Minister Al-Shanfari refused to discuss PDO restructuring.

As far as PDO's general manager Rudi Jaeckli was concerned, Oman had the choice of remaining in the hands of PDO or going the way of other countries by restructuring the agreement. Jaeckli told Patrick Maley in an off-the-record conversation one evening that he felt the government should accept more responsibility in the planning, price setting and sales related to its oil. Shell had gone as far as it would go. If Oman wanted a higher price, it would have to decree it. And if it did, Jaeckli said it had better hit the right level or Shell would be compelled to decrease liftings and/or cut back capital expenditures in Oman. Maley thought that Jaeckli was absolutely sincere in what he was saying and that he personally would like to see Oman grow up, so to speak, and take its place among its oil-exporting neighbors.[1]

Was Shell looking for a situation wherein it would operate the production facilities for a fee and make no further capital investment in Oman? This was a critical question, because Shell said it was not interested in an accelerated program at Amal or Marmul, the heavy oil fields in southern Oman, although both fields were part of the PDO concession.

The oil fields of southern Oman primarily contain oil that is heavier and more viscous than the oil discovered in northern and central Oman as well as in most of the major fields in the Arabian Peninsula. Huge investments are required for any large volume heavy-oil production.[2]

[1] James H. Critchfield, *Oman Papers, 1968-1991.* D. Patrick Maley and Associates, *Oman Oil and Gas Priorities – February 1976.*

The history of the these heavy oil fields in southern Oman goes back to 1953, when the first concession for exploration in Dhofar was granted to Wendell Phillips, who agreed to forego an initial bonus in favor of an experimental work program on the Marmul reservoir.[3] It was done by Cities Service. Oil was discovered in 1956, and in 1958 a resident Cities Service geologist estimated recoverable reserves to be 800 million barrels.

In 1976, PDO discovered oil at Rahab, 16 kilometers southwest of Marmul.[4] This caused the government to look once again at Marmul heavy crude as a possibly viable project. Dr. Omar Al-Zawawi, Sam Patterson, Ken Bodine and Bruce Edmonds all endorsed a stepped-up program for Amal and Marmul and were putting together estimated costs to do so over the next three to five years. If Shell was unwilling to invest capital to produce Amal heavy crude, new sources of outside capital would be needed.

A number of oil companies had shown an interest in exploration. At the time, Elf/ERAP, Sun Oil Company, Elf Sumitomo, and Quintana were engaged there. A number of other companies had expressed an interest in Oman, such as Husky, Amoco, Phillips, Tenneco, Texaco, BP, Gulf and many others, but these companies wanted to see the data before seriously pursuing any effort. And regardless of outside interest, as long as Royal Dutch Shell controlled PDO, it did not look like new capital would be coming in.

TTI's request for data from PDO continued to be ignored. It was TTI's plan to apply the Tetra Tech methodology used in the NPR-4 (Office of Naval Petroleum Reserves in Alaska) to Oman. But before this could be done, it needed a massive data transfer from Shell and the ministry of petroleum to Houston. Two Tetra Tech geologists, Jordan Petsoff and Kirby Gowan, arrived in Oman in April 1976 to begin a review of the data, but there was nothing for them to work with. The two men were simply stonewalled. At one point, Critchfield told Al-Shanfari that he planned to send Petsoff and Kirby back to the States, but Al-Shanfari said no. It took the intervention of Sultan Qaboos to finally get the data transferred to the ministry.

[2] James H. Critchfield, *Oman Papers, 1968-1991*. Society of Petroleum Engineers, *Development of Heavy Oil Reserves in South Oman*, Ministry of Petroleum and Minerals, 1983.
[3] See Chapters One and Five.
[4] Ibid. *PDO Annual Report*, 1976.

PDO Restructuring Proposal

Not unexpectedly, on May 5, 1976, the Joint Management Committee formally presented a proposal to the ministry to make PDO a limited liability company. Under the former agreement, which dated back to 1967, IPC and now PDO (Shell and minority shareholders Compagnie Francaise des Petroles and Partex) was obliged to pay a royalty of 12.5 percent of the posted price of the oil plus 50 percent of the new profit after deducting operating expenses from the gross revenue.[5]

In January 1974, when Oman became a 60 percent shareholder, a quasi fee-type arrangement was established, wherein Shell's 40 percent equity oil profit was adjusted with each oil price increase. In 1976, this formula yielded a net cash flow to Shell and partners of 26¢ per barrel on all barrels produced. PDO had continually complained that it could not carry on with this arrangement and, in particular, that it could not participate in the Marmul development nor could it carry out secondary recovery efforts in northern Oman.

The Shell proposal, which was clearly meant to increase profits, came at the same time that the government was pushing PDO to develop new oil projects in southern Oman. It appeared that Shell was beginning to see a series of rising costs that would erode its profit under the concession and that any appreciable capital spending program in excess of depreciation would further reduce its cash flow.

Shell, apparently representing the minority shareholders, was asking either for better terms under the concession or for repayment of the $133 million investment in Oman, after which it would simply work as a contractor. On May 12, the Shell team returned to London with the most recent draft comments produced in the ministry.

At a meeting on May 16, Critchfield told Minister Al-Shanfari that he did not think the proposal provided a long-range solution to Oman's situation. The government owned 60 percent of the venture but was effectively barred from exercising its equity position in management. According to his calculations, in 1975, Shell had made a profit of 40 percent on its equity; this was approximately three times higher than the 10-15 percent the five major U.S. oil companies had

[5] See Chapter Five.

made elsewhere during the same period, and more than twice the worldwide Shell return on equity of 18 percent.

Critchfield pointed out that Oman needed outside capital. Shell had made it clear that it would not provide it. Evidence suggested that there was commercial potential in the Amal area in southern Oman. Shell was not willing to invest any capital that it could not recoup from current production. Nor was it willing to provide the government with technical and financial data to make any independent judgments on operations and development in the PDO concession area.

The value of Shell to the government was perfectly clear and should not be discounted. However the government, which faced an extremely serious financial situation in the years immediately ahead, could not afford to permit Shell to play an obstructionist role designed to maintain a distinctly advantageous financial position in current oil operations.

An alternative for the government to consider would be to initiate planning to take over 100 percent ownership of PDO and negotiate a service contract with Shell for current production, a production sharing agreement with Shell and other companies for development of the south PDO area, a long-term crude sales agreement for Shell at market prices, and another service contract to develop the gas infrastructure and operate the pipeline and related facilities on behalf of the government. All of this would require new injection of capital, possibly from Arab and/or European sources. This was probably more than Minister Al-Shanfari was prepared to hear at that time.

Discussions would continue with Shell throughout the year and into 1977. Noting that it took Saudi Arabia four years to negotiate a buyout agreement with the Aramco partners, Critchfield believed there would be plenty of time for the Oman government to negotiate its buyout from the strongest possible position. Unfortunately, this would not turn out to be the case.

In the final analysis, Critchfield asked, "What is the advantage to the sultanate in negotiating any agreement along these lines at this time?" His advice was for the sultanate to take its time to identify and study the variety of other arrangements that were evolving in the prolonged negotiations in all of the other oil exporting nations before negotiating any agreement with Shell.

Oil Production Issues

Another important oil issue that was beginning to surface was the subject of declining oil production in Oman's major fields. In May 1976, normal curiosity caused Bruce Edmonds to plot some very rough curves on production by the various fields. There appeared to him to be a sharper decline in the Fahud field than would normally be expected considering the rate of production. He requested production data from PDO, which he forwarded on to Houston for study. The August 1976 PDO production report suggested that four fields – Fahud, Yibal, Natih and al Huwaisah – exhibited decline curves, and because these four fields contributed some 240,000 bpd, Edmonds felt the rate of decline could be significant. At the beginning of November, Edmonds prepared a trend line and presented it to Khalifa al Hinai, the ministry's director of technical affairs, with the cautionary statement that such curves were only estimates but could be diagnostic.

On November 30, 1976, while Edmonds and Tetra Tech Houston were working on this, PDO engineer Herb Spatschek met with ministry officials and warned there had been a very preliminary downward revision to the oil production forecast. This confirmed Edmonds's concerns. On December 8, Spatschek briefed Minister Al-Shanfari; Joint Management Committee members Muhammad Musa, Khalifa Al-Hinai, and Dr. Sharif Loutfi; and Tetra Tech advisors. Dr. Loutfi, who was very concerned about the impact of this situation on revenues, said he would report this turn of events to Sultan Qaboos as soon as possible. He asked Spatschek to follow up with a report on the validity of the data, particularly the projection that over a six-year period production would be reduced by 100 million barrels.[6]

The report's cover letter notified the ministry that "PDO will continue to produce all petroleum reservoirs at the maximum rate consistent with good oilfield practice. Field performance in recent months, however, has shown that production rates previously forecast for 1977 and thereafter will not be fully attainable. A preliminary downward revision was therefore made and submitted to the ministry

[6] James H. Critchfield, *Oman Papers, 1968-1991*, PDO Petroleum Engineering Department, *A Note on PDO Production Forecasts*, December 22, 1975.
[7] Ibid., letter from PDO Acting General Manager B. A. Lavers to Minister Said Al-Shanfari, December 26, 1976.

in November 1976. Intensive reservoir engineering studies are currently in progress based on recent production performance and we shall prepare a full report on the outcome for presentation during January 1979."[7]

An independent review of PDO's monthly reporting of producing wells did show that in the previous two years, a dramatic decline in production had taken place. While average daily production of oil was dropping, the average water cut was rising. It appeared that PDO was approaching the point where it could be producing more water than oil.

Tetra Tech advisors strongly felt there was a need for a conservation program as well as improved reservoir maintenance procedures. The time had come for the Oman government to request an independent study by a reservoir engineering specialist to examine Oman's 260 wells and 64 reservoirs. But TTI had not convinced the government of this. The company began to look for an expert reservoir engineer to send to Oman, but had not yet found the right man.

10

SO MUCH TO DO

Tetra Tech International's exposure in Oman was expanding rapidly. Its central focus was still in Said Al-Shanfari's ministry, simply because he had such a broad mandate: oil, natural gas, minerals, agriculture and fisheries. But as time passed, the TTI people on the ground, such as Kirk Agon, were getting more involved in the wider issues of economic development. During the years 1977-78, TTI would be dealing not only with oil and gas issues, but with water resources and the strategic Musandam Peninsula.

As the pace of activities in Oman had begun to broaden, TTI Rosslyn, which backstopped efforts in Oman, needed more focus. Critchfield decided it was time to reorganize the home office. He divided the staff into three teams: Team 1, headed by Patrick Maley, would handle all oil and gas matters; Team 2, headed by Paul Debrule, a hydrologist on loan from Tetra Tech Pasadena, would be in charge of water engineering and technology; and Critchfield would be in charge of Team 3, economic development and long-range planning.

Oil and gas issues would remain the central focus for TTI as it attempted to represent Oman in its dealings with PDO at a time when pricing of oil and ownership of the oil resources were still under negotiation. To aid in this effort, TTI added a new member to the team in the ministry. Dr. Ernest Murany had a diversified background in petroleum geology and exploration; prior to joining TTI, he had worked extensively in Venezuela, both in the private oil sector and with the Venezuelan national oil company. He was also a Marine Corps veteran of World War II. His focus in Oman would be to assist in the development of an exploration program.

While these advisors were working on building relationships with PDO, plans were under way for a visit from former Aramco chief Tom

Barger. Barger arrived in Oman on March 25, 1977, and spent a full week in Muscat before going to Salalah to meet with Sultan Qaboos. He spent time with Minister Al-Shanfari, met the staff at the petroleum ministry, visited PDO and met with most of the key PDO people, including the new manager Frank Jetses. He toured the oil fields by air. Undersecretary for Foreign Affairs Yousuf bin Alawi gave Barger an extensive briefing on UAE–Saudi Arabia–Oman border matters. He visited the copper deposits courtesy of the Prospection Ltd. plane. He talked with Elf officials about its drilling of their concession in the Hormuz Strait. He also met with Remy De Jong on the water projects under way. There were numerous social events in the evenings, some including the American ambassador and Americans from TTI and other companies, and on two separate occasions he had private dinners with Qais Al-Zawawi, Dr. Omar Al-Zawawi and Brigadier Tim Landon.

The first thing Tom Barger reported, because it was so unusual in this semi-arid region, was that it rained every day, heavily at times. These were good omens. In fact, the April 3 flight to take Barger and Minister Al-Shanfari to Dhofar to meet with the sultan was cancelled because of heavy rain in Salalah. The trip was rescheduled for the next morning. When they arrived, Al-Shanfari gave Barger a short tour of his hometown. He drove by his new farm to see what effect the rains had had. The farm was a foot deep in water. A bit further on, they passed two men busily watering new trees from a municipal tank truck. "You see," Al-Shanfari said, "the regulations call for them to water the trees, so that's what they are doing."

Barger was fascinated by the minister. He learned during this visit that Al-Shanfari had been born in Salalah and that, at the beginning of monsoon season, his father would take the family into the mountains to live among the *jebalis* (mountain people) for the summer. Al-Shanfari's father traded sardines for ghee, the clarified butter of the cows of the region.

Frustrated by the inability to get an education under the old sultan, Al-Shanfari made his way by dhow to Qatar and eventually to Saudi Arabia, where relatives helped him get a job with Aramco. When he was working at an Aramco refinery in Ras Tanura, Tom Barger was running the show in Dhahran. Al-Shanfari told Barger that when Sultan Qaboos called on him to become the minister of petroleum, he accepted with great trepidation because he knew nothing about oil. He said he had two sleepless nights worrying about the job and his inadequacy, but that he could not say no to the sultan's request.

Al-Shanfari was due to meet with Shell a month after his appointment. He decided to prepare for this meeting by asking some major oil companies to come to Oman to see if they were interested in working there. He did not expect anything to come from this immediately, but thought it was a good way of informing himself about the oil business before meeting with Shell. He sent telexes to Exxon and some other companies, all of whom sent representatives to Muscat. They talked a lot about oil, and he soaked it up like a sponge.

Al-Shanfari, with reference to the current negotiations regarding PDO restructuring, said he told Shell to make up its mind about developing the heavy oil fields in Marmul and Amal, because another company was willing to put up $400 million to do the job. He revealed to Barger that the other company was Deminex, a German firm. When Shell agreed to go ahead with Marmul and Amal, Al-Shanfari commented, "The devil you know is a lot better than a new devil you don't know." Barger considered Al-Shanfari to be a very shrewd minister indeed.

Barger commented that Al-Shanfari put him in his place when he remarked, "Said, if you had stayed with Aramco, you would possibly be the refinery manager today." In response, Al-Shanfari said, "Do you think that is a better job than the one I have now?"

On that note, the two drove to the palace to have tea with the sultan. The meeting took place in the garden where they sat around a small table. The initial remarks between Sultan Qaboos and Tom Barger were small but interesting. Barger told the sultan that when he first went to Saudi Arabia he worked as a geologist in the western Rub al Khali (Empty Quarter) and that one of the very few books available at that time had been written by Bertram Thomas, who had started his journey across the Empty Quarter from Salalah.[1] Sultan Qaboos spoke of the exploits of Wilfred Thesiger, the famous explorer who wrote the classic *Arabian Sands,* relating the story of his crossing of the Rub Al Khali in 1946.

[1] A British civil servant and explorer, Thomas, author of *Arabia Felix*, served as finance minister to the Sultan of Muscat and Oman from 1925 to 1932. During this time, he made a number of excursions into the desert and became the first European to cross the Rub Al Khali.

He said that Thesiger had recently been in Oman and requested permission to climb the Jebal Al Akhdar.[2] He had come to Salalah to recruit some of the bedouin who had accompanied him across the Rub Al Khali. When the group arrived in the north and found they were supposed to climb up the Jebel Al Akhdar, they thought Thesiger was out of his mind. "Why would anyone want to climb to the top of the Jebel Al Akhdar when there were now helicopters to take you there?" The sultan was amused by this.

They then got down to business. Sultan Qaboos asked Barger what he thought was going to happen to the price of oil. Barger said he thought the price would rise slowly. Al-Shanfari briefed the sultan on his current negotiations with Shell on pricing.

Barger then launched into a substantive analysis of Oman's oil, based on his visits to the PDO producing fields the past week. His general impression was that their operations were efficient, well managed and without extravagance on non-essentials. As with oil fields throughout the world, production in Oman would decline in the future, and it would be forced to look to new sources of energy. Oman's problem would be to bridge, or at least narrow, the gap between the time of the exhaustion of its oil and gas resources and the development of new sources of energy.

Barger told Sultan Qaboos that he saw two possibilities open to Oman. The first was continued exploration. From what he learned about the geology of Oman, Barger thought it unlikely that any very large oil fields, such as those in Saudi Arabia or Abu Dhabi, would be discovered. On the other hand, it was likely that smaller fields would be found. It was true that nearly all of Oman territory likely to contain oil and gas had been explored, but the exploration had not yet approached the intensity of exploration carried out in the United States for example.

PDO, because of the length of time it had worked in Oman and the great area its work had covered, undoubtedly had more information on the geology of the country than any other company and as much expertise as any oil company in the world. Oman at the time had only four companies actively engaged in exploration. Barger thought there were probably others out there that would be willing to try to find oil if land were made available to them, and he encouraged bringing new

[2] Jebel Al Akhdar is the highest mountain in Oman, standing more than 7,000 feet above sea level.

companies in. In the history of the oil industry, he said, there are many examples of the discovery of oil in areas previously explored and abandoned by the most competent companies.

The second method of increasing Oman's supply of oil was to try to increase the percentage of oil recovered from the reservoirs. The current estimate used by PDO provided for the recovery of about 20 percent of oil from the reservoirs rocks, meaning 80 percent would remain in the reservoirs when the fields were exhausted. This amount was so great that it seemed worthwhile to see whether more oil could be squeezed out of existing reservoirs. Barger encouraged the sultan to obtain the best possible talent from among the expert reservoir management companies.

He credited Shell, the operator, with being the second largest oil company in the world with great experience and highly competent management and technology. However he emphasized that the predicted decline in production was such that Oman, because it depended so heavily upon the production of oil and gas for the greater part of its income, should consider having an independent study of reserves and procuring practices on its behalf. Such a study would be both expensive and time consuming and would require the complete cooperation of PDO, as it had gathered most of the basic data required to make the study. The idea was not to prove or disprove the accuracy of PDO estimates, but rather whether they could be improved by the application of different ideas, backgrounds and experience. There were many ways to operate oil fields, and there was no sure scientific way to decide which way was best.

Barger also recommended conservation of the associated gas by reinjecting it back into the fields so that it could be used at a later date. This surprised the sultan, who did not know that the gas could be recovered a second time.

The sultan brought up the subject of the Keyline project, which would bring the oil and gas from the Shaibah field in Saudi Arabia out through Oman rather than the Saudi port at Ras Tanura.[3] Qaboos favored such a project. It would provide an alternate route for shipping Saudi oil through the Strait of Hormuz, if an emergency safety valve was needed. In 1977, King Khalid bin Abdul Aziz of Saudi Arabia and Sultan Qaboos had agreed to survey a pipeline route from Saudi Arabia through Oman.

[3] See Chapter Seven.

It was Barger's impression that Aramco preferred the Ras Tanura option for various technical reasons, but would obviously not oppose a decision to bring the oil out through Oman if this were considered desirable by the Saudi government for political reasons. It was Qaboos's view that the Saudis were not going to consider the Oman option at that time.

The subject of boundaries between Saudi Arabia, the UAE and Oman was discussed briefly. Barger quite correctly pointed out that boundaries should be fixed before oil was discovered. He noted that all Aramco maps currently in use showed the same borders drawn by the British in the 1950s, when Britain represented Oman in its border discussions with Saudi Arabia.

At the conclusion of their meeting, the sultan accompanied Barger and Minister Al-Shanfari on the long walk back to their car. Barger overheard Al-Shanfari remark in Arabic that "Tom Barger was a very good man." After the farewell, the minister drove like a wild man to the airport where the plane had been waiting for some time to take them back to Muscat. On the way back, Al-Shanfari invited Barger to return to Salalah with his wife after the monsoon and spend a month there at his expense. Barger seemed to have won him over.

Following Barger's visit, Sultan Qaboos directed Minister Al-Shanfari to consult with Critchfield on reservoir engineering. In May 1977, Al-Shanfari formally requested that Tetra Tech prepare a detailed reservoir engineering study. Thus, one more small step was taken by the Oman government to take charge of its economic resource base. TTI began looking for a reservoir engineer of a caliber sufficient to deal with the PDO counterparts.

After his visit, Barger began to think about "enhanced recovery" in Oman. He felt he might not have adequately covered this subject when he was with Sultan Qaboos and Said Al-Shanfari. Several months after his visit, he wrote to Critchfield about this. He admitted that when he was working in Saudi Arabia, the concept of enhanced recovery never entered into discussions of production methods. "We could get all the oil there was on the first time around."

However, Oman was different, and in the months since his meeting with the sultan, Barger concluded that Shell's interest in the Oman fields might depart widely from the government's interests. If the government were to exploit its oil at rates that would furnish the optimum return to

Oman, it would almost certainly have to settle for lower rates of production. While this might seem unpalatable, it could potentially create a greater total income over a longer period than currently seemed likely. Shell was producing at the highest possible short-term rates consonant with the investments being made. Barger commented that Shell officials would not be human if they did otherwise. He added that he could be wrong on this analysis, but if he were right and new measures were not taken soon, the government might well lose billions of barrels of oil – irrecoverable billions.

Agreement Signed with PDO

On April 11, 1977, Oman entered into a new agreement with PDO. Had Barger's thoughts been shared with Sultan Qaboos and Minister Al-Shanfari earlier, they might not have been so quick to sign the new agreement on restructuring. Critchfield had to admit that he was taken by surprise by the haste with which a deal was made. Neither Sam Patterson, returning from the Joint Management Committee meeting, nor Tom Barger, returning from his visit, had any understanding that an agreement was imminent.

Critchfield said he would do some soul searching on what went wrong with TTI's communications with the government on that one. Both Ken Bodine and TTI Rosslyn had been working on a counterproposal on behalf of the government. In the final analysis, TTI's input might not have made any difference. The government, familiar as it was with the Critchfield penchant for extensive study of a problem before commitment of resources, clearly felt it was the right time to make a move, and it was probably correct in this case. What disappointed Critchfield was that he had hoped the Marmul and Amal fields could be peeled off for new companies to invest in. Unfortunately, that was not to be.

The 1977 agreement kept the PDO private shareholders as investors. They would be responsible for advancing 40 percent of the capital needed to find new oil reserves, as well as to produce the ever-declining existing oil reserves. In return they were given incentives. They gave up their higher, non-guaranteed 41¢-per-barrel profit for a lower but guaranteed fee of 31¢ per barrel. An accelerated depreciation schedule was added wherein PDO would use deferred income tax payments to finance its share of the capital costs of accelerated exploration and production. Thus, instead of receiving its full investment back in cash, PDO would receive it in installments. It was estimated that the PDO investment of $133 million would be down to $50 million in four years. The agreement stipulated that these terms were renegotiable at the end of 1979.[4]

The agreement was a hybrid between a service contract, such as used in Qatar or Saudi Arabia, and a tax arrangement. While the government would collect most of the profits of oil production, it still would not have control over the operation of PDO. And the operator was not subject to financial disciplines. Looking down the road, the government had two choices for the future. It could move back to a tax plus royalty system, or it could buy out the private shareholders' equity and convert PDO into a genuine national oil company.

After the agreement was made final, Minister Al-Shanfari appointed Salem Shabaan undersecretary for technical affairs and chairman of the Joint Management Committee. TTI advisors thought that Shabaan, who had been director general of agriculture in the ministry, was a very capable and strong leader with whom they could work closely. He was performance directed and a person of action. This would be a turning point in the ministry's dealings with PDO.

In conversations with TTI advisors, both the minister and Shabaan said they wanted to take an active role in formulating oil and gas policy and were going to depend heavily on advice from TTI. On numerous occasions, they mentioned they were tired of being led by PDO down the "primrose path" without questioning whether PDO programs were in the best interest of the Oman government. As an example, they pointed out the ineffectiveness of the government at the recent Joint Management Committee meetings. The government did not have an opportunity to question production planning and the new exploration drilling schedules for the remainder of 1977. It would now vigorously plan for the next sessions, and it wanted TTI support.

TTI's exploration expert Ernie Murany advised Khalifa Al-Hinai, the director of technical affairs, that in order for the ministry to carry out its job, the government would need essentially the same data as

---

[4] TTI interoffice memo from Ken Bodine forwarding the English text of the agreement between Oman and PDO, dated April 11, 1977, PM/102-3/81/77.

[5] Petroleum geologists (including Tom Barger) have generally agreed that opening areas to small- and mid-sized operators has had a positive impact on exploration. One such

PDO had. He suggested and it was agreed that ministry representatives be authorized to call counterparts in PDO to obtain data or interpretive information. The ministry needed seismic and other geophysical data so that its personnel could study it prior to the government's approving its 60 percent of the cost of drilling. Once again, the issue of PDO data acquisition had raised its ugly head, but this time it was resolved once and for all. From that time on, data flowed fairly freely between PDO and the ministry.

Both Bruce Edmonds and Dr. Murany had been acutely aware the PDO was production oriented. The 1977 budget was 70 percent production and 30 percent exploration. The overall tendency was to phase out exploration. Murany felt that if exploration continued its downward trend, it might be best to have PDO relinquish all acreage except for its producing fields and give other companies an opportunity to obtain profits from smaller fields.[5] He was in favor of having TTI take over exploration He believed – based on the old oil field axiom that "the best place to look for oil is where there is oil" – that central Oman deserved more exploration.

TTI did not take over exploration as Murany suggested, but it did assist the ministry in putting forward a new exploration drilling schedule, which was accepted by PDO, and all sides were pleased with what seemed to be a new atmosphere of cooperation between PDO and the government. And PDO did revive its exploration effort.

And Now to Gas

In early 1976, Critchfield made yet another approach to the government concerning gas, pointing out that over the past three years, Oman had invested in excess of $60 million on materials and services in anticipation of a gas utilization project. It was losing $3-5 million a month in revenues from natural gas liquids and $1-7 million a month from sales of natural gas. Representatives of many respected international companies had visited Oman in those three years to study the problem, but no progress had been made toward the construction of facilities necessary to implement a gas program.

geologist pointed out in 2005 that the United States was an extreme example where, in addition to the major oil companies, thousands of small- to mid-sized operators had been able to keep production levels consistently high over the past 100 years.

Critchfield's personal view was that Oman was drifting into serious financial troubles. Infrastructure development in Muscat and Dhofar was outrunning income-producing economic activities. He felt that rapid and intelligent development of a program to use associated and non-associated gas offered the single most promising economic action that the government could undertake.

The first gas project in Oman, which was completed in October 1978, was the 345-kilometer, 20" pipeline from Yibal to Gubrah near Muscat. The gas would fuel the power plant and desalination plant in the Greater Capital Area. As the price of oil went up, it had become obvious that using gas instead of diesel oil to fuel electrical generation plants was the economical way to go.

In a meeting with Sultan Qaboos in Salalah in early February 1977, when the Yibal-Gubrah pipeline was still under construction, Critchfield recommended that the gas pipeline be extended from the Greater Capital Area up the Batinah coast to Sohar, not only to fuel the copper project under way but to provide electrical power generation to the population there in anticipation of furthering development in this region.

Sultan Qaboos acted quickly on this recommendation. On February 7, 1977, at a meeting of the Development Council, he made the decision to develop the Seeb-Sohar Corridor, using the copper project and the gas pipeline as the focal point of the development plan. Critchfield considered this a significant accomplishment that would have a major influence on development in the area. Subsequently, the Ministry of Petroleum and Minerals ordered TTI to prepare reconnaissance surveys and economic feasibility studies on the entire area, most of which were completed by late 1978.

Oil companies were not geared to look for gas to be used in stand-alone economic ventures. Any non-associated gas that had been found was an accident of oil exploration. PDO used non-associated gas for oil field operations and showed no interest when the government discussed possible projects with other companies to use this gas. Dr. Murany thought there was sufficient non-associated gas for a modest petrochemical industry. He noted that other countries actually levied a retroactive tax on companies for flaring liquid natural gas. However, the government made no move to explore this possibility.

TTI continued to study what needed to be done to develop a gas exploration program separate from oil exploration and whether it made sense for the government to direct its own gas exploration, making gas a government-owned monopoly from the outset. There were many aspects to be considered, including substituting gas for diesel fuel in power generation, using gas as a fertilizer feedstock, and even exporting gas to neighboring states such as the UAE. Also, there were several pipeline systems being considered, the economics of which needed to be carefully studied.

Critchfield met with Minister Said Al-Shanfari on several occasions to discuss the complex problem of gas utilization, including regulation, marketing and physical distribution systems. He noted that virtually all oil producing nations had dealt with this by establishing a national gas company, and he strongly urged that the Oman government follow this course. It was important that the gas system be run efficiently as a business enterprise with sound financial management from the outset. Such an authority was an indispensable part of the administrative machinery required by any nation that has a national gas system and dispenses gas to a variety of customers – public utilities, private industry, government-owned industry and the domestic and commercial consumer.

The technology of gas utilization was changing rapidly, and the price of energy faced enormous challenges in the years ahead. A sustained supply of gas over a very long period could become the single most critical element in Oman's economy. This would be significant if and when oil production went into a sharp decline. Critchfield hammered away on this subject, but the minister avoided making any decisive move in that direction.[6]

It was 1979 and Oman's development was moving ahead rapidly. In the broader Middle East, historic changes were taking place. Momentum for a Middle East peace was building with Anwar Sadat's visit to Israel in 1977 and the signing of the Camp David Accords in 1978. But these positive developments were soon overshadowed by events that would haunt President Jimmy Carter until the end of his administration. Mohammed Reza Pahlavi abdicated his throne and left Iran in January 1979. Ayatollah Khomeini returned from exile in

[6] Action to do this was taken in August 2000, when the government formed a closed joint stock company called the Oman Gas Company. It is 80 percent owned by the Ministry of Oil and Gas and 20 percent by the Oman Oil Company. It owns and operates the pipelines that deliver gas to power generation plants and other small consumers. The first gas sales to the UAE, delivered by pipeline, took place in 2004.

February 1979 to lead the revolution that resulted in the establishment of an Islamic republic. In November 1979, the U.S. Embassy in Teheran was overrun and its employees taken hostage.

The Iranian Revolution led to the so-called Second Oil Shock, when crude oil prices jumped to $34 per barrel. While this event caused economic disruption worldwide, the oil-producing nations in the Middle East, including Oman, were making record profits. Thus once again, Oman found itself in the enviable position of being able to afford what it was buying.

11

TTI ROSSLYN ACTIVITIES

In 1977, Critchfield began searching for additional staff for the Rosslyn office. He would soon lose Patrick Maley, who closed down his consultancy business and joined one of the Seven Sisters, Mobil Corporation, where he would spend the next ten years at the company's headquarters in McLean, Virginia, and as general manager of Mobil's Saudi affiliate in Riyadh. While it was a good career move for Maley, he would be missed at Tetra Tech, both in Muscat and in Rosslyn. His contribution to the effort in those early days had been extremely valuable.

Before Maley's departure, Critchfield brought in John Sasser, a promising young staff economist who had been in the Tetra Tech Systems Group since 1974 and whom Critchfield co-opted to work part-time on specific projects. A graduate of Gettysburg College with a degree in physics, Sasser soon became a full-time TTI employee. His principal responsibilities were to be the economic aspects of gas utilization in Oman; however, after Maley's departure, he took over all issues related to Oman's petroleum business and became head of Team 1.

At about the same time, Josee Carre joined the Rosslyn staff. Josee had been working for Yehia Omar, first in London and then in Geneva. Born and educated in France, Josee was an extremely efficient administrative assistant who might possibly still be in Europe had she not had a small encounter with the Swiss authorities. The story goes that she had a minor one-car collision with a telephone pole and that when the Swiss police arrived on the scene, she did not have the papers required for employment in Switzerland. The Swiss authorities told Omar that Ms. Carre must go. Yehia asked Critchfield if he could use a bright, efficient secretary on his staff. She had been paid through the remainder of the year and he would donate that to the TTI cause. Ms Carre arrived in Rosslyn, with the proper papers of course, and began her career in the

United States. What Josee and John did not know at the time was that they would be spending the next quarter century in Oman and the Arabian Gulf together.

Another new face at the Rosslyn office, and a man who was becoming a star performer, was Arthur Rypinski. Arthur was 23 years old when he joined TTI in 1978. A graduate in economics and international relations from American University in Washington, DC, he had just returned from England where he had studied at the London School of Economics. He was barely off the plane when TTI staff economist Dixie Sokolosky, who had taken classes with Rypinski at American University, brought him to the attention of TTI. Critchfield snapped him up before another potential employer had a chance, and Arthur was happy to have a job and an income.

In the beginning, Rypinski reported to John Sasser. His first assignments were short-term oil price forecasting, in support of Oman's oil price negotiations and natural gas pipeline planning in the sultanate. It was not long before Critchfield realized how blessed he was to have this young man on the team. Despite the age difference, the two thought and worked very much alike. They both had a Darwinian approach to research, in that they could take an immense amount of data, disappear from the crowd and immerse themselves, sometimes for days, and reappear with a finished product that was clear, concise and sometimes even brilliant. Critchfield was not about to let Arthur Rypinski get away, and after a short period of time he raised his very minimal entry salary.

An Extra-Curricular Contract for Tetra Tech International

In an audience with Sultan Qaboos in early 1978, the sultan remarked to Critchfield that he thought his young officials needed more exposure to the United States. While most of them had been to England and parts of Western Europe, some for study and some for holidays, too few had been exposed to American history and culture. Would Tetra Tech International be willing to create a short course for a select number of Oman officials, ones he personally planned to put on a fast track. Critchfield, of course, said he would be delighted to do this.

Each Omani who came to the United States under TTI's sponsorship stayed for several months, and a tailored program was developed to meet their specific fields of endeavor. The first such Omani was Ahmed Suwaidan, a young official in the Palace Office. His interest was in telecommunications. He spent from early March to early June 1977 in Washington, California and Texas. All TTI employees and consultants took part in the program. Tutors were also engaged from Johns Hopkins University and other academic institutions in the area. He also met many Americans from both the private and public sectors. In private tutorial sessions, Suwaidan was taken on a geopolitical tour of the USSR, Western Europe and the Middle East as seen from American perspectives. TTI employees lectured on the potential of economic development in Oman and on systems engineering and modern problem-solving techniques. He spent a week on the West Coast, with visits to San Francisco, Los Angeles and Tetra Tech facilities in San Diego. He had a complete tour of Tetra Tech Houston. When he returned to Oman, he went back to his old job, but before long Sultan Qaboos appointed him minister of post, telephone and telegraph.

In April 1978, Colonel Salem Al-Ghazali, at the sultan's request, spent several weeks in the United States as a guest of TTI. Although he was not there in any official capacity, Critchfield arranged for him to meet many government personalities, such as CNO admiral William Crowe, who had been regional naval chief in Bahrain, and Hal Saunders, assistant secretary for the Middle East; as well as several retired ambassadors and CIA officials, oilmen, bankers, lawyers and businessmen. He also made the rounds to California and Texas. He received lectures from Middle East experts. He traveled extensively, meeting oil company officials and other personalities with ties to Oman. This was in preparation for his assignment to take over as the number-two person in the new Ministry of Defense under Sultan Qaboos, who was his own defense minister. Later, Al Ghazali would become the minister of commerce and industry.

Colonel Ali bin Majid al Ma'amari, a Dhofari, likely had the most exposure to American military practices and a big dose of geopolitics from Critchfield himself. He was put through a fairly heavy schedule that began with his arrival in Washington on September 16, 1979, and lasted three months. He visited all the government institutions in Washington, saw the U.S. Congress in action, visited Harvard and Woods Hole Oceanographic Institute, participated in the airborne deployment of the new 155 mm artillery at Fort Bragg, visited the Kennedy Space Center (and Disneyworld), was exposed to the American revolutionary era at Yorktown, Jamestown and Williamsburg, and attended a several-day program in southern California and San Francisco, including a visit to a Chevron refinery center. He had lectures on geopolitics, the USSR, and systems analysis; there was a minimum of wasted motion in his schedule. He returned to Oman in December and shortly thereafter replaced Tim Landon as equerry to Sultan Qaboos, head of the Oman Directorate of Intelligence and head of the Palace Office, where he remains today with the rank of major general.

Landon had said repeatedly to Critchfield that his goal was to work himself out of his job. Landon moved permanently to London, but he continued to serve as a personal advisor to Sultan Qaboos. When Critchfield visited Oman from January 15 to 27, he called on Ali bin Majid at the Palace Office and found him fully installed in what had been Landon's office. He proceeded to do business with him on the assumption that he would serve the same function that Landon had. In fact, Ali bin Majid fairly rapidly scaled his function back to concentrate on national security affairs. He had limited interests in the development areas TTI was working on, but Critchfield maintained a close relationship with General Ali bin Majid, who continued to be the principal go-between in arranging meetings with Sultan Qaboos.

Critchfield, during this same period, spent several weeks in Oman making sure that TTI was meeting all its contract commitments. A letter to his wife dated January 21, 1979, reveals how he viewed the performance of his company. This was before the era of email, and expensive international phone calls were used only for business purposes.

January 21, 1979

Dear Lois,

Russ Dalton will leave tomorrow night to return to Washington for a crash redo of parts of the pipeline reports for Oman and Saudi Arabia. So of course I am using the opportunity to communicate with you. Chuck Koberger brought your letter which I have read and re-read – enjoying every line over and over.

I am impressed with the size and complexity of what I have created here. Many things to sort out and everyone needs attention of some kind. Kirk continues to grow as the competent chief executive. I will announce before I leave that he is the new vice president of TTI.

I saw Salem Al-Ghazali privately at home soon after I arrived – a very good talk. The morning of the 15th, Kirk and I met with Hamoud Al-Harithy, the fairly new Minister of Water and Electricity. We have a marvelous relationship with him. He is also chairman of the Musandam Development Committee and works as closely with Kirk as I do. Later that morning, I met with Qais Al-Zawawi in his office. Kirk and Yousuf bin Alawi also present.

Early on the 16th, I met with Salem Macki, who brought me up to date on his week in London with Charles Black – a successful venture. Later in the morning a meeting with Tim at the Palace Office – tour d'horizon and some specifics too. At 1 PM Kirk, Nga and I went to a lunch at Salem Al-Ghazali's home – a farewell for Rob Browning whom he replaced. Frank Jetses, PDO general manager, got me off in a corner and congenially gave me a hard time about how unnecessary it is to have Tetra Tech looking over their shoulder.

Later on the 16th Sam Patterson shows up at the office. He, Brad Dismukes and I dine with the Agons.

On the 17th at 8 AM Kirk, Yousuf bin Alawi and I lifted off from the police helicopter pad for a day all over the Musdandam Peninsula, meeting with the *walis* (governors) of Khasab and Bayah, visiting isolated tribes in the hinterland, landing on huge peaks to look at impossible ideas for roads. Lunch on a rug under a tree in the desert produced like magic from a village that almost escaped my notice. Later we had the full treatment with lamb, rice et al with the *wali* of Bayah before heading back. A very good day.

The morning of the 18th I had a good hour with Mohammed Zubair, another hour with Qais in his office. The Intercontinental crowd has arrived and are in his waiting room when I leave. I see them at (U.S. Ambassador) Marshall Wiley's residence for cocktails and again at Mohammed Zubair's for dinner the next night. Although Friday is a holiday, I worked in my room all morning, sat in the sun and read for an hour or so at noon and went to the beach to run late afternoon.

Our compound is two adjacent villas – one two story, one a single story. The former is the office on the lower floor and the Agons live upstairs. Their apartment has been redone and is cheerful. Kirk, Russ, Nga, Daud and Ishaq staff the former. Daud is the cook and major domo of the transient quarters. I have a bedroom and bath. Joe Callahan has the same. Amen, a tall Sudanese draftsman, has the third bedroom. We have a dining room, a kitchen, an engineering and drafting working office and a sitting room with sofa and chairs. Daud and Ishaq are two old Pakistanis. Ishaq is jack of all trades, driver, messenger, airport greeter, etc. Daud has a little less status but they compete. Each has a small air conditioned room that Kirk ingeniously added and they share a bath. Between them, we are marvelously taken care of. I have my work all spread out on a well-equipped and large desk in my room. I slip into proper attire for meetings and slip back into slacks the moment I return. Except for one day when I was late getting back, I have run three miles on the beach in front of the Intercontinental Hotel – wide, flat and hard like Daytona Beach.

The water contract has been in a snarl since it expired last July 31. We are in a second extension but papers have been lost. Al-Shanfari is never here and we have not had a cent for months. I am determined to unsnarl this before I leave and tackle Qais head-on with the whole mess today. Also, I am engaged in a fairly massive sorting out of water problems in the hope that I will have a new two-year contract fairly well along before I leave. Substantively, I think we are now on top of things. Kirk as VP will have the follow up job when I leave. I am optimistic.

The oil and gas business is going great. Our recommendation to the government to put it to dear old Shell for $14.03 per barrel prevailed, although Shell went through great gnashing of teeth, charges of blackmail etc. $14.03 was exactly what Sasser and Rypinski calculated.

I have spent much time on Oman-Saudi pipelines, borders, et al, and will spend more. I must go to Saudi Arabia from here, have my visa application in (routine since the Oman Foreign Office is sponsoring) but no firm flights yet.

After all the confusion dies down, it appears that [former President] Gerry Ford and David Rockefeller will be here about the same time on the 26th. Qais is furious since it was DR's schedule that got all fouled up working through the Oman Embassy. Also Betty has been shifting around a little too.

I am going to Salalah on the 24th to meet with His Majesty and give him my ideas about what all this means. I have been invited to a strategy session tomorrow morning that should be interesting. I have pulled my thoughts together and will sleep soundly tonight.

The minute that I have a new water proposal in the mill and have done all I can to make the visits of the VIPs go well, I will shove off to Saudi Arabia. Then it is an open agenda. I do not have any idea who I will see.

This is, I think, probably a landmark visit. This is where all the action is centered and Kirk is month by month growing into the man that can hold most of it together. He needs to pace himself and ease off – I can see too many little signs of overwork and will give Nga and him some guidance before I leave. Once I am home, I need to sit down and look at where our TTI budget is at half point. Then I will turn my attention to other matters. Home, the beach house etc. with you in the middle of it all looks good to me. If things go as well as I think they will, I will leave here with a definite sense of having things in hand. Saudi Arabia is an open question and it is there I will have to form some effort in the months ahead.

Qais is coming to Washington next month – relations with the U.S. are obviously a key issue. As I left the foreign ministry a few days ago, the Chinese ambassador was getting out of his car at the front door. Changing times!

I go through your letter describing the house furnishings for our new beach house. It is a marvelous warm, exciting vision that gives me a great feeling of happiness and anticipation. Don't become discouraged, my love. Sooner or later your husband will tire of riding choppers to Hormuz, running on the beach in Oman, and remaining deeply involved in the future of the world's economic stability. I did a marvelous briefing map for Gerry Ford last night – loaded with lots of good political action in my old tradition. We expect to see that map get around a good deal in the months ahead.

I have worried about your Mother and have, of course, no word of how your weekend in Florida went. You can plan to get one more letter to me here if you find out when Russ Dalton returns, on the 28th I think.

Well, I have been at this for most of the evening. As you may gather, this is a benign, well organized life that I lead here – vaguely reminiscent of the army. The Omanis are lovely people and it is a pleasure to work with them – if one does not expect too much too quick. I have the feeling that my role here will be going through a gradual change now. The appointment of Kirk as vice president and getting over the hurdle of renewing the water contract would set his course through mid-1981. Much of the pressure will be off, I think.

I am very anxious to finish the current job and be getting off the plane in Dulles. But this trip was a must – so many critical loose ends. I love you very much and appreciate so well all that you do to make it possible for me to carry out this side of my life.

Lovingly, Jim[1]

[1] James H. Critchfield, *Oman Papers, 1968-1991.*

12

WATER, WATER – NOT EVERYWHERE

There Are No Rivers or Lakes in Oman

One cannot say that it never rains in Oman, but the fact is that Oman lies in an arid region of the world. It is hot and dry; in the interior, very dry. Only in the south, in the Dhofar region, is there benefit from regular summer rain, known as the monsoon, and even there rainfall rates are low. Elsewhere, there can be sporadic rains, heavy at times, but rainfall is sparse and there are long periods of drought. This makes the art of exploring for water extremely important.

For thousands of years, the Omanis obtained their water from an ingenious system known as the *aflaj*, a series of man-made underground and surface channels originating in the mountains and flowing to populated areas, where the water they carried would be gathered for irrigation and domestic use. In areas not served by the *aflaj*, water would be drawn from wells either by hand or by animal power. After 1955, the first mechanical well pumps using diesel fuel were introduced.

Water supply depends on both the amount of rainfall and the percentage of rainfall that can be channeled into aquifers for storage. The goal in a semi-arid climate, such as Oman, is to divert the maximum amount of rainfall into these working aquifers. Most aquifers are natural; they are phenomena of nature, not man made. But structures can be built to increase the amount of water that reaches the aquifer: dams, retardation structures, flood control and water transports systems, such as canals, pipelines, ditches, and *aflaj*.[1]

As the flow of *aflaj* varied from year to year, depending on rainfall, villages in Oman developed a system of concentric zones of cultivation.

---

[1] For an authoritative study on water in Oman, see J.C. Wilkinson, *Water and Tribal Settlement in South-East Arabia: A Study of the Aflaj of Oman*, London, Oxford University Press, 1977. For the reader not familiar with the terminology, aflaj is the plural of *falaj*.

In the heart of the village were the date gardens, which were generally watered even in dry years. Around the fringes of the villages, crops such as vegetables or alfalfa were grown during years of large *aflaj* flow, and the land was allowed to lie fallow during years of low flow.

The nature of agriculture changed with the advent of oil. Despite the fact that there was little profit in growing dates, the price of land and water rights in date gardens had risen rapidly. It appeared that some Omanis were using the income derived from the oil boom to purchase date gardens in their home villages for reasons related to stature and social security rather as an economic investment. By contrast, the economic value of the fringe crops had steadily risen because of increased demand from both Muscat and the neighboring United Arab Emirates. While the demand for water in Oman was potentially infinite, supplies, even under the best of circumstances, were relatively limited.

The early water policies in Oman were based on traditional Islamic law. Under this law, water was free for all, but its legal status was governed by effective possession. In general, the person who dug the well became the owner, whether or it was on his land or on unowned land. The government also owned wells.

The *aflaj* were generally owned by a community of users or perhaps by a leading family. Its use for irrigation was reserved by the owner, and he could draw down as much as he wanted. Sultan Qaboos realized that the time had come to re-examine these traditions in light of increased demands for water not only for agriculture, but also to support the rapid expansion of development projects in Oman. The issuance of royal decrees by the sultan containing written regulations on water utilization would soon replace tradition.

When Tetra Tech arrived in Oman, there was no ministry of water, nor was there any structure for the administration of water resources. The Tetra Tech team from Pasadena, which conducted a survey in 1975, had been there as guests of Dr. Omar Al-Zawawi.[2] Theirs was not the first company to come to Oman. Many others had conducted water resource surveys, but there was no coordinating body in Oman to analyze the data and make decisions on Oman water policy.

Sometime during the summer of 1975, the sultan moved the responsibility for water resource management from the Ministry of Communications to the Ministry of Agriculture, Fisheries, Petroleum

[2] See Chapter Six.

and Minerals, headed by Said Al-Shanfari. A Water Resources Council was formed under Royal Decrees No. 26/75 dated June 28, 1975, and No. 45/75 dated September 18, 1975. Al-Shanfari added a water resources department to his burgeoning ministry. The initial council members were Minister Al-Shanfari, who was chairman, Minister of Communications Abdel Hafidh Rajab, and Minister of Interior Mohammed bin Ahmed.

At the same time, Sultan Qaboos told his ministers that TTI would be the primary consultant to the council on all matters related to water. TTI was well aware that the subject of water requirements for domestic and commercial use had been addressed by Sir Alexander Gibb & Partners.[3] Although most of their studies had been made available, they did not include data on agricultural irrigation, which made up an important percentage of the total water requirements of Oman. Another major problem was that the outline of water needs for commercial and industrial use appeared to be inconsistent with the most recent development plans of Oman, which had grown considerably since the original study was done.

A year later, on June 15, 1976, Tetra Tech International signed a two-year water resources contract for $900,000 to provide technical services to the Water Resources Council. The council, however, had yet to hold its first meeting. Was the subject of water so overwhelming that the Omanis in charge could not face up to the challenges ahead of them? Whatever the answer to this question, TTI did not wait for the council to get organized. As a starting point, it built its planning on the water survey results done in March 1975 by Tetra Tech engineers Drs. Le Mehaute and Sonu.[4]

TTI hired Dr. Thad McLaughlin, a geologist, to be the technical director of the effort. He visited Oman on June 15, 1976. Dr. McLaughlin had retired from the USGS in December 1975 after a prestigious career. Just prior to his retirement, he had served as chief of an American team studying water supply problems in Saudi Arabia. While most of his career was spent on projects in the Rocky Mountain region of the United States, he had also performed work in Jordan and Greece. As TTI technical director he would travel frequently to Oman. Assisting

[3],Ibid., Sir Alexander Gibb & Partners, *Water Supply to Muscat and Mutrah*, November 1974; and *Water Resources Survey of Northern Oman*, April 1974.
[4] See Chapter Six.

him would be Dr. Remy de Jong, a Dutch hydrologist, who went on the TTI payroll in 1977. De Jong's previous experience had been entirely in the academic world.

The TTI plan, and Dr. de Jong's first task, was to establish a technical secretariat whose initial work would be to determine the present and future requirements for water in Oman and to assist the availability of surface and ground water, i.e., establish demand and supply. Based on these forecasts, the secretariat could then determine the size and nature of the infrastructure that was needed. This would involve building storage reservoirs, water distribution networks and desalination plants. The secretariat would report its findings to the Water Resources Council when it met.

In fact, the first meeting of the council did not occur until February 2, 1978, a year and a half after the TTI contract was signed. In the interim, de Jong devised ways to get things done, such as drafting preliminary letters for the minister, discussing the letters with the minister, and putting them in final form for the minister's signature, which gave him the mandate to continue his work. At the same time, he worked on organizing a data library for the ministry and writing a water code.

In 1976, the United Nations Development Program, Food and Agriculture Organization (UNDP/FAO) produced a water resources development report based primarily on work done by private consultants over previous years.[5] The report's conclusions were generally negative. It had several recommendations pointing to improving water resources, and went into considerable detail on the types of projects that could be carried out in the various regions of Oman. According to the report, there was an urgent need for water legislation and the establishment of a national water policy. It recommended that the newly established Water Resources Council establish a database and begin to identify potential water development projects.

All this advice was well and good, but Dr. de Jong could not do much more than add the report to his newly organized library. He represented the entire water resources staff in the ministry.

As time passed, it became apparent that the terms of reference of the Water Resources Council needed to be spelled out in greater detail.

[5] James H. Critchfield, *Oman Papers, 1986-1991,* UNDP/FAO, *A Summary of Water Resources and Agriculture Development Reports in the Sultanate of Oman, October 1975- January 1976,* Bo G. Appelgren, Consulting Water Resources (Spain/Sweden).

Thus Royal Decree No. 76/77 dated November 2, 1977, promulgated the Water Resources Development Law, which gave the council the authority to issue permits and licenses to dig and operate wells and to prepare a water code.[6]

The first formal meeting of the Water Resources Council on February 2, 1978, was a get-acquainted session. The ministers attending did not need to get acquainted; they knew each other well. It was clear, however, that they knew little about what had been going on regarding water planning. Attending the inaugural meeting were Ministers Said Al-Shanfari, Abdul Hafidh Al-Rajab, and Mohammed bin Ahmed; Dr. Remy de Jong, acting as technical secretary; and Dr. Thad McLaughlin, who had flown in from the United States earlier that week.

Minister Rajab wanted to know at the outset if there were any Omanis on the staff, to which de Jong had to respond that there were none and this would be a pressing issue when they started issuing permits and licenses. He said he and Dr. McLaughlin were the staff. McLaughlin was there to provide expert assistance in setting up the secretariat under the terms of the TTI contract.

Rajab asked which came first, the TTI contract or the formation of the Water Resources Council. In actual fact, the council came first, but no work had been done until, under the terms of the contract, TTI set up the secretariat. Rajab also wanted to know what had happened to all the water resource studies the government had contracted for at great expense since 1971. He was assured that they were all available in the secretariat and would be used as references as specialists moved forward.

These reports did not, however, provide all the answers. More data on how much water was available and where and how it could be used was needed. Furthermore, before a plan could be formulated to allocate water resources, a policy had to be established at the top government level, i.e., the Development Council and Sultan Qaboos. The Water Resources Council would remain an empty shell until water policy was seriously addressed. In short, the development of a water plan for the nation was moving ahead at a snail's pace.

Dr. de Jong, using extensive maps and charts, briefed the ministers on the basics of water preservation. He pointed out that most of the

[6] Ibid., from Royal Decree No. 76/77.

water in Oman originated in the mountains and flowed either to the coast or toward the interior. Most of the rainfall in the mountains went into the sea, with little opportunity to recharge the water in the ground and ultimately the *aflaj* system; thus, water was being lost. To recharge this water, retardation structures (dams) needed to be built between the mountains and the sea. Most of the ministers at that point became dam experts, relating personal experiences from the areas in which they had lived.

Thad McLaughlin told them about a plan that had succeeded in Los Angeles. Water that had been flowing quickly to the sea was successfully harnessed by a rock barrier, which lessened the velocity and enabled them to use or store most of the water. The types of dams to be built in Oman would vary from one valley to another. This approach had been used in Saudi Arabia and was recommended for Oman. The council members agreed that visits to the various areas needed to be done prior to the next meeting.

There was also curiosity about the use of satellite photography. De Jong told them that the satellite passed over Oman every eighteen days and that the images it took were available from Landsat – at a price, of course. Satellite photographs could be extremely useful in these early planning stages.

Before the meeting ended, the ministers got down to basics, with Minister Al-Rajab taking the lead. He recommended that no new wells be dug without permits from the council and that these permits be issued by the newly established water resources department in Al-Shanfari's ministry. The meeting came to a close with Minister Al-Shanfari stating that he would notify the Development Council that they had decided that recharge dams would be built on a case-by-case basis and that general guidelines for issuing permits and licenses for well drilling would be prepared. Everyone agreed that the local *walis* would be informed before visits were made to any site. That was an important afterthought.[7]

During the next few months, efforts to organize a water plan continued. The secretariat sorely needed a qualified staff, and de Jong engaged the services of UN agencies to help train staff members in administration and hydrologic evaluation techniques.

[7] James H. Critchfield, *Oman Papers, 1968-1991, Minutes of the First Meeting of the Water Resources Council,* February 2, 1978.

The Greater Capital Area

Water supply in the Greater Capital Area came mainly from the new desalination plant at Gubrah. What did not come from there was pumped from wells in Wadi Samail. When the desalination plant was shut down for maintenance, more water had to come from the wells; as more water was pumped, the salinity content went up. If an accidental interruption of the desalination plant occurred, this could lead to increased salinity of the groundwater supplies and there could be a serious threat to the Greater Capital Area's water supply.

As a result, a moratorium was put on well drilling in the Wadi Samail until a water recharge program could be developed for the critical Greater Capital Area. These were the kind of issues discussed at the level of the Water Resources Council and subsequently sent up the chain of command to the Development Council. The Greater Capital Area always received priority attention on all matters.

The Batinah Coast

TTI always gave the water situation in the Batinah, the strip of coastal plain beginning at the Seeb airport and continuing to Oman's northern border with the UAE, immediate attention. The Batinah was a heavily populated region that contained about half of the total land under cultivation in Oman. The salinity of the ground water in the Batinah coastal area was of particular concern. The area was under development for copper mining and potentially the exploitation of other minerals. It was being looked at as a future site for light industrial development and agricultural pursuits. And the more affluent Muscatis, who aspired to be weekend farmers, were building second homes there.

The availability of sufficient water resources was far from known. What was known was that salt water was beginning to seep into the fresh water. Inland encroachment of salty water from the coast had already occurred along a strip of the Batinah west of Seeb. This encroachment, resulting from heavy pumping inland with declining fresh groundwater outflow to the sea had led to salinization of the soil and the death of many trees. Concentrated pumping near population centers had resulted in local concentrations of brackish water and deterioration of water quality.

From very early days, the Batinah coast has been a place of romance and intrigue. Sumerian tablets refer to a country named Magan as a source of copper. It seems certain that they were referring to Oman, and more specifically, the Batinah. Evidence from excavations near Sohar shows that the copper mining and smelting industry was well developed by the year 2000 BC.

Sohar, the major village on the Batinah coast, dates back to the first millennium. A settlement was unearthed there in which buildings from the first century AD were found, indicating a flourishing settlement. The artifacts discovered show that Sohar was a significant trading center at the time. Archeologists found merchant seals and a type of fine terracotta earthenware, possibly imported from India.[8] Water for the region came from shallow wells.

In the year AD 853, "on a Sunday night and for three nights, a destructive flood overspread the region. Many houses were destroyed and many people drowned. Sohar was destroyed and the water reached very high levels. And because of hunger and homelessness, many people left their homes and spread throughout the country."[9]

The Batinah region eventually became resettled, and through the nineteenth century, the production of dates increased. The water used for irrigation came from wells that employed mules or bullocks pulling a rope connected via a pulley to an animal-skin bladder that lifted the water from deep wells into reservoirs that were directed through channels to date plantations. These worked much like the *aflaj* did in the interior. These wells operated around the clock, and Western visitors in the nineteenth century reported hearing the deafening sound of the squealing pulleys throughout the entire Batinah coast 24 hours a day. By the 1880s, date plantation owners were expanding production in order to meet a growing American demand. This was prior to the development of the California date industry, which was created in part from offshoots of the Omani date palms imported and planted by the University of California in the early 1900s.[10]

---

[8] Ministry of Water Resources, March 1995.

[9] Abdullah Humayd Al Salmi, *Tuhfat Al Ayan: bi Sirat ahl Oman (History of Oman)*, vol. 1, p. 161 (Al Istikama Bookshop, Oman).

[10] Matthew Hopper, "The African Presence in Arabia: Slavery, the World Economy and the African Diaspora in Eastern Arabia, 1840-1940" (PhD dissertation, UCLA, September 2006).

What particularly troubled Critchfield was the high volume of diesel water pumps introduced in the past five to six years, not only in the Batinah but also in Salalah and the Greater Capital Area. These pumps were rapidly threatening the ecology of the coastal plains of Oman. Many of the coastal aquifers were already out of balance in some areas, and the solution, Critchfield believed, was to regulate use and maximize the recharge of aquifers to maintain a balance. The current organizational structure was not capable of dealing with this serious problem in the Batinah or elsewhere. The system was not working.

A Push for Reorganization

The TTI effort on the ground in Oman, led by Remy de Jong, wandered down a variety of dead end roads, and there was little tangible progress. By June 1978, it was clear to Critchfield that TTI was in real trouble for lack of performance in the water resources arena.

He enlisted the help of Joseph T. Callahan, the director of TTI's water resources staff in Rosslyn and for many years a senior USGS water specialist, in launching a rescue operation. Callahan recruited and brought to Oman Joe Rousseau, Charles Reed, Coyd Yost and Bobby Gaddis, all experienced hydrologists. Rousseau seized the initiative and produced a superior and creative report on the Batinah plain.

Rousseau's effort demonstrated how much data could be collected in two months by qualified experts willing to work. They tested one thousand wells, and their report dramatically revealed a rapid deterioration in the Seeb area.[11] This went right to the heart of the current policy debates about the Greater Capital Area water supply.

Yost and Gaddis also went to Dhofar and produced reports that put the company's work in Salalah in a much improved position. Their findings, however, were not encouraging. Unless additional sources of groundwater were found in Salalah and the surrounding region, they believed it would not be possible to carry out all of the agricultural

[11] Ibid., Tetra Tech International, J. P. Rousseau, *Ground Water Salinity Survey of the Southeast Batinah Coastal Plane*, 1978.

[12] Ibid., Tetra Tech International, B. L. Gaddis, *Effect of Ground Water Use on Quality and Availability in Salalah Coastal Plain*, 1978 , and *Model of Shallow Aquifer, Salalah Plain, Sultanate of Oman, 1978.*

work projected in the next five-year plan.[12] Kirk Agon did a fine job of pulling all these reports together.

If a new contract was signed, Joe Rousseau would stay on in Oman. TTI had specific recommendations for further work to be done in the most critical areas of the Greater Capital Area, the Salalah plains and the Seeb-Sohar corridor. As a result of the efforts of the Callahan, Rousseau and Agon team, TTI was back on firm ground with the Water Resources Council.

Meanwhile, on July 29, 1978, Sultan Qaboos issued a decree announcing that Hamoud Al-Harithy, the Minister of Electricity and Water, would replace Abdel Hafidh Rajab, the Minister of Communications, as a member of the Water Resources Council. Shortly after this announcement, the sultan appointed Rajab as Minister of Agriculture and Fisheries, carrying out the long expected split off of these activities from the Ministry of Petroleum and Minerals. Rajab then replaced Al-Shanfari as chairman. Minister Al-Shanfari then returned to his world of oil and gas.

As far as TTI was concerned, Hamoud Al-Harithy's presence on the scene was extremely welcome. Kirk Agon began working with him immediately, and together they put together a report to Qais Al-Zawawi on how to turn policy into action. Qais, as deputy chairman of the Developmental Council, would be the man to approve the financing of ongoing projects. Agon also made a special effort to brief Abdel Hafidh Rajab on council matters. He was regarded as a tough, able and sometimes difficult minister. It was important that he be well informed on these activities.

At this juncture, Critchfield felt that, despite the changes in the Water Resources Council, there were important organizational changes that needed to be made. He met with Sultan Qaboos on October 31, 1978. The briefing took place in a desert tent in the interior of Oman, where Sultan Qaboos was visiting local tribal dignitaries. Critchfield was flown in by helicopter to meet with the sultan on the subject of water. Psychologically, it could not have been a more perfect setting. There was no water in sight. The caravan of ministers waited outside while Critchfield presented Sultan Qaboos with his ideas on how the water resources program should be drastically changed.

After formal greetings, Critchfield said,

> Your Majesty, the Batinah coast is headed for an ecological
> disaster, because of oil money and diesel pumps. The
> introduction en masse of the high-volume diesel water pump
> in the past five or six years presents a rapidly developing threat
> to the ecology of the coastal plains of Oman, including Salalah,
> the Batinah plains and the Greater Capital Area. We think most
> of the coastal aquifers in some areas are already out of balance
> with their use exceeding recharge. We are convinced this is true
> in Salalah. We see signs that it is the situation in the Batinah.

Critchfield explained that over-pumping by government, business
and private landowners had resulted in the intrusion of salt water, which
was damaging the wells. There were no regulations to stop this, and the
Water Resources Council, which Sultan Qaboos had formed in 1975,
had failed in its job, not only in the Batinah but in all of Oman. TTI,
which was operating the secretariat, had also failed. He had some ideas
for change. The immediate solution was to regulate use of the wells
and maximize the recharge of aquifers to maintain a balance.

Critchfield recommended that a regulatory agency be developed to
carry out policies on the use of water. He thought that the Water
Resources Council, as it currently existed, should be scrapped and a royal
decree issued to establish a new council, with Sultan Qaboos as chairman.
It would then truly be a policymaking body. In this way, the sultan
would have the opportunity to influence and direct his vital national
water program.

This regulatory agency would become the key organization
responsible for developing and recommending sound water policies and
for seeing that they were carried out. He also recommended establishment
of a separate Oman water authority, with its own personnel, budget and
administration. It would function as the executive arm of the government
in developing and carrying out national water policies.

It would have primary responsibilities for developing the data,
the technology and the technical basis for water policies approved by
the new Water Resources Council. Critchfield handed the sultan
a diagram outlining how a new water council and authority
might look.

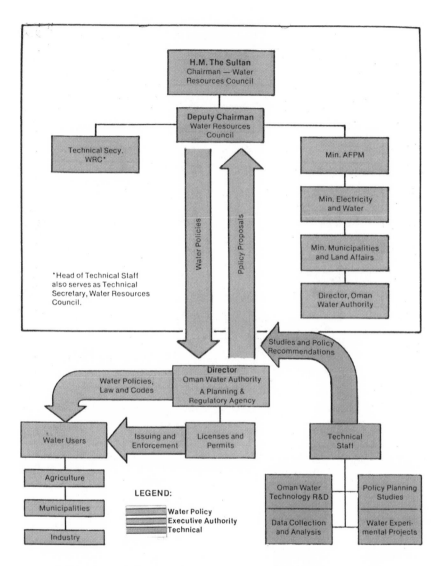

Organizational Diagram for a Water Council and Authority –1978

If the sultan would implement this change and give TTI the responsibility for organizing and staffing some form of water authority, Critchfield would personally accept the responsibility for seeing it succeed. Sultan Qaboos listened thoughtfully.

By the end of 1978, Dr. de Jong was replaced by Dr. Robert H. Dale, an experienced American hydrologist with a USGS background. It was about that time that TTI, disappointed with the support it was getting from Tetra Tech Pasadena in finding appropriate personnel to send to Oman, began to use its USGS connection for technical help and expertise. Most of the hydrologists that followed Dale to Oman would come from the USGS pool of former or retired employees.

TTI also maintained the connection with Glen Brown, an important role model for them all. USGS had carried out more than thirty years of water resources work in Saudi Arabia, amassing a great knowledge of the water problems of the Arabian Peninsula. There was a real advantage in making these former USGS specialists available to Oman.

Also in late December 1978, Agon forwarded to Ahmed Suwaidan, who at this time was director of the Palace Office, drafts of two decrees reorganizing the agencies related to water resources. The general concept followed that proposed to Sultan Qaboos during Critchfield's desert visit in October. Letters were also sent to Brigadier Tim Landon and to Qais Al-Zawawi, whose support he would need to bring about any major change. Water Resources Council members were also briefed on these proposals.

On Critchfield's next trip to Oman, in January 1979, he met with Sultan Qaboos. The sultan made the unsolicited remark that he had not acted on his proposal, but that he would. Whether or not that had any influence on ministerial foot-dragging concerning renewal of the TTI water contract, by then six months overdue, a new contract was signed on April 1. TTI's contract was extended until December 31, 1980, when it would be placed into the Oman five-year-plan calendar.

Satellite imagery delivered from TTI Team 2 (Water Engineering and Technology) in Rosslyn to Dale's new team provided fairly spectacular support for planning and action. In cooperation with the Ministry of Electricity and Water, three wells were drilled in the Hajjar limestone formations on the outskirts of Muscat in the Wadi Adai. The first of these showed that they could produce water equivalent to 14 percent of the Gubrah desalination project. Dale believed that the Hajjar limestone formations, many of them extending into the outcrops in the central mountains and Musandam, were heavily charged, fairly old limestone aquifers not sensitive to variations of periodic drought.

Encouraged by these factors, Critchfield had Dale and his team prepare a study for Sultan Qaboos using the hydrological maps, the new enhanced imagery and a slightly modified version of the organizational proposal Critchfield had presented to the sultan a year before. In September 1979, Critchfield asked Brigadier Landon to arrange an audience with Sultan Qaboos in Muscat.

Critchfield met with Sultan Qaboos on October 20. He told him about Dale's drilling of the three wells and his belief they would be capable of producing a sustained production of water that could significantly supplement the production of the Gubrah desalination plant. When he again presented the concept of a water authority and delivered Dale's latest report, he asked for three years to prove out theories about Oman water. Sultan Qaboos agreed. Critchfield could not have imagined the bureaucratic and managerial obstacles that lay ahead. Some came from outside, including decisions made by the US/Oman Joint Commission, and others from within.

Far away from the Greater Capital Area, a bit of good news came along when a drilling rig working in the Musandam-Rawdah area on October 23, 1979, hit water. Rawdah was located in a mountain-locked valley with a flat floor of several thousand acres and a rapidly dwindling population. Scarcity of water was the problem. Earlier in the year, Yousuf bin Alawi, Critchfield and Agon had explored this area by helicopter.

They had examined a 90-foot dug well that was bone dry in the center of the alluvial valley bottom. The residents still living there were desperate for water. Landing on the 8,000-10,000-foot-high mountain peaks that surrounded the Rawdah bowl was dramatic but, in terms of finding a feasible access road in which to truck in supplies, proved to be a fruitless exercise. In the end, the imperative of some action by the government to provide water led to a decision to fly in, piece by piece, a water drilling rig and, barrel-by-barrel, the water needed for drilling.

Finding water in Rawdah was very encouraging. Up to that time, the only way the government was getting water to the villages was by truck to the interior, by boat to the coastal areas or by operating a few expensive and very small desalination plants. The TTI water team in Oman was optimistic that success was in its reach. If the team was correct in its estimates, the Oman water situation would be transformed.

If the Musandam's vast mass of limestone peaks and cliffs, viewed as barren and dry until then, should prove to hold reservoirs of ancient water, the character of the Musandam Peninsula would change. The initial strike was just a first step, but Dale and his team were optimists, perhaps dreamers. Only time would tell.

The Public Authority for Water Resources

On December 4, 1979, Sultan Qaboos signed Royal Decrees No. 62/79 and No. 63/79 outlining the new administrative structure to expedite the development of the water resources in the Sultanate of Oman. And thus the Public Authority for Water Resources (PAWR) was created.[13] Its chairman would be Hamoud Al-Harithi, the Minister of Electricity and Water. He would report directly to Sultan Qaboos as chairman of the Water Resources Council. Critchfield, Agon and TTI's Team 2 had turned another corner and were optimistic that the PAWR would be the vehicle to get a water plan under way.

Finding water and storing it was to be the work of the PAWR. The Water Resources Council had been reduced to a policymaking body. Since 1970, there had been considerable *aflaj* repair in the interior and southern Oman as well as flood control work. What was needed now, and had been needed for a long time, was an extensive water plan for the nation.

The first order of business for the PAWR was to establish a secretariat to be operated and staffed by TTI. The PAWR was divided into five districts:

Al Batinah District Office – Sohar
Interior District Office – Nizwa
Southern District Office – Salalah
Sharqiyah District Office – Mudayrib
Capital Area District Office – Seeb

One of the primary problems that had plagued the sultanate throughout its recent history was the inability to establish a long-term, reliable data gathering program in the rural areas. Historically, government efforts had been conducted from Muscat. The district offices would change all that. They would also act as liaisons between the PAWR and the public and private interests within the district.

[13] Ibid., Royal Decree No. 63/79 *Concerning the Formation of a Public Authority for the Water Resources Council* and Royal Decree No. 62/79 *Concerning Reformation of the Water Resources Council,* December 4, 1979.

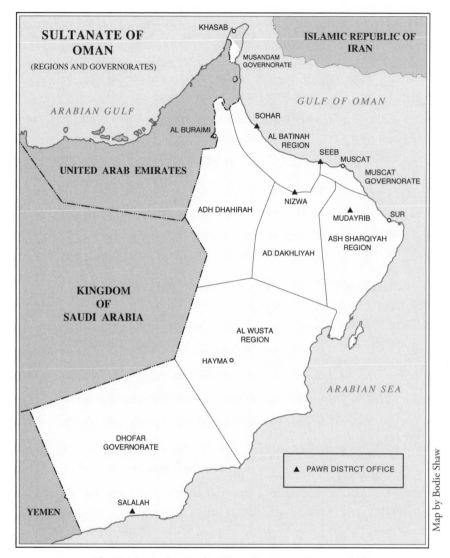

The Public Authority for Water Resources District Offices

Because the geology of Oman was so diverse, the problems facing each district varied. The Salalah district officer concentrated on collecting data required to construct a computerized groundwater simulation of the Salalah Plain. The Seeb district officer placed emphasis on long-term water supplies for the Greater Capital Area and actions needed to prevent or retard salt water intrusion along the southern Batinah coast. The Sohar district officer, also concerned with salt water intrusion, dealt with problems related to potential groundwater contamination resulting from the Oman Mining Company. He was also responsible for dealing with the complexity of finding water in the Musandam. In the interior regions of Nizwa and Mudayrib, the district officers were challenged with the mountainous areas where most of the towns and villages were located as well as the difficulties associated with work in the vastness of Oman's desert. Seminars were held every six months for the staff to discuss common techniques of data gathering and analysis.

The PAWR secretariat also established a scientific laboratory to carry out needed analyses of water and other related activities. The initial operation of this facility got off to a poor start when the scientist hired for the job had to be let go for lack of performance. In mid 1981, an experienced water chemist, Soloukid Pourian, was put in charge of organizing the laboratory. Pourian, a naturalized U.S. citizen of Iranian descent, was multi-lingual and had worked in Iran, Germany and the United States. Before pulling up stakes and moving his family to Oman, he had been working with the County of Los Angeles and doing consulting work with Tetra Tech Pasadena.

Dr. Bob Dale was extremely enthusiastic about the work and, if somewhat disorganized, carried with him an aura of optimism that was catching. His team soon was augmented by four hydrologists – all from the USGS pool of talent. The professional staff sometimes referred to themselves as Dale's "hydro-commandos." Failure was not an option.

The work of the PAWR continued at a rapid pace for those on the ground, but there did not seem to be a sense of urgency within the government about the water program. Critchfield, who had been pushing TTI Rosslyn and Dale to get operational as quickly as possible, was concerned that the PAWR would not be ready should an emergency occur. He pointed out that storms, floods, drought and other natural phenomena that inflict great hardship on a town or state in the United States were dealt with by the U.S. president's "declaring it a disaster area," thus triggering availability of money and immediate actions by various agencies. In principle, the Water Resources Council would be in charge of how to handle such crises in Oman. In practice, the PAWR would have to do the job.

In general, Critchfield felt that Oman had moved at too leisurely a pace to get a meaningful water program under way. And he knew who would shoulder the blame if the PAWR were not able to perform when needed. It would be Tetra Tech International.

As a result of the U.S./Oman Joint Commission established in 1980, the U.S. Army Corps of Engineers and U.S. Agency for International Development (USAID) were brought in to get programs under way. What had been slow motion up to then suddenly became a flurry of uncoordinated activity.

The ground water exploration program was run along lines similar to an oil exploration program. First, the PAWR identified a number of aquifers throughout Oman, drilled and tested exploration wells, established programs to collect data on what happened to rainfall once it falls on Oman soil, studied stream flows and started on the long process of studying Oman's principal water reservoirs.

In keeping with the tested principle of petroleum engineering that pilot projects should precede large-scale investment in production schemes, a proposal was made in 1979 to enhance recharge of the aquifers above Seeb. This was the area upon which the Greater Capital Area was dependent. Drilling a number of exploration wells in the vicinity of Wadi Aday proved to be very successful and demonstrated that the aquifer formation near the Greater Capital Area would yield large quantities of fresh water. The water from Wadi Aday was blended with the water from the Gubrah desalination plant before being distributed to users. The cost of the desalinated water, which provided the Greater Capital Area with 73 percent of its water, was some four times that of ground water.

The exploration effort was later extended to include drilling sites in Wadi Mijlas and Wadi Mayh south of Muscat. It was hoped that extending the exploration program would identify water resources that could be available to supply domestic water to the Greater Capital Area over the next 10-15 years and thus lessen the dependence on desalinated water.

One of the more successful groundwater exploration projects was undertaken near the Salalah plain in the south. Virtually all the wells drilled led the PAWR to conclude that there was significant potential in this area for groundwater development. And during the monsoon from May-September, the area received enough rain to support agricultural development and a population of about 50,000.

This kind of exploration drilling was done in every district, and about 1,350 wells and *aflaj* were monitored for water quality on a weekly or monthly basis. In addition, inventories were made of more than 10,000 wells countrywide.

At the same time, the PAWR was structuring a surface water program. It constructed gauging stations to measure the flow past a point on the stream. These stations needed to be designed to withstand floods for many years. Reliable flood information would assist in the development of designs for civil works such as recharge structures, flood control devices and roads.

As time passed, preliminary engineering designs for groundwater recharge were completed. The staff evaluated the reservoirs that were suitable for recharging. By the end of 1980, PAWR hydrologists had completed the design for Wadi Al Khawd and were working on the design for Wadi Aday, both serving the Greater Capital Area.

While undertaking these tasks, the PAWR was also training Omanis to eventually replace the foreign experts. This was an important endeavor, because Sultan Qaboos was adamant in pursuing a policy of Omanization. The PAWR contributed in a significant way to this program.

Virtually every task and project undertaken by the PAWR was designed to provide the sultanate with the tools necessary for water resources planning and management. TTI advisor Dr. Thad McLaughlin was assisting with interviews of hydro-geologists for tours of duty in Oman. Ten additional professionals were in the pipeline to arrive in Oman in the months ahead. Kirk Agon would provide on-the-spot support and guidance for the program. By the end of 1980, the full complement of twenty technical advisors was complete, and Omani civil servants were joining every day and being trained for fieldwork. PAWR's clerical and technical assistant staff had increased to thirty-five. It was looking like a thriving organization.

13

FOCUS ON THE MUSANDAM PENINSULA

When Dr. Omar Al-Zawawi and Yehia Omar were briefed on Tetra Tech in Rosslyn in January 1975, they were impressed by the ports and harbor work Tetra Tech Pasadena was doing. They wanted the company to do a survey in the most strategic area in Oman, the Musandam Peninsula. Separated from the rest of Oman by part of the United Arab Emirates, the Musandam Peninsula is located in the northernmost part of Oman. Its mountainous coastline extends into the Strait of Hormuz.

When he took over the reins of government, Sultan Qaboos thought of his country as a maritime nation by both tradition and geography. He considered the western Indian Ocean and the security of the maritime routes from the Arabian Gulf to both Europe and the Far East to be of critical importance. Once the land war in Dhofar was over, the sultan hoped to develop the maritime potential of Oman, including a small but credible navy. Very early on he spoke of his interest in establishing a relationship with the U.S. Navy, but nothing official had yet been done. Getting the Tetra Tech team to look into port development was clearly a precursor to moving in that direction.

The Strait of Hormuz and its strategic implications interested Critchfield immensely. He predicted that OPEC production by the end of the 1970s would be up to ten million barrels per day, and a high percentage of this would be going through the strait. There were also serious environmental issues to examine. Traffic and pollution problems would only grow. This would have a big impact on TTI's thinking on the Musandam Peninsula, the Strait of Hormuz and the need to keep the Keyline pipeline project alive.[1]

Out of that interest came a contract to survey the area and to present a proposal for the development of a maritime facility in the Musandam.

[1] See Chapter Seven.

Dr. Choule Sonu, a port design specialist from Tetra Tech Pasadena, headed a second mission to Oman and traveled over the entire Musandam Peninsula. He was specifically tasked to look into the possibility of developing a small port on the northern coast. The final report, dated May 16, 1975, laid out a plan for development, which over time could result in a complete air, land and water development program for the area. Yehia Omar presented this report to Sultan Qaboos in June 1975.[2]

The report identified several potential sites where the oceanographic environment (currents, tides and waves) would permit the location of a harbor and further maritime development. As a result of the site survey and analysis of available data, Tetra Tech recommended that the government undertake a four-phase maritime development program that would result in a complex of air, land and water facilities.

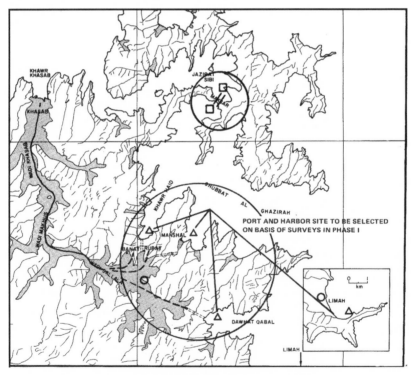

Map Detail of Four Phase Development Proposal

[2] James H. Critchield, *Oman Papers, 1968-1991,* Tetra Tech Report No. TT-A-041, *Development of a Maritime Facility on the Musandam Peninsula in the Sultanate of Oman,* May 16, 1975.

Phase 1 would establish Khasab as a facility around which the complex would be developed. This phase of work would include constructing a mooring wharf, enlarging the airstrip and building a small breakwater and/or dredging into Wadi Khasab to insure protection for ships.

Phase 2 would establish an anchorage in the Khawr Kuwai on Jazirat al Ghanam Island, with a helipad and a wharf at Salib, and if feasible, a landing strip on Jazirat al Ghanam.

Phase 3 would establish a harbor and port at one of the three sites in the southeastern part of the Musandam Peninsula, the selection to be determined after bathymetry (water depth measurements), land and preliminary soil surveys, and an evaluation of the relative cost of building a connecting road from each of the sites to Khasab. In addition, an airstrip would be built in Khasab, and a road connecting the Khasab port with whichever site was selected.

Phase 4 would, if feasible, connect the Gulf of Oman and the eastern side of Musandam with the Arabian Gulf and the western side of the peninsula via a canal, with or without gate locks, through the Al Maksar Isthumus.

As a first step, the report recommended that the government establish an ocean-oriented presence at Khasab in order to facilitate the step-by-step development of a Musandam maritime complex. The remainder of the report contained technical details to support the four-phase proposal.

While there was not going to be immediate action by the Oman government on the recommendations of this report, Critchfield foresaw that any future development in the Musandam Peninsula would include TTI. In September 1975, Qais Al-Zawawi, then Oman's Minister of State for Foreign Affairs, told Critchfield he would entertain a specific proposal for further development of plans for the Musandam Peninsula. Critchfield's instincts were correct: TTI's future in Oman would be on many fronts.

While some borders drawn in the Middle East seem strange to outsiders, the Oman/UAE border on the Gulf of Oman defies imagination. The Musandam border only begins to make sense when the earlier tribal history is understood. The predominant tribe in the Musandam was the Shihuh, which had its own Arabic dialect. The tribes of the area defined their territories – the Shihuh pledged allegiance to Oman; the other tribes of the region to the UAE – and the result was that the strategic Musandam Peninsula became separated from the rest of Oman by the UAE. Fujairah, one of the six emirates, lies on the eastern side of the UAE on the Gulf of Oman. Ras al Khaimah and Sharjah are on the Arabian Gulf. The Hajjar mountain range divides the UAE in two, separating Fujairah from Ras al Khaimah and the other emirates. In 1977, the only practical way to get from Muscat to Musandam was by flying over the UAE.

At the time, the population of the Governorate of Musandam was about 15,000. Most lived in the coastal villages historically dependent upon the sea for food, income and access to trading centers. Subsistence agriculture, primarily date palms, complemented fishing as a source of income. A few family settlements existed within the upper reaches of Musandam's *wadis* and *jebals,* where they had been able to trap enough water and silt runoff to maintain rudimentary agriculture. In the summer months, most of these people migrated to the coastal areas due to lack of water for their farms. While there, they earned income from fishing. As certain elements of change were introduced, such as health clinics and schools, the people began to aspire to more than fishing and subsistence agriculture. With the local presence of the government and the military, new employment opportunities were gradually created.

The Musandam Development Committee

On May 1, 1976, Sultan Qaboos issued a letter of instruction to form a committee to take care of all related activities in the area bordering the Strait of Hormuz. It was to be called the Musandam Development Committee (MDC). The MDC would be chaired by Minister of Communications Abdel Hafidh Rajab, with one representative each from the ministries of agriculture, fisheries, petroleum and minerals; defense; and foreign affairs. The letter instructed the chairman to ask TTI to appoint a qualified advisor/secretary for this committee. A separate letter from the Ministry of Defense appointed Robert Browning, director general of the Ministry of Defense, as its representative on the committee.[3] Periodic meetings were to be held every six weeks, or more often if necessary.

[3] Ibid., Sultanate of Oman, Ministry of Diwan Affairs, No. S/2-2/76/91 May 1, 1976, and Department of Defense, No. DMD/DEF/I-14-B, May 10, 1976.

In October 1976, TTI submitted a contract outlining the general scope of work it would undertake. The contract was making its way through the various bureaucratic channels, but TTI's work had already begun. When the MDC met with Sultan Qaboos in Salalah on February 20, 1977, he told them he wanted a progress report every three months.

On March 22, 1977, Kirk Agon was officially appointed MDC secretary. In return for services performed, the committee would pay TTI a fee of $115,000 for 1977 and $128,000 for 1978.[4] The committee met fairly frequently. Most of the meetings were at the Ministry of Communications office in Muscat, but they also visited Musandam, together and separately, on frequent trips. While development projects were going on all over Oman, action in Musandam was special. It was not easy to get there, travel was always by helicopter, and, as there were no overnight accommodations, all visits had to take place in one day. On one occasion, Agon and Critchfield were stranded in Kumzar due to weather; Critchfield's bunk was a pile of boat lines curled up by the dock near the desalination plant.

Khasab urgently needed a hotel/guesthouse to make life easier for commuters from Muscat and for prospective investors and businessmen. Agon was in touch with Muscat hoteliers to obtain cost information, a first step in getting this project off the planning board and into construction. The next important step was construction of an airport in Khasab. However, a critical conflict surfaced immediately. The Ministry of Social Welfare was soon to begin construction on 72 low-cost housing units in the same area as the planned airport. Because of the confining nature of the mountains surrounding Khasab and a limited amount of level area on which a landing field could be built, the MDC was faced with a serious problem. A contractor was scheduled to begin construction on the housing project shortly; but the director general of civil aviation had not yet obtained funding for the airport. It was not even in the five-year plan.

Everyone agreed that the airport would eventually be built, but in the meantime, the space must not be developed for any other use. This was an urgent agenda item at the April 28, 1977, MDC meeting. The outcome was that the Ministry of Social Welfare would hold its project in abeyance for 30 days and an ad hoc committee of representatives

---

[4] Ibid., Sultanate of Oman, Musandam Development Committee, *Contract to Supply a Secretary to The Musandam Development Committee*, February 22, 1978.

from the Ministry of Defense, the Oman Air Force and the Directorate of Civil Aviation would launch a site survey for the airport and obtain funding for its construction from the Defense Ministry. Robert Browning was put in charge of this activity. No one wanted to see an extended delay of the housing project, but the airport took precedence. As it turned out, Browning's committee visited Khasab and decided that the housing project as planned would not interfere with airport development. While thirty days were lost, much was gained by forcing the airport issue to be addressed. Building a new military/civilian airport was a matter of urgency.

There were many other problems to address in dealing with Musandam Peninsula's development. There were questions related to road building, electrification, port development, water supply, commercial enterprises and town development. The ministers serving on the MDC all had other responsibilities to attend to, and there were only so many hours in a day. But evidence shows that they gave a lot of their attention to the Governorate of Musandam and to their role in the MDC.

For example, the MDC was soon made aware that local citizens in the Musandam Peninsula, who were heavily dependent on the UAE for staple foods and commercial goods, had been experiencing difficulties in getting what they needed. The MDC calculated that if it could support local merchants in opening stores in Khasab, the citizens would be less dependent on the UAE. The MDC was also instrumental in building a cold storage facility to permit fishermen to deliver their catch to market in Khasab. This would be the beginning of establishing a viable commercial community in Khasab.

As instructed, the MDC delivered its first quarterly progress report to Sultan Qaboos in June 1977.[5] It outlined what would be a very aggressive program for the rest of the year:

Construction of electrical power plants was under way at Khasab, Bukha and Bayah; the first would be completed in July and the final one in October. Still to be resolved was who would be responsible for connecting electrical power to individual residences.

Sixteen villages were scheduled to receive water supply systems. This included a desalination plant for Kumzar and Shaisah and wells to supply Bukha, Ghumda, Limah, Qidah and Bayah. The remaining villages

[5] Ibid., *Musandam Development Committee Quarterly Report to His Majesty Sultan Qaboos bin Said*, June 1977.

152

would be supplied with water delivered by tanker ships. This project was expected to be completed by the end of August.

In order to improve the supply of water for agricultural purposes, concrete-block water tanks would be constructed in 32 strategic locations. Residents and local contractors would do the work. Once completed, trucks would deliver water to these tanks as needed.

Contracts had been awarded to build 72 low-cost housing units in Khasab and 60 units in Bayah.

Design-and-tender documents to build a modern all-weather jetty at Khasab would be completed by the end of September.

The citizens of Bukha requested that a road be built to connect them with Ras Al-Khaimah in the UAE. The MDC decided the project was not politically feasible at that time and suggested instead that a survey be done on the cost of building a road from Bukha to Khasab. Although Bukha was closer to the UAE, it made more sense to improve communications between the Omani villages of Bukha and Khasab.

Funds had been budgeted to build the cold storage and ice plant in Khasab. Plans were under way to build clinics and schools in Kumzar and Limah and a youth hostel in Khasab, which would house students who lived too far to commute each day to school.

Private businesses were beginning to take note of investment opportunities in the Musandam Peninsula. There had been queries regarding creation of a transshipment facility at Khor Ash Sham, the inlet between Khasab and Kumzar, to be used by cargo vessels headed for the Arabian Gulf.

The MDC's role was to coordinate all these and future projects with each ministry or agency that would be doing the actual work. The process thus far seemed to be working. The MDC secretary did what he could to ensure that the left hand knew what the right hand was doing. It was not an easy task.

By the end of 1977, projects were moving along, some of them on schedule and others not. The three electrical plants had been completed but were not yet in operation. On the water scene, one of the three tankers had been delivered and was in service. The wells to smaller villages had been completed, but the desalination plants at Kumzar and Shaisah were not operational, pending availability of qualified personnel to run them. The people of Shaisah, who annually went to Sharjah in the UAE to harvest dates, threatened not to return until the plant was operational.

The people in Rawdah, isolated in the central part of the Musandam province, obtained their water by tanker trucks from Ras Al-Khaimah in the UAE. Alternatives included digging wells and/or constructing a road between Rawdah and the east coast Omani village of Limah, where sufficient groundwater was available. Still, given the rugged terrain in which the work was being done, what had been accomplished was dramatic. To the MDC, these were matters of national security and were considered a priority.

The MDC realized there were other major gaps in the region's development. There was a significant lack of communication between Khasab and the outer world. In addition to no airport, there was no commercial sea transportation, no roads, no telephone and telex facilities, and no television. There were no commercial banks. If commercial shops were to be opened in Khasab, they would need at least a branch office of one or more banks in Muscat.

In July 1978, Minister of Electricity and Water Hamoud Al-Harithi replaced Rajab as MDC chairman. He and Kirk Agon had worked very closely together on water issues. They now met frequently on MDC questions. The big projects on the agenda were the new jetty for Khasab, the airport, and roads. Offshore oil exploration taking place in the Strait of Hormuz would need to be taken into account. If oil and/or gas were found, a supply base would be needed in Khasab. The new jetty would have to be large enough to handle oil rig supply boats and tanker ships delivering fuel to a storage depot for various consumer needs. These factors were taken into account when designing the jetty project. The final design was sent to the directorate general of finance in July.

The MDC continued to expand. In October, three new members were added to the committee: Ministry of Communications Undersecretary Abdullah Al-Qatabi; Ministry of Agriculture, Fisheries, Petroleum and Minerals official Muhammad Al-Kassim; and Development Council Secretary Sharif Loutfi. Dr. Loutfi's presence was particularly important. Having a good understanding of all projects under way in Oman, he could put into perspective what the MDC could realistically do for the Musandam. He could also provide ideas on how to attract private investment to this remote but increasingly strategic area.

Everyone on the committee agreed that the government needed to continue with its effort to provide electricity, water, health and educational services, and communications to a greater number of citizens. They realized that although they had been very active for almost two years laying the groundwork for future development in the Musandam Peninsula, the results of this activity had not been visible to the local population. Some public relations work was needed here. The committee members suggested that Agon, the MDC secretary, prepare an article for the local Oman press tracing the recent history of Musandam development and giving insight into the MDC's strategy. They asked Agon to follow up with regular press releases.

In late November 1978, the Palace Office notified the MDC that Sultan Qaboos would chair the next meeting on December 23 in order to address the many outstanding decisions related to development in the Musandam Peninsula. The committee, of course, welcomed this opportunity to meet with the sultan, and all were present that day. Also attending was Minister of Defense Undersecretary Colonel Salim Al-Ghazali, who was designated to replace Robert Browning on the committee.

The first item on the agenda was political. The MDC needed to establish the extent to which lines of communication would be established with the UAE and, by implication, the extent to which the Musandam province should depend on the UAE for its economic well-being, not only for consumer goods but also for employment opportunities. The most basic question in this regard was whether a road should be built between Musandam and the adjoining emirate of Ras Al-Khaimah.

Although the sultanate was able to provide infrastructure to improve communications and quality of life in the Musandam Peninsula, a more difficult task was to provide a means of employment for its citizens. At that time, the fisheries industry offered one of the best potential sources of employment and was being expanded. But Musandam citizens continued to travel to the UAE for jobs. There were pros and cons to this issue. Some felt that a road connection to the UAE through Ras Al-Khaimah would only encourage the exodus of Musandam citizens.

Sultan Qaboos's decision was not to pursue building a road at this time. Relations between Oman and Ras Al-Khaimah were still unsettled; a road connection between the two was premature. What he wanted to see were road connections between Khasab and the isolated west coast villages of the province. This would make Khasab a center whose facilities would be more readily available to a greater number of Musandam's citizens. In light of this, he directed that the ministries of communication and defense give priority consideration to the construction of a road connecting six outlying villages, including Bukha, with Khasab. He also ordered a ferry service connecting Khasab with the coastal villages of the province and from there to the northern Omani port of Sohar.

The MDC then turned to the subject of offshore exploration of the Henjam reservoir in the Strait of Hormuz and the impact this would have on the port facility at Khasab should production become a reality. Sultan Qaboos's view was that an enlarged port facility could not be justified based solely on the possible exploitation of Henjam, but at the same time he thought it was better to build a facility large enough to serve future requirements of all kinds, such as handling ships carrying petroleum products, construction materials and heavy equipment. He directed planning to be implemented with this in mind.

The MDC acknowledged that one of the basic requirements not yet met was in the field of telecommunications. As a short-term solution, the committee proposed using high-frequency radio to connect Muscat with Khasab; this was how Salalah communicated with Muscat. Of concern to Sultan Qaboos was the fact that people in the Musandam Peninsula were watching television broadcasts originating in the neighboring states and did not yet have access to Oman television. He wanted to see that situation remedied.

The sultan wanted to know what steps were being taken to make commercial goods from Oman available to the Musandam citizens. He was informed that a warehouse facility in Khasab would be built for goods transported from Muscat at government expense to be sold on a wholesale basis to existing retail merchants.

On a final note, the MDC chairman raised the subject of MDC command and control. Committee members were concerned about becoming involved in activities for which ministries had been established. Was Sultan Qaboos concerned about this?

The sultan's response was that first, the MDC must establish that there was funding available for a particular project, and second, it should notify the ministry concerned of its recommendation regarding this project. Thereafter, the MDC should follow the project all the way through to the end. If difficulties arose, then the MDC should raise these problems with him. The sultan closed the meeting by noting his pleasure with the progress of the MDC to date. He stated it was his intention to meet with the committee every six months. He was optimistic concerning the future development of Khasab and all of the Musandam Peninsula.[6]

After the sultan's participation in the MDC's meeting, the momentum picked up measurably. Of particular importance was the responsibility assumed by the Ministry of Defense. Colonel Al-Ghazali informed the MDC on January 10, 1979, that engineers from the Ministry of Defense would be taking over responsibility for construction of access roads in the Musandam Peninsula, a decision that was greeted with enthusiasm by the committee. During the last half of January, the Ministry of Defense dispatched a survey team to Musandam to determine a tentative routing for the roads, a schedule of work and a projection of funding required for each road construction project.

It was of course understood that the Ministry of Defense would have a direct interest in development in the Musandam area. The ministry would see to it that civil development projects, such as the airfield at Khasab, telecommunications and roads, also met military requirements. Colonel Al-Ghazali notified the committee that there would soon be a military governor assigned to Musandam. The military governor would have authority over the local Musandam *walis* and would become a member of the MDC. Subsequently, on May 16, 1979, Lt. Col. Rashid Al-Azeedi was appointed the new military governor and a de facto member of the MDC.

Another official visit to Musandam in June was made by Minister of Communications Sayyid Salim bin Nasser, who had replaced Rajab. He met with the governors of Khasab, Bukha and Bayah. They no doubt were marveling at the attention they were receiving from the Muscat ministers, who were promising all sorts of good works for their people. At the same time, Muscat officials knew all too well how important it was to have good relationships with the local authorities.

The MDC continued to work on all the issues on the table. In the month of June alone, Kirk Agon had made three full-day trips by helicopter to Musandam to address the problems of infrastructure, remoteness from Muscat, an expanding program involving many ministries, and the stress this put on the Omani bureaucracy to deal with the responsibilities immediately at hand in Muscat – let alone those

[6] Ibid., Musandam Development Committee, *Minutes of the Extraordinary Meeting of the MDC,* December 23, 1978.

in the inaccessible region of the Musandam Peninsula. The MDC had given TTI huge responsibility, and, happily, it had an excellent track record in Oman. The lesson painfully learned, however, was that Oman probably would have to go for a centralized authority in the Musandam province.

The MDC Secretariat at Work

As MDC secretary, Kirk Agon had almost single-handedly taken care of the tracking and coordination of the dozens of projects under way. One such project was the introduction of a ferryboat system to connect Muscat with the Musandam Peninsula.

In November 1979, the MDC leased a ship called the *Al Nims*, which arrived in Mina Qaboos, the port serving Muscat, on November 2. The initial use of the vessel would be to deliver gas and oil supplies to the electrical generating facilities in Khasab and to the Ministry of Defense engineers at Bukha. Its first voyage was successfully completed in mid November, arriving first in Khasab and then visiting other potential landing sites on its way back to Mina Qaboos. A longer-range plan for the ferry service was to upgrade the landing sites to handle passenger traffic.

Many other projects had been completed but were not yet operational. For example, the power plants at Khasab, Bukha and Bayah were finished in 1978, but it was not until June 1979 that sufficient fuel was delivered to put them into operation. Initially, the plants would operate six to eight hours per day. For more than a year, the citizens had been so close to having electricity but yet so far. Largely due to Agon's efforts over many months, these power plants became operational in June 1979 – bringing the first electricity of any significance and reliability to the three largest villages in the province.

Neither of the newly constructed desalination plants at Kumzar and Shaisah, small villages only accessible by boat, was working. These seemingly small problems were beginning to loom large. The citizens were complaining about what they considered to be government neglect and tended to compare their situation to that of their more well-off neighbors in the UAE. The last thing the Oman government wanted was to have its citizens emigrate to the UAE.

A Change in Course

Eventually word of these problems got to Sultan Qaboos. He decided to give more centralized authority to the MDC to get projects completed and operational more quickly. On Oman National Day, November 18, 1979, Sultan Qaboos issued a decree that the MDC would be given administrative, executive and financial responsibility for development of the Musandam Peninsula, including, significantly, the Strait of Hormuz traffic lanes that were within the Oman territorial waters.[7] Kirk Agon and John Sasser, who was in Muscat on temporary duty at the time, immediately began to prepare plans for TTI's role in the new MDC, one that would have some teeth. With the exception of the ministries of defense and education, the new MDC would take over the functions of virtually all ministries represented there.

Perhaps the significance of the Musandam Peninsula and the Strait of Hormuz can best be described in Sultan Qaboos's own words on the occasion of the ninth Oman National Day celebrations. This was the first time he publicly talked about the strategic Strait of Hormuz since he assumed power. The following are excerpts from his speech:

My Dear Countrymen,

No doubt you have heard a lot about the Strait of Hormuz, which as you know is part of our national waters and one of the most important sea lanes of the world through which passes a huge proportion of the world's oil supplies. Should the present instability in the Middle East result in an interruption of this flow, the results would be disastrous; not only would immense hardship be caused to millions of people, but the economies of many countries – countries whose own strength and stability is indispensable to the defense of freedom – would be gravely damaged. Oman is pledged to defend the right of all peaceful shipping to pass through this Strait. This is not only our duty under international law, it is also our duty to humanity and to our friends in the free world.

Should the strait be exposed to danger, Oman will not hesitate to act in defense of our national sovereignty and the

[7] James H. Critchfield, *Oman Papers 1968-1991*, Royal Decree No. 60/79 *On Additional Powers for the Musandam Development Committee*, November 18, 1979.

safety of international navigation. We believe it is the responsibility of all countries that are beneficiaries of this traffic – oil producers and consumers alike – to contribute to the protection of this vital waterway against the dangers of terrorism or other forms of aggression, and urge them to do so. Oman does not call for the intervention of foreign forces for this purpose; given the means, the sultanate is fully capable of undertaking necessary measures; but the means must be provided.

The cooperation of our brother states in the area is also essential to the security of these waters. It is for this reason that the irresponsible attitude of certain states, long noted for their mischievous and disruptive activities, is particularly to be deplored. Indulgence in such manifestations of political immaturity cannot be permitted to endanger world peace and stability and the lives of millions. The vital geopolitical importance of the Gulf as an area underlines the absolute necessity for the fullest cooperation between our states. Much has been said in the past in favor of this. But very little has been done. Certainly, there have been consultations and joint action in limited spheres, but consultation in the political and security fields has now become of the highest importance to the stability of the region and its continued immunity from foreign interference.[8]

It is clear that at this moment in time, Sultan Qaboos was placing great emphasis on this area. Saddam Hussein had just taken over as President of Iraq. The Shah of Iran had been deposed and Islamic leader Ayatollah Khomeini was in charge in Iran. Tensions in the region were high.

On December 1, 1979, Kirk prepared a TTI in-house report on what the seven ministries were doing in the Musandam Peninsula, activities that, as a result of the sultan's decree, would now be directly administered by the MDC. It was intended as a planning document to prepare for its role under the new mandate.[9]

---

[8] Ministry of Information, Omnet, Speeches by Sultan Qaboos bin Said, November 18,1979.

Ministry of Electricity and Water

The Ministry of Electricity and Water built the electrical power plants at Khasab, Bukha and Bayah in 1978. This was part of a larger project that included 26 rural electrification power plants throughout northern Oman. Identical in design, they were constructed by the UK firm Hawker Siddeley Power Corporation in 1975 and 1976. Hawker Siddeley was also responsible for putting in the distribution lines throughout the villages. In the initial stages, not all villagers received electrical power. This was particularly true in Khasab and Bayah. Distribution and capacity would have to be increased to reach those not yet served. In Khasab, distribution lines needed to be extended to the Khasab airport. Planning was also needed for construction of power plants in other areas, such as Kumzar, Limah and Rawdah.

With regard to water, there were two desalination plants and five well sites supplying domestic water for the entire Musandam Peninsula. The rest of the villages were supplied water by tanker ship. There were currently two such vessels in operation, the M/V *Khasab* and M/V *Kumzar*. The water was offloaded to an overhead water tank which fed a small distribution system connected to public water points throughout the villages.

Six other villages in the Musandam relied on groundwater for their supply and the quality ranged from excellent to acceptable. The most critical water supply situation in the Musandam was at Khasab, where the water quality was poor and pumping appeared to be causing further deterioration of water quality.

As he inventoried projects, Agon made notes on things the MDC should give priority attention to when it became operational. It was clear to him that more water and fuel tanker ships would be needed and a port captain should be hired to run the tanker fleet and establish a delivery schedule. Water supply systems needed to be provided to villagers not being serviced. The exploration effort in Khasab should continue with the hope it would be successful and improve the existing supply.

Ministry of Land Affairs and Municipalities

The Ministry of Land Affairs and Municipalities had built a temporary administrative facility in Khasab at the north end of the Khasab airstrip. There were no other facilities in the rest of the province. Unfortunately, the building in Khasab would have to be demolished, because its location would not comply with safety regulations.

A new headquarters building was needed in Khasab as well as in Bukha and Bayah. The ministry had placed one Land Rover-type vehicle in Khasab, Bukha and Bayah for refuse collection and had only one driver and helper in each location to support this effort. The ministry also had a small landing craft called the M/V *Musandam*, which operated from Khasab delivering fresh water to coastal villages where draft limitations were such that the M/V *Kumzar* and M/V *Khasab* could not provide this service. Agon hoped to use the M/V *Musandam* as a general workboat for the MDC.

Except for the airport and the port facilities in Khasab, there had been no steps taken on infrastructure projects. A master plan was needed for Khasab, Bukha and Bayah and the west coast villages, which would eventually be connected to Bukha by road. A town planner would be needed at a very early stage to work on this project. When surveying sites, first priority would be given to government-owned lands upon where no development had taken place. Registration of privately owned lands, except in cases where easements were needed for roads and utilities, would be postponed.

The public works department had designed and was working on various construction projects. These included low cost housing in Khasab and Bayah, the Ministry of Education dormitory in Khasab, schools in Limah and Qidah, and mosques in Bayah and Bukha. The MDC would be taking over the development of these projects from the public works department. A school/clinic at Kumzar, an extension of the Khasab hospital, and civil facilities in Rawdah would be among the early projects.

Ministry of Communications

The Ministry of Communications was in charge of airports and port facilities in the Musandam. It normally would also have handled road building had not the decision been made to have the Ministry of Defense take over the construction of all graded roads in the area. Once completed, however, the Ministry of Communications would take over the maintenance responsibility.

The first of the roads to be completed would be the Khasab-Bukha road, scheduled for January 1, 1981. Therefore, planning was needed for obtaining capital equipment, such as graders, and personnel to handle road maintenance.

In 1978, the Ministry of Communications engaged Techno Consult International of Pakistan to design a jetty for Khasab and possibly to supervise construction. There had been several fits and starts in this design project. First, the requirement was for a depth of three meters at low tide; then the company was asked to re-design the jetty to provide for seven meters of water at low tide and a berth of 100 meters in length so as to accommodate petroleum products tankers normally used by British Petroleum and Shell. Techno Consult promised the design documents by March 1980. The port facility for Khasab was funded at RO 5.6 million ($16 million).

There was tremendous political pressure to design and construct a small fishing jetty for the village of Bayah. Bayah residents had been denied access to the Fujairah (UAE) jetty adjacent to Bayah unless it was for the purpose of landing fish for sale in the UAE. That meant that all cargo designated for Bayah had to be offloaded at a spot some eight kilometers from the village. Agon noted that while there might not be an economic justification for construction of a jetty in Bayah, he thought a budget estimate for it should be included in the next five-year plan in the event it was decided to proceed with building a jetty. This was just one example of the awkwardness of separation of the Musandam Peninsula from the rest of Oman.

The MDC had been working for some time with the Ministry of Communications regarding the upgrading of the existing airfield at Khasab to meet civil aviation requirements to enable the commencement of a Gulf Air Skyvan service between Seeb International airport and Khasab. The requirement to upgrade the facility was urgent if development in the Musandam were to proceed.

Ministry of Commerce and Industry

The Ministry of Commerce and Industry up to that time had not been active in the Musandam province, but there were three proposed projects. One was the construction of commercial distribution facilities. One idea was to construct a warehouse in Khasab that would be turned over to a commercial operator who would purchase goods in Muscat, have them transported at government expense to be sold wholesale to existing retailers in Khasab and environs. One of the more urgent needs was for a hotel in Khasab so that contractors, consultants and government representatives could spend more than one day in the area. And finally, in connection with port development, there was need for a storage facility to handle petroleum products (fuel oil, gasoline and A-1 jet fuel) offloaded at the port for onward distribution.

Ministry of Agriculture and Fisheries

The Ministry of Agriculture and Fisheries had been active in the Musandam province since 1978. It had distributed boats and outboard motors to fishermen and was building a cold store and ice plant in Khasab that was expected to be open in February 1980. This was a highly visible project that could be expanded to improve both the agricultural and fisheries programs in the Musandam. What was needed were agricultural and fisheries advisors to enhance the viability of both industries.

Ministry of Posts Telegraphs and Telephones

The Ministry of Posts Telegraphs and Telephones had a challenge in the Musandam. The only communication with the outside world was by high frequency radio networks established by the Ministry of Defense, the Royal Oman Police, the Governor's office, the Ministry of Electricity and Power and the MDC. And none of these networks talked with one another. After many meetings to discuss the improvement of communications from the Musandam to Muscat, all conceded that what was needed was a satellite communications system. Muscat already was using satellite communications; all that was needed was to install an earth station in the Musandam. This would not only provide communications, but also television coverage. Actually, funding had been appropriated for an earth station in Khasab in 1979 at a cost of about $2 million. Pressure was then on to implement the program. The MDC needed to find a first class satellite communications expert to help supervise construction. It would take only four or five months to get the program up and running, once the contract had been awarded.

Ministry of Information and Youth Affairs

The only reason that the Ministry of Information was involved in MDC affairs was with regard to the installation of a television and radio transmitting facility in the Musandam Peninsula. Once the earth station was established in Khasab, television and radio transmissions could begin. It would also be possible to extend this service to outlying areas by installation of a small television transmitter on one of the high mountain peaks.

As for youth affairs, it was thought that youth clubs should be established in the three major villages in the Musandam. These would be patterned after facilities constructed elsewhere in the sultanate, consisting of mainly a football field and a clubhouse.

The first meeting of the MDC to discuss its new executive role was held on December 6, 1979. Using a slide presentation, Kirk Agon outlined the plans for 1980. He reviewed all current activities related to water resources, electrification, town planning, commercial development, agriculture and fisheries, satellite communications, radio and television and civil construction. He pointed out those projects that needed the immediate attention of the committee and what steps should be taken to begin the transfer of operations to the MDC.

Agon also pointed out to the group that his role in the past year had expanded from administrative secretary to operational project manager. For example, in the previous year, TTI had conceptualized and managed the development of the ferryboat service and the fuel delivery program, the establishment of the commercial warehouse, preparation of bids for the well drilling program in Khasab, and other activities needing consultant studies. As a result, two additional TTI staff members were assigned to the MDC secretariat. All this, he noted, would be reflected in an amendment to the TTI contract asking for additional funding.

Back in Rosslyn, Jim Critchfield wrote to Nicholas Boryatinski about this new development. He pointed out that Sultan Qaboos had converted the MDC from a monitoring and coordinating body to an executive authority with direct operational responsibility for activities that had up to that time been carried out by the ministries. The sultan had given a higher priority in Oman's development planning to the Musandam Peninsula and the Strait of Hormuz, and TTI had been propelled overnight into a major operational role. It had, in fact, assumed responsibility for management of the program to develop the entire

Musandam infrastructure. He realized that performance of this contract would be exceedingly difficult because of the nature of the work, the remoteness of Musandam, the lack of reliable transportation and the extreme hardship conditions that prevailed. He was alerting Boryatinski that TTI would need various kinds of support from Tetra Tech Pasadena; and he was already in touch with the engineering division on the Khasab port project. He did not tell Boryatinski that he had been less then pleased in recent months with the help he had or had not received from them. The new three-year contract with the MDC totaled $6 million. Critchfield felt it was time for the Pasadena office to take notice.

At the end of 1981, the MDC submitted a formal report to Sultan Qaboos chronicling the progress made since the MDC assumed management of the Musandam's development projects.[10] At the outset, the sultan was reassured that the MDC had retained its line of communications with the various ministries and had actually become a sort of clearinghouse for development planning. Development in the Governorate of Musandam was more efficient, and duplication of efforts had been minimized. The citizens, while still complaining, expressed the view that the government seemed to demonstrate a new awareness concerning their needs.

The MDC secretariat had also assumed direct responsibility for town planning. By mid 1980, it had completed town plans for Khasab, Bukha and Bayah. Each plan, which was developed on the basis of population projections through the year 2000, included areas and plots for housing, schools, hospitals, government offices, commercial centers and public services. Aerial surveys of all areas within Musandam had also been done to identify locations that might be expected to develop by the year 2000.

Construction of the road system to link the major villages of the Musandam was well under way. When completed, Kumzar would be the only major village not served by a road. The airport at Khasab, a 600-meter gravel strip, was being rebuilt by Oman's air force; when completed in mid 1982, it would include a 2,000-meter-long airstrip plus a parking ramp and airport facilities. This would allow larger aircraft to serve the area.

[10] Ibid., Musandam Development Committee, *Report to His Majesty Sultan Qaboss bin Said*, 1980/1981.

One of the major goals of the MDC was to draw the people of the Musandam Peninsula closer to the rest of the sultanate. In November 1980, the first satellite earth station was commissioned in time to provide telephone, radio and television communications for the occasion of the tenth Oman National Day. Khasab could then communicate with Muscat and the rest of Oman. This service would be expanded to other locations within the province.

By the end of 1981, the MDC had two offices, one in Ruwi (outside Muscat) and one in Khasab, with an auxiliary office in Bayah. The Ruwi headquarters employed 60 professional and administrative personnel, who handled the budgeting, accounting, purchasing and personnel administration tasks. The Khasab office, responsible for 425 personnel throughout the province, handled the operational tasks. It took two years for the MDC to become operational as a centralized unit, and its accomplishments were beginning to become apparent. Most of the major projects were well under way, and communications between Muscat and Khasab were vastly improved.

1

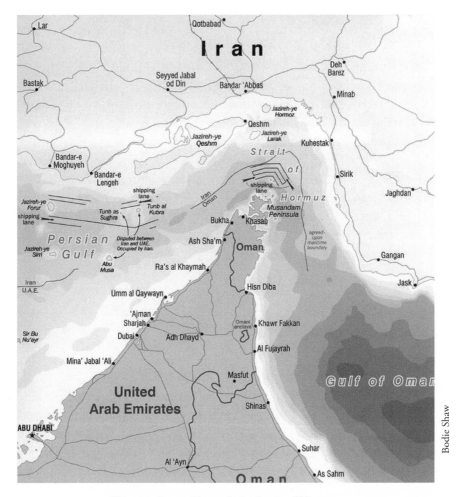

Shipping Lanes Through the Strait of Hormuz

14

THE STRAIT OF HORMUZ

The effort to develop the Musandam was only partly a result of the noble desire to bring a better quality of life to the 15,000 residents there. The pragmatic reason for developing the Musandam was its strategic location. The Strait of Hormuz, one of the most important maritime passages in the world, is also one of the most congested routes in world oil trade, with dozens of tankers passing through every day. It is the only sea passage available for Saudi and other Gulf states oil exporters.

The Oman government was well aware of the strategic importance of the Strait of Hormuz. Even though its own oil production did not flow to market through the strait, it bore a great responsibility in seeing that it remained a safe, secure and free passage for movement of more than two-thirds of the world's oil supply. Oman also had an important interest in protecting its mainland from adverse offshore events.

There had been some early efforts to deal with legal matters related to the international waters. The first was a Royal Decree issued on July 17, 1972, on Territorial Waters, Continental Shelf and the Confined Region for Fishing. This decree extended territorial waters 12 nautical miles, defined the continental shelf for exploring natural resources, and declared a 50 nautical mile exclusivity for Omani fishing. In 1974, Oman and Iran, after some months of negotiation, concluded a median line agreement in the Strait of Hormuz, which was ratified on May 28, 1975.[1]

Starting in 1977, TTI began to recognize that the Oman government was going to have to address several critical issues related to the strait. On one of his regular visits to Oman in February 1977, Critchfield met with Sultan Qaboos and members of the MDC in

[1] See Chapter Four.

Salalah. He told them there were several problems with the oil tanker traffic through the Strait of Hormuz. One was oil pollution along the coastal areas that was probably coming from tankers emptying ballast and tank washing before entering the strait. Effects of this were being seen on the Omani shoreline in the Batinah and Dhofar. Tighter regulations had to be developed and enforced. Also, the narrowness of the channel, five to seven kilometers, created the danger that one of the tankers could run aground and leave a great spill on the rocky coast of the Musandam Peninsula. One solution to ease these potential dangers would be to move the tanker traffic away from the coast.

As a result of this meeting, Critchfield took on the role of informal advisor to Yousuf bin Alawi, the deputy foreign minister. When he returned to Washington, Critchfield got in touch with TTI consultant Charles Black and attorney Richard Young, who specialized in maritime law. He asked both if they would address the subject of shipping routes through the Strait of Hormuz. In addition, the Oman government was looking into the feasibility of extending its fishing zone out to 200 miles in order to exercise more control over the growing foreign fishing fleets in the area. Before they could do that, however, they had to complete the definition of the baselines along its entire coastline.

The Oman-Iran median line drawn in 1974 was prior to any effort to establish an Oman baseline. The Oman-Iran agreement concerned only that part of the median line that was a continental shelf and was intended to apply only to mineral rights. This was now becoming relevant because the Henjam reservoir being explored by Elf-Aquitaine sat right on the median line as drawn in the agreement.

TTI began pulling together all its data from previous years. It proposed that Tetra Tech Pasadena's Dr. Choule Sonu carry out an oceanographic study of currents in the Strait of Hormuz in order to have sufficient data upon which to base a contingency plan for oil spills and pollution in the strait. Sonu had been in Oman in March 1975 and did the survey of potential sites for construction of a maritime facility in the Musandam.[2]

Sonu had also headed a team in 1976 that studied the currents on the Iranian side of the Gulf near Kish Island. With logistical assistance provided by Kirk Agon, he carried out another study in April 1977, working out of Khasab on a motorized dhow with an Omani crew. He

[2] See Chapter Seven.

and one additional scientist completed the project in fifteen days. This was the first such effort at data collection in the Strait of Hormuz. Sonu's report was delivered to the government in January 1978. Dr. Sonu later prepared a formal report for the U.S. Department of Navy's Office of Naval Research combining his Kish Island study with that of the Strait of Hormuz, and that too was sent to the Oman government.[3] But as of that time, there was no Oman government repository for this type of scientific data, so the report was kept in the TTI Muscat office, with a copy going to the Ministry of Foreign Affairs for its information.

In June 1977, Yousuf bin Alawi asked Critchfield to take on three tasks: examine the possibility of rerouting Hormuz traffic to put more of it outside of the Quoin Island group (Salama Wa Banata); to assist in defining the Gulf of Oman and Arabian Sea baselines; and to examine the possibility of establishing a 200 mile fisheries zone. With this move, the traffic separation scheme was born.

The Oman government did not delay in issuing a decree on fishing rights. On June 15, 1977, Royal Decree No. 44/77 amended the 1972 decree by extending the region for fishing to 200 nautical miles.[4] This action was in line with worldwide practice. To deal with the proximity of Iran, a paragraph was added to the new decree noting that if there were a state facing the Oman coast, limits for fishing would be determined by a median line.

In July 1977, Yousuf bin Alawi requested that TTI hire a cartographer to plot the baselines of the Omani 200 mile fisheries zone. This was done, and the original map was delivered to the Ministry of Foreign Affairs in October. The cartographer noted that the agreed Iran-Oman median line at many points appeared to be in Iran's favor. The single geological petroleum structure, the Henjam reservoir, was on both sides of the median line. This could impact oil operations in the future. The question arose whether Oman and Iran should revisit the 1975 median line agreement, but that question was set aside for the time being.

---

[3] James H. Critchfield, *Oman Papers, 1968-1991*, Tetra Tech, Final Report, *Oceanographic Study in the Strait of Hormuz and over the Iranian Shelf in the Persian Gulf*, TC-3675, March 1979.

[4] Ibid., Sultanate of Oman, Royal Decree No. 44/77, *Amendment to Royal Decree on Territorial Waters, Continental Shelf and the Sultanate's Confined Region for Fishing*, June 15, 1977.

On May 30, 1978, Critchfield reviewed the situation with Ardeshir Zahedi, the Iranian ambassador to Washington. He told Ambassador Zahedi that Tetra Tech was doing some cartographic work for Oman, and that the State Department had also done some independent studies on the Oman-Iran agreement. He alerted the ambassador that this would come up in the future, when the development of resources in the Strait of Hormuz might be conducted jointly. Critchfield commented that there was a consensus that errors, primarily in Iran's favor, existed in the current median line. He suggested that at some point Iran, being the larger of the two parties, might find it appropriate to propose a reexamination of the original work. The State Department studies alone, copies of which he gave to the ambassador, provided a reason for such action by Iran. But first, Critchfield noted, it would be essential for both countries to finalize and agree on baselines. Until that was done, any effort to modify and extend the existing median line agreement could not go forward. Critchfield learned later that Ambassador Zahedi did forward a report to Teheran outlining the content of their meeting.[5]

Traffic Separation Scheme

It wasn't until early in 1978 that the traffic separation project got moving. Charles Black was asked to represent the Oman government in its negotiations for a new agreement with the U.N. Inter-governmental Maritime Consultative Organization (IMCO) in London. But first, new charts had to be drawn. The traffic lanes through the Strait of Hormuz were based on an old assumption that the strait was in international waters. Charts showing the traffic schemes under current use had been published by IMCO in September 1968. After studying the situation, Richard Young, the lawyer on retainer to TTI, pointed out that these waters were in fact within Oman's territorial area; IMCO had no precedent or legal jurisdiction, and Oman could set whatever exclusions or separations it saw fit. It was in Oman's national interest to establish a safer traffic scheme, and it had the legal right to do so.

Once everyone agreed that Oman was justified in going ahead with revising the 1968 IMCO traffic charts, Charles Black put together a

[5] Ibid., letter from James H. Critchfield to Minister of State for Foreign Affairs Qais Al-Zawawi, June 26, 1978.

proposal and suggested a timetable to deal with IMCO in getting a new traffic separation scheme approved. To justify the need for change, Black referred to a June 22, 1977, report published jointly by the UNDP and the Arab Fund for Economic and Social Development, which concluded that the existing traffic separation in the Strait of Hormuz was hazardous and recommended prompt review.[6] The Oman government had also begun to report directly to IMCO, citing foreign vessels for noncompliance with the established scheme in violation of navigational safety and protection of Oman's rights in its territorial waters.

With nothing more than the existing charts in hand, Black went to London on February 25, 1978, and began a series of meetings with IMCO principals. He informed IMCO that the process would be slowed down by the necessity of clearing each step with the Oman government, which would then have to coordinate the new plan with the appropriate neighboring countries, in particular Iran. Black and TTI would be doing the basic work on the new effort, but the Oman Ministry of Foreign Affairs would have to give its stamp of approval at each step before the plan was officially submitted to IMCO.

And that was what happened. After meeting with IMCO officials in London, who incidentally had no problems with the concept of Oman putting forward a new and safer traffic separation scheme in the Strait of Hormuz, Black began work on the project. He went back to the Berkeley Hotel, where he was staying, armed with the navigational charts, a set of rulers and overlay paper. He did the first draft on the floor of his hotel room that very evening.[7] He met again with IMCO officials and then returned to Rosslyn, where he presented the draft to TTI. This was then sent to Muscat, and Kirk Agon began working with Yousuf bin Alawi and his designated Ministry of Foreign Affairs official, Sadek Jawad Suleiman, to determine whether the proposed changes met with government approval.

The proposed new scheme placed the traffic lanes north of the Salamah Wa Banata, literally "Salamah and her daughters" (the Quoin Island group), but still within the boundary limits of the continental shelf of Oman. The scheme consisted of one eastbound and one

---

[6] A. A. Sbaiti and H. G. Kallafallah, *Status of Navigation through the Arabian Gulf,* UNDP and Arab Fund for Economic and Social Development, Tokyo, Japan, 22 June 1977.

[7] Telephone conversation between the author and Charles Black on June 18, 2005.

westbound traffic lane, each two miles wide, separated by a zone two miles wide and an inshore traffic zone between the southern boundary of the scheme and the coast of the Musandam.

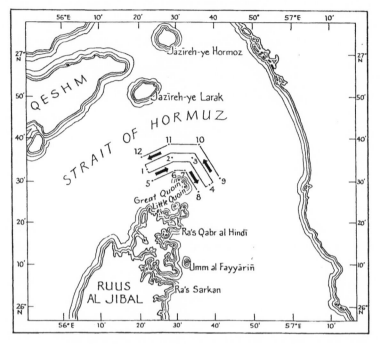

A Detail of the Strait of Hormuz Shipping Lanes

Sadek Suleiman, who had been deeply involved in the new traffic separation scheme project and did most of the contact work with the Iranians, told Agon on June 22, 1978, that the Oman government had recently received a note from the Iranian government, which not only agreed with the change in location of the traffic plan, but also promised Iran's support for it.[8] The government would be taking the proposed new scheme to other neighboring Gulf states, but only on the basis of furnishing information and not for consultation or consent.

[8] Ibid. Black remarked that he felt he could take some credit for Iran's support of the traffic separation scheme. When work was under way on establishing baselines and revisiting the median line agreement between the two countries, Black suggested to Yousuf bin Alawi that the navy send a patrol boat out to one of the rocky Quoin islands each morning and raise the Oman flag and then take it down each evening. They did this for a period of weeks, until it was apparently accepted that this island was Oman territory – at any rate, the Iranians never challenged that this was Omani territory.

174

Once the cartography work was completed, Charles Black and the Oman Embassy First Secretary Hussain Mohamed Ali in London submitted the proposal in October 1978 to the IMCO Subcommittee on Safety of Navigation. In September 1979, the formal presentation was made, and the IMCO General Assembly adopted it in November 1979. The new traffic separation scheme was published in the U.S. Defense Mapping Agency "Notice to Mariners" on November 3, 1979.[9]

Shortly after IMCO approved the revised scheme, the world press took note; one article praised Oman for making the Strait of Hormuz a safer seaway. It quoted Sadek Suleiman, by then Oman Ambassador to Washington, as saying this was "a service Oman is providing to the international community."[10]

Office of Ocean Affairs

It was becoming increasingly clear that the Oman government needed to establish an office that could deal on its behalf with the myriad of issues related to offshore activities. Critchfield had discussed this with Tim Landon in mid 1978. In September 1978, he wrote to Qais Al-Zawawi and urged him to put such an office in the foreign ministry. Qais agreed and requested that TTI be in touch with Yousuf bin Alawi on this matter. Bin Alawi in turn asked Kirk Agon to prepare a proposal and terms of reference both for the office itself and for TTI's role in such an office. Bin Alawi also appointed Salem Makki to take responsibility for the office in the foreign ministry. Salem Makki had returned from studying in the United States and was at this time an undersecretary at the Ministry of Foreign Affairs.

It was March 1979. Momentum was building and bin Alawi wanted the work to be completed yesterday. Agon told TTI Rosslyn that he intended to present a document in the next few days unless TTI saw any reason for delay. It did not. The course of events was exactly what Critchfield had been pushing for.

[9] Notice to Mariners, No 44, November 3, 1979, published by the U.S. Defense Mapping Agency, Washington, DC.
[10] "Vital Mideast Oil Route Made Safer" by John Cooley, Christian Science Monitor, October 30, 1979.
[11] See Chapter Five.

In the beginning, the newly named Office of Ocean Affairs would have one Omani senior foreign service officer (Salem Makki), one contract consultant (to be hired), a secretary, and a draftsman. The office would serve as regional and international liaison for questions pertaining to marine pollution; it would exercise policy supervision over vessel traffic systems; take responsibility for defining, drafting and publishing appropriate marine boundaries to include baselines and median lines; and attend regional and international conferences concerning Law of the Sea, pollution control, and related ocean matters. The Ministry of Foreign Affairs announced the creation of the Office of Ocean Affairs on May 1, 1979.

Status of the Elf-Aquitaine Concession

As noted earlier, the Elf/ERAP offshore concession had been awarded on December 4, 1973.[11] Subsequently Elf teamed with another French company, Aquitaine, to explore this area. Elf-Aquitaine was working both sides of the Strait of Hormuz, having previously obtained the concession in offshore Iran. The government of Oman was hoping for success in this venture, since success offshore would have a direct impact on the overall economy of the Musandam Peninsula. Production of offshore oil and/or gas could change the area's economy, then totally limited to fishing and agricultural pursuits, into one of substantial gain. if Khasab were to become a crude oil storage and export facility. Furthermore, the oil companies involved would invest capital for the support projects.

Elf began drilling on the Oman side in September 1976. As it turned out, the Henjam structure where drilling was taking place was on both sides of the Oman-Iran median line, with only about 22 percent on the Oman side. And almost half of the hydrocarbons contained in the Henjam structure was not oil but gas, meaning that a market for gas would have to be found. These factors complicated plans for actual drilling and production.

Iran had not shown any interest in developing the Henjam structure for oil or gas, and their agreement would be necessary. Elf-Aquitaine had not indicated it was prepared to go ahead without further exploration

[11] See Chapter Five.

on the Iranian side, and there were issues involved if Oman were to deliver associated gas to markets in the UAE. Even within the government of Oman, many agencies would need to get involved, especially the Ministry of Petroleum, Ministry of Foreign Affairs, and the MDC. It would be some time before the Oman government would be in a position to make a decision on this complex but potentially profitable activity.

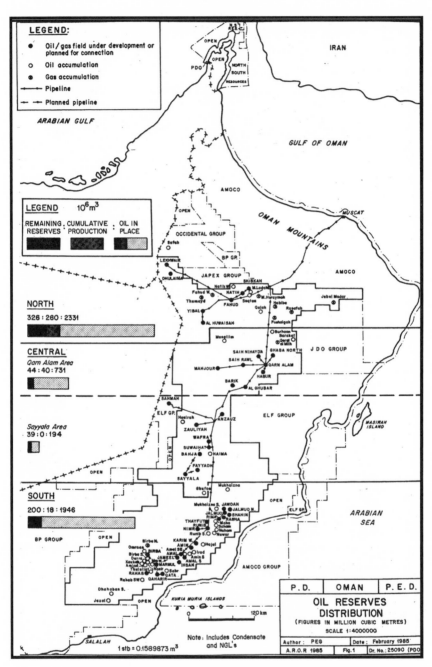

A Survey of the Distribution of Oman's Oil Reserves–1985

15

DEVELOPING OMAN'S
ENERGY RESOURCES

As advisors to the government of Oman, Tetra Tech International had consistently recommended a policy on exploitation of oil and gas resources that would find a middle ground between maximizing current revenues and conserving resources for the future. When Tom Barger visited Oman in 1977, he identified the adoption of a conservation policy as the single most important objective of the Ministry of Petroleum and Minerals and urged the ministry to do an independent reservoir engineering study to update the estimates of Oman's oil reserves.

This issue more than any other proved to be the most explosive and unpleasant in TTI's dealings with PDO and Royal Dutch Shell, but TTI never once faltered in trying to convince the Omanis that their oil reservoirs and production programs had to be examined in light of declining production. PDO, on the other hand, used every device it had to delay any independent reservoir engineering study. TTI considered this strategy to be very short sighted and damaging to both the government's and Shell's interests from almost every point of view. Sultan Qaboos, Minister Al-Shanfari and the Development Council were caught in the middle of this debate. But forcing PDO to become involved in reservoir engineering would probably prove to be the most important and lasting contribution TTI was to make in its thirteen years advising the Oman government.

On Barger's recommendation, TTI obtained the consultancy services of Brad Dismukes, a Texas-based reservoir engineer of established reputation. He was highly intelligent and a tough negotiator. PDO would be forced to take notice. He made his first trip to Muscat in December 1978, and then traveled between Muscat and Houston for most of 1979. While he maintained an office in the ministry, he worked independently. Some of the TTI staff in the ministry, put off by his forceful personality and method of operating, began siding with Shell on how the task of reservoir engineering should be tackled. Eventually, Critchfield instructed his Muscat petroleum engineers to stand down and let Dismukes do his job.

One of Dismukes's first observations was that the ministry did not have the cost data from PDO needed to assess the efficiency of its petroleum operations. This withholding of information was new to Dismukes but not to TTI. Since the government was paying all the costs, it certainly had the right to the information. In his talks with PDO, Dismukes did not discern any disagreement with this; the information just never got from PDO's office to the ministry. More pressure was needed here. He also noted at the outset that many of PDO's technical practices served almost exclusively to accelerate oil production at the expense of total ultimate recovery. PDO strategy appeared to be to minimize current spending and avoid short-term production cutbacks.

Oman's financial interests were simply not identical to those of Royal Dutch Shell. Prior to April 1977, it was clear that Shell was basically refusing to invest in Oman. Its production strategy was to get as much oil as possible out of Oman at the lowest possible cost. However, after the April 1977 agreement revision, the Omani government basically paid the capital and operating costs and Shell received a fee. If the Oman government wanted to invest in producing more oil, Shell should have had no objection. They were not paying for it. But it was some time before Shell came around to that view.

Dismukes wanted the extensive data from PDO necessary to begin a systematic study of production practices and costs. He was the first to comment that even a highly skilled major operator such as Shell could sometimes get into habitual operating procedures, and he was certain that procedures could be improved by exposure to a fresh view. In January 1979, he presented a list of 24 types of data the ministry should request from PDO. They ranged from geological maps to drilling data, well logs and costs of works carried out by the various operating units.

At the same time, Critchfield told Sultan Qaboos about Brad Dismukes, adding that his presence was a direct response to the sultan's request to Minister Said Al-Shanfari to follow up on Critchfield's and Tom Barger's recommendations about reservoir handling. He wanted to be sure that the sultan was up to date on what was being done in the event there were any repercussions related to Dismukes's work.

PDO strategy during 1978–79 was to maintain maximum off-take with minimum investment. This was also Oman government policy. Shell almost certainly saw its own interests served by this tactic; it had, in fact, already benefited greatly. As Brad Dismukes pointed out, "There is no right or wrong in oil field depletion rate as long as it met the needs of the government. The Development Council and the Finance Council should be made aware, however, that there was an option to at least examine the possibility that a lower production rate might result in higher revenues over the long term." No one had shown any inclination to seize this thorny issue. The sultan had been the only one who had taken any action to face the problem.

As time passed, Dismukes told Critchfield he thought it was important to brief the government officials dealing with oil policy. He proposed that key officials be alerted to the possible economic consequences of over-production, pointing out that PDO's reports indicated that several reservoirs in northern Oman had decline rates in excess of 20 percent per year. Furthermore, oil recovery efficiency in Oman was abnormally low compared to oil field practices worldwide. He wanted the briefing to emphasize that the concept of "maximum efficient recovery" (MER) was preferable to the current practice of "maximum off-take."

He defined MER as "the highest producing rate that could be sustained for an appreciable length of time without damage to the reservoir and which, if exceeded, would lead to underground waste through loss of ultimate oil recovery." He hoped such briefings would lead the government to support independent reservoir engineering studies and back the ministry's request for data from PDO. Dismukes attached urgency to this effort, because the 1980 PDO production program book called for "all fields to be produced at full potential...."[1]

In March 1979, Dismukes produced two reports for the Ministry of Petroleum and Minerals, copies of which went to Team 1 in Muscat and Rosslyn for presentation to the Oman government. Working with him was H. J. Gruy and Associates, Inc., a respected petroleum engineering consulting firm based in Dallas. The first report analyzed the oil reserves and PDO's production forecast assuming the policy of "maximum off-take" was followed. The second report assumed a policy

---

[1] James H. Critchfield, *Oman Papers, 1968-1991*, memorandum from Dismukes to Edmonds dated June 5, 1979.

of producing at a rate near to "maximum efficient recovery," which would increase future oil recovery substantially.[2]

In defense of PDO, Dismukes pointed out that PDO's job was not to provide economic justification to the government for production programs. It carried out government policy and was not expected to know the government's requirements for income. But no one disputed that Shell was definitely benefiting from this policy.

Team 1 Muscat threw this hot potato to Team 1 Rosslyn, asking for a decision on how to handle the reports with the Oman government. Ministry officials Khalifa Al-Hinai and Salem Shabaan were aware there was something in the works, and Kirk Agon, in a meeting with Minister Al-Shanfari, informed him that important decisions lay ahead for the government regarding reservoir engineering. The thought in Muscat was that Dismukes should present such a briefing at the May meeting of the PDO Joint Management Committee.

Dismukes's work prompted Critchfield to write a rather philosophical letter to Sultan Qaboos in April 1979 about planning a future that takes care of the social and economic needs of the current generation as well as those of their children and grandchildren. "In some ways," he said, "the choices to be made were easier because of rising world oil prices. Brad Dismukes's recent work clearly shows that a policy of reduced PDO production would increase the volume of oil that could ultimately be recovered about the time the young children in Oman became young adults. It was probable that some oil that was originally recoverable had been lost, but there was still time to address the issue."[3]

Critchfield added that the operating oil company was not necessarily at fault. Only the government could say what it needed for revenue today against demand for oil revenues in the future. However, he did not believe the sultan had been presented with well-defined options from which to make a choice. He urged him to ask his advisors for a full economic reappraisal of existing production policies.[4]

Brad Dismukes attended the Joint Management Committee meeting in The Hague in May. In addition to briefing the government

[2] Ibid., *Reserve Estimates and Production Forecast*, March 25, 1979, and *Rate of Production, Ultimate Oil Recovery, and Economics*, April 4, 1979.
[3] Ibid., letter from Critchfield to Sultan Qaboos, April 17, 1979.
[4] There is no record of a response to Critchfield's "children and grandchildren" letter.

members of the committee, he handed Khalifa Al-Hinai and Bruce Edmonds handwritten notes indicating a potential loss of 250 million barrels of recoverable oil in Yibal, Oman's first oil field. He estimated that this loss would become irreparable in the future.

When Dismukes returned to the states and studied the situation more closely, he wrote to Bruce Edmonds in Oman that upon further study, he felt that he had greatly underestimated the possible future loss of oil. He thought further reservoir studies were needed, and soon. He said that PDO had steadfastly refused to carry out reservoir studies that would show the efficiency of recovery under their present plans. The current PDO plan called for increased water injection, a plan Dismukes said would affect only about half the oil in place. Alternate methods would recover more oil over a longer period of time.

Back in Texas, Brad Dismukes wrote to Critchfield on May 27, 1979, commenting that the year had not been wasted. The PDO 1980 program book had been published and included a different water injection plan for the Yibal field. "At least," Dismukes commented, "it was a start towards improving oil recovery."[5]

In July 1979, Dismukes prepared an extensive report on the exploitation program for Yibal based solely on PDO information.[6] The report compared two methods of recovery: peripheral and pattern flooding.[7] His conclusion was that a peripheral flood would recover some 400 million barrels more oil than the pattern flood that was currently under way. He recommended that his report be subjected to numerical simulations to validate the estimates, and then presented to the ministry for a decision as to later actions. He also pointed out that a complete reservoir study of Yibal was long overdue.

The ministry reacted almost immediately to Dismukes's recommendation, and in August 1979 it contracted with Gruy and Associates of Dallas to prepare mathematical reservoir simulations of the Yibal field.

---

[5] *A Comparison of Peripheral and Nine-Spot Flooding in Yibal Shuaiba*, prepared for Tetra Tech by Brad Dismukes, July 1979.

[6] Ibid.

[7] Ibid. In the words of Brad Dismukes, "An operator sometimes has several options available as to where and when to inject water in a flood. He may choose a pattern arrangement or a peripheral flood with edge and/or bottom water injection."

A Target of Opportunity on Long-Term Planning

In September 1979, John Sasser, who quite by accident found himself sitting next to Muhammed Zubair, the Minister of Commerce and Industry, on a Gulf Air flight from London to Muscat, took advantage of the five-hour trip to exchange views on public finance. Zubair, a close friend of Sultan Qaboos, was a member of the Development Council and the Oil and Gas Council, and was part of the Omani elite.[8] Sasser had a captive audience and made the most of it.

In discussing the budgetary process, Zubair pointed out to Sasser that the year 1979 was the first time government budget submissions spanned a five-year period rather than a single year. This was the beginning of the five-year plans, and it was an important step toward longer-range planning. This led to a discussion of what the Oman government planned to do with its surplus funds resulting from the dramatic rise in oil prices. Sasser, picking up on the TTI mantra, commented to Zubair that the best investment the government could make was in an oil conservation program. He repeated the concern that PDO's production policy was not in the best interests of the country and that in fact it might be causing damage to certain fields because of overproduction.

He specifically pointed to the northern Oman fields, such as Yibal, where practices were sub-optimal and damage might have already been done. It was the view of TTI that the petroleum law needed to be rewritten to include strict regulations governing certain production ratios, i.e., oil/gas, oil/water, injection rates and reservoir pressures. Such a law would produce the desired production conservation and restoration of good oil field practices. The value of oil left in the ground would not only appreciate but would have the added benefit of increasing ultimate recovery. The minister acknowledged this and said that the higher levels of government were already leaning in this direction. He said the sultan and other policymakers were receptive to a production policy as long as it would provide sufficient revenues to cover the targets. Sasser expressed surprise. This was the first time he had heard that the government was examining an alternative production policy.

Zubair said there was concern from some quarters that a conservation program might discourage additional exploration by other potential concessionaires. Oman needed to continue an aggressive exploration

[8] See Chapter Three.

effort. There needed to be a balance between the two.[9] At the very least, this conversation showed that the ministers were beginning to think through some of these critical decisions regarding Oman's future.

Dismukes Forges Ahead

By October 1979, Critchfield found that all this discussion within the ministry of a conservation policy was causing tremors in Muscat. The government was aware that they could afford the revenue loss from cutting back 50-75,000 bpd. Furthermore, there appeared to be a consensus among the chief policymakers that conservation was a worthwhile investment.

In warm-up sessions to prepare for the October 17 Joint Management Committee meeting in Muscat, Brad Dismukes brought up with Salem Shabaan several technical issues related to the Yibal and Lekhwair fields. He recommended that production be reduced until further technical adjustments were made. There was a PDO proposal for a water injection project for the Lekhwair field that totaled $60 million. Dismukes advised that this not be approved until a much less costly $6 million pilot program was carried out. There were also large cost overruns that needed to be discussed.

At the Joint Management Committee meeting, Shabaan followed the agenda as rehearsed. Dismukes tabled the April 1979 Gruy and Associates Yibal study, which estimated that past production practices had resulted in reservoir pressure declines and that over the last ten years, an estimated 63 million barrels of oil had been lost. He offered an alternate program that would enable the government to maintain the production rate for six years beyond 1995, when it would otherwise commence its decline. Other items in this report spoke of technical improvements that could enhance the performance at Yibal. PDO's only response was that it had recently initiated its own Yibal study. According to Dismukes, the scope of this study was entirely different from his.

At the post-meeting luncheon, PDO manager Frank Jetses, who had been clearly embarrassed in front of his management, let both Bruce Edmonds and Dismukes know he did not think this was the forum to raise these issues. His reputation had been hit hard by the ministry's

[9] James H. Critchfield, *Oman Papers, 1968-1991*, report of John Sasser's conversation with Zubair, September 1979.

decision to go for an independent reservoir survey. He accused Dismukes of poor communications with PDO over the problem. Dismukes responded that for the first three months of his assignment, he made every possible attempt to get the data he needed and attempts were cut off with a PDO response that he was taking up too much of their time. Jetses retorted that Dismukes was using the wrong terminology and the wrong data. Furthermore, reservoir studies in general had little validity. When Dismukes made a move to walk out, Jetses's temper cooled somewhat.[10] Dismukes later noted, with some satisfaction, that shareholders CFP and Partex were highly complimentary of his presentation.

Critchfield met with Jetses the next day at Bruce Edmonds's home and tried to cool things down. Jetses told Critchfield that, as a personal matter of conviction, he was skeptical of the value of reservoir simulation studies. But he acknowledged that there had been production malpractices in the past that had left permanent marks on the fields.

Critchfield reviewed with Jetses TTI's interest in the subject of reservoir management, going back to the initial visit of Tom Barger and the subsequent hiring of Brad Dismukes. He also said that Dismukes's work was not the effort of an individual, but that of the entire advisory staff. He expressed regret at Jetses's personal exposure, commenting that it was partly due to the fluctuating circumstances of the oil market.

He reminded Jetses that he had signed a formal agreement with Minister Al-Shanfari two years previously to establish a technical committee and that, to Critchfield's knowledge, the committee had never met. PDO had had the opportunity to get it started but had failed to do so.

Critchfield said he would pour oil over the troubled waters for Jetses if he would agree to a full and constructive exchange of data. Jetses agreed. Critchfield noted, however, that TTI would not back off the promotion of a conservation policy. Jetses acknowledged that Oman's income was in excess of its needs, but also noted that Shell had crude deficiencies, adding that "it was not part of the Aramco gang."[11] In Critchfield's opinion, Shell's thirst for crude should have no bearing on Oman's conservation policy.

[10] Ibid., TTI minutes of the JMC meeting, October 17, 1979.
[11] Ibid., TTI report of Critchfield's meeting.

Critchfield told his staff that he would recommend to the sultan that if Shell followed through with the agreement to exchange technical data, then he would not ask him to play any further role on this tired and worn subject. In discussions with Qais Al-Zawawi and Muhammad Musa, deputy chairman of the Development Council and the director of finance, respectively, Critchfield urged them to implement the conservation policy on technical grounds.

The Gruy simulation study of Yibal, the primary purpose of which was to determine the plan of water injection that would result in the highest oil recovery, had been completed and forwarded to TTI Rosslyn on February 6, 1980.[12] Dismukes sent 18 copies along with a cover letter to the technical director, Khalifa Al-Hinai. The study, a 58-page compilation of text, tables, charts and maps, showed a 26.8 percent increase in oil recovery (an additional 400 million barrels of oil for the life of the field) by changing from the current waterflood method to a recovery mechanism known as "peripheral water injection."

The following week Brad Dismukes sent Al-Hinai his economic analysis based on the results of the Gruy recommendation to blend a peripheral waterflood injection method into the present scheme. Dismukes predicted net profits of $6-8 billion at $30 per barrel; at $40 per barrel, net profits would be $9-11 billion. He recommended that fieldwork proceed to provide the additional reservoir data needed to optimize a development program. There was no question in his mind that these field expenditures were justified. Dismukes then touched on a sensitive subject: the possibility that the objectives of the government to conserve natural resources could conflict with the operator's apparent need for maximum production.[13]

Early in 1980, Sultan Qaboos announced that Oman's national policy was to produce oil and gas within the framework of a conservation program, and Minister Al-Shanfari advised both PDO and the ministry staff that a conservation program was now policy. But nothing appeared in writing. The road was paved with good intentions, but somewhere between April and June 1980, Minister Al-Shanfari began to equivocate, and other ministry officials were also sidestepping the issue. In May, TTI Muscat learned and reported to Rosslyn that the sultan had set the

---

[12] *Mathematical Simulation Study of the Shuaiba Reservoir in the Yibal Field of Oman for Tetra Tech International*, H. J. Gruy and Associates, Inc., February 6, 1980.

[13] Ibid., *Yibal Field Waterflood Economics*, February 13, 1980.

production level for 1981 at 350,000 bpd: 340,000 bpd to be produced by PDO, and 10,000 bpd by Elf-Sumitomo. This effectively eliminated any possibility of a conservation program. The sultan's decision was reportedly linked to the pressing need for revenues to meet expanding defense costs.

It was also during this time that PDO was converted to an Oman company, finalizing an agreement that had been under negotiation for three years. On May 15, 1980, PDO registered as a local Oman operating company called Petroleum Development Oman, LLC. However, the ownership remained the same: 60% Oman government; 34% Shell, 4% Total and 2% Partex.

About this time, minister Al-Shanfari informed TTI that he had made the decision to have all reservoir engineering studies done by PDO using its own Royal Dutch Shell engineering capabilities in The Hague. TTI could only speculate on what was behind this reversal. The Minister also told the TTI staff in Muscat that he planned to direct-hire reservoir engineers. Ads were currently being run in the London newspapers. Critchfield was planning a trip to Oman in June and would explore this with the minister and others. Until then, the only thing that could be done was to accept the decisions gracefully and see how they worked out.

Al-Shanfari had put on ice any further plans to have outside reservoir engineering companies do the work. In Critchfield's opinion, all the benefits to the government of a second opinion were lost. He had to admit that TTI did not have a particularly good record on reservoir engineering staffing. Brad Dismukes, its most qualified engineer, was a consultant, not a full-time staff member. But, in the following months, PDO did step up to the plate. It added to its own reservoir engineering staff and began investigating secondary recovery techniques in its existing fields.[14]

Dismukes also did related work on the consequences and costs of not pursuing a conservation program. PDO was not enthusiastic about this program, but, drawing on the Shell organization, it had become more active in reservoir work. It continued to challenge Dismukes's recommendations on many points. TTI had full confidence in Dismukes but believed it was important for the ministry to seek a second expert

---

[14] Later on in the 1980s, after extensive reservoir studies, the Oman government did make the optimum investments, and both Shell and the government realized substantial additional income out of fields that Shell had written off in the late 1970s.

opinion. Despite Al-Shanfari's edict about additional outside consultants, on June 1, 1980, he signed a letter of agreement authorizing a computer simulation of the Yibal reservoir. He made note that he was requesting this study because of Dismukes's previous report suggesting that as much as 400 million barrels could be gained in ultimate recovery of oil from the Yibal field if a peripheral waterflood was "combined with the current PDO practice of inside pattern waterflood."[15] Dismukes contracted with Gruy and Associates to do this additional work.[16]

Communications with the Boss

When Critchfield met with Sultan Qaboos in June 1980, the sultan stated not once but twice in the course of the audience that he had the impression that production could reach the level of 350,000 bpd without jeopardizing the conservation program, since current capacity was 500,000 bpd. Production at that time was 279,000 bpd.

Critchfield's response was that production could probably be pushed up to 350,000 bpd, but that was the limit. The sultan insisted that PDO manager Frank Jetses and Al-Shanfari had told him that production could go up to 500,000 bpd. Was Critchfield sure of his position? Critchfield said he was. The sultan was clearly puzzled.

The sultan told Critchfield that contrary to what was being said, Oman did not require the revenue from 350,000 bpd. It could cut its spending to fit its revenues. Critchfield could only conclude that Sultan Qaboos was still committed to the principle of conservation, but needed a clearer picture of what was involved.[17] In a later discussion during the same visit, Qais Al-Zawawi also expressed the opinion that Oman did not then have high-priority revenue requirements for production at the level of 350,000 bpd.

The confusion about the 500,000 bpd capacity figure was soon explained. It turned out to be only an estimate on paper. PDO had gone back to the drawing board and determined that it could extract twice as much oil out of the Yibal/Fahud/Lekhwair reservoirs as it had previously told the government. But upgrading these reservoirs would require

---

[15] James H. Critchfield, *Oman Papers, 1968-1991*, letter of agreement from Minister Said Al Shanfari to Tetra Tech International, MOO/3/11/247/80, June 1, 1980.
[16] Ibid., *Inverted Nine-Spot Waterflood Study of the Yibal (Shuaiba) Field, Oman*, H. J. Gruy and Associates, Inc., September 23, 1980.

investment from either PDO or the government, a decision that had not yet been made.

By September 1980, it appeared that Sultan Qaboos and his ministers had in principle adopted a conservation policy. In practice, however, oil production was being pushed to the maximum based on capacity and "good oil field practices." This did not equate to a real conservation program, and policy remained confused.

An Oil Refinery for Oman

In July 1979, Orin Atkins, president of the Kentucky-based Ashland Oil Company, Inc., at the suggestion of Yehia Omar, phoned Jim Critchfield at his office in Rosslyn to express interest in purchasing crude. Jim told him the ministry in Muscat handled all crude sales. Later in the fall, Critchfield met Omar, Atkins and Ashland officials in London. Atkins again expressed interest in crude. Once more, Critchfield explained that TTI's advisory role precluded any business association with outside companies and that Ashland should approach the ministry directly. That ended any further discussion of business between Atkins and TTI regarding crude oil sales. But Critchfield was instrumental in helping Ashland promote its interest in building a refinery in Oman.

In late 1979 and early March 1980, Bill E. McKay Jr., president of the international company Ashland Development Inc., a subsidiary of Ashland Oil, went to Oman at the invitation of Minister of Petroleum Said Al-Shanfari. Critchfield had recommended that Al-Shanfari meet McKay when the minister started thinking about building a refinery in Oman. This was Ashland's specialty.

In his first meeting with Al-Shanfari, McKay described Ashland Oil Company as one of the largest independent petroleum refiners and marketers in the United States. Ashland also manufactured chemical and petrochemical products, including carbon black. It was also a producer and marketer of coal. Ashland was definitely interested in opportunities that would be of mutual interest to Oman and Ashland, particularly the new petroleum refinery project. Ashland was also interested in talking about gas recovery systems, gas utilization projects, several pipeline projects, terminal improvement projects, and environmental conservation projects, including water supplies and food supply projects. Clearly Ashland saw a future in this developing nation.

Tetra Tech's endorsement of Ashland and McKay's subsequent visits resulted in an invitation by Minister Al-Shanfari to bid on a technical services contract related to the construction and start-up of Oman's first oil refinery. All negotiations were carried out directly with ministry officials. Ashland's bid of $1.7 million came in considerably lower than Shell's bid of $6.7 million. Beyond the strict economics, the Omanis favored Ashland because its unique processing capabilities netted more gasoline from a barrel of crude oil than the conventional refiners.

An agreement to oversee the construction of a 50,000 bpd refinery was signed on October 1, 1980. The agreement called for 20,000 bpd of Oman crude at the official price in exchange for technical services on construction and start-up of a refinery. The refinery was built by Mitsui and operated by the Oman Refining Company, with Ashland providing the staff. It was of the hydroskimming type and processed a fairly light (35 degrees API) Oman export blend of crude oil. Its products were fuel oil, gas oil, motor gasoline and jet fuel. It was anticipated that by 1987-89, the market for Oman products would surpass the supply. There was talk of building a separate refinery in the future rather having to import from elsewhere in the Gulf.

Critchfield also provided written introductions for McKay to Minister of Electricity and Water Hamoud Al-Harithi and Minister of Commerce and Industry Mohammed Zubair during McKay's March 1980 visit to Oman. Although Ashland would be dealing directly with the petroleum ministry, Critchfield thought it would be useful for both parties if Ashland were to find a role in Oman's developing economy.

Status of Oman's Natural Gas Development

Back in 1977, when Sultan Qaboos approved a plan to expand the gas pipeline from Seeb to Sohar, Critchfield met with Minister Al-Shanfari to discuss plans with regard to natural gas use. These were complex problems for the government. Gas needed to be regulated, marketed and distributed from the point where PDO transferred the gas to the government. The gas system could then be run efficiently as a business enterprise, in which gas would be dispensed to a variety of customers: public utilities, private industry, government-owned industry and the domestic residential and commercial consumer. Virtually all oil producing nations had established a national gas company to solve these problems. Critchfield recommended that the Oman government do the same

In early 1980, Critchfield asked Arthur Rypinski to summarize what had been done on gas policy. His response was revealing.[18] "Gas policy had generated more paper than any other single issue that TTI had been involved in," Arthur noted. TTI had two-and-a-half legal-size file drawers stuffed with paper on one aspect or another of gas policy in Oman. Most of this paper, he added, had no current value.

The reality was that when PDO began producing from Oman's fields in the early days, no provision was made for gas recovery in any form. Then when energy prices rose, various parties began to realize there was money to be made from stripping the liquids from Oman's flared gas. Each of the various parties undertook to engage a firm to either invest in Natural Gas Liquids (NGL) production or to prepare a feasibility study. The Oman government made and cancelled several agreements on gas utilization. It was soon overrun with feasibility studies. From 1973-78, no less than eight companies had submitted studies. They ran afoul of PDO, which refused to either batch liquids in the PDO pipeline or blend them for export. However, by 1977, PDO, recognizing the value of associated gas, agreed to begin a program of liquids stripping and gas re-injection rather than flaring. PDO expected to further reduce flaring of associated gas and to increase liquids recovery in 1980.

When the Yibal-Gubrah pipeline became operational in mid 1978, it marked the completion of a major milestone in the plan for "putting out the flares" and the beginning of a long-term plan for developing a natural gas economy. The availability of this gas would provide a major stimulus to the economic development of the areas surrounding the pipeline and would lead to development of an electric power grid throughout the region. Extending the Yibal-Gubrah pipeline at Murayrat to the copper project at Sohar expanded the scope for development in the Batinah region of Oman. And the prospect of large amounts of natural gas being made available near coastal export facilities produced a number of gas utilization proposals. TTI participated in the review and evaluation of many of these.

[18] James H. Critchfield, *Oman Papers, 1968-1991*, TTI interoffice memo, *Gas Policy in Oman*, February 13, 1980.

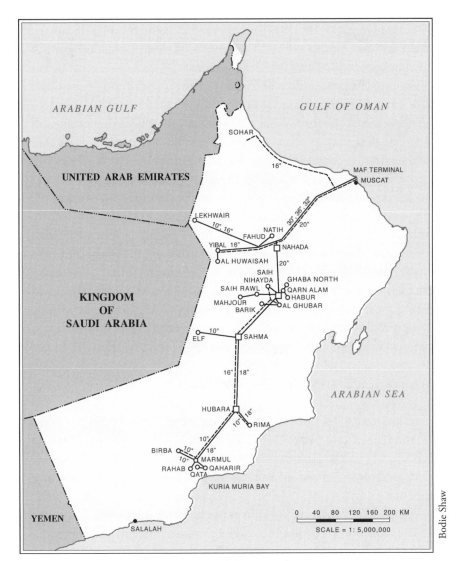

Oman's Pipeline Network

As for non-associated gas, Oman had about 4 trillion cubic feet of reserves, found almost entirely as a byproduct of oil exploration in the PDO area. This was used for the oil fields and for the pipeline from Yibal to Gubrah. It would also be used when the pipeline to Sohar was completed in 1981 or 1982. The government could deliver gas anywhere from Yibal to Gubrah/Muscat to Sohar by simply turning on the taps.

Companies other than PDO were also finding gas. The Gulf-Quintana group, the Elf offshore concession in the Strait of Hormuz, and the Elf-Sumitomo group in western Oman all identified gas but suspended operations for lack of a gas market.

Among the proposals TTI did not support at the time were those related to the building of large-scale petrochemical plants. It had prepared a lengthy report on industrial gas utilization two years before and concluded that such projects would divert too much natural gas that would be needed elsewhere.[19] The Oman economy in the future would become heavily dependent upon internal supplies of natural gas for the generation of power and electricity needed for the continued economic and social development of the country.

It was absolutely imperative that Oman remain as free as possible from dependence upon external sources of energy. Perhaps building a petrochemical industry would work in the future, but at this time, particularly when the industry itself was in a depressed state, TTI advised that operation of a large petrochemical complex in Oman would severely restrict available gas supplies for power and electricity and lead to a great dependence on alternative sources of energy.

Contribution to the Five Year Plan 1981-1985

In late 1979, TTI turned to examining the Ministry of Petroleum and Minerals's "Five Year Plan 1981-1985." Arthur Rypinski headed this project from the Rosslyn end and worked with Brad Dismukes on recommendations that would eventually be packaged and sent to Minister Al-Shanfari.

Rypinski felt that this was the perfect opportunity to demonstrate TTI's capabilities in economic analysis to all of the senior people in the ministry. He wrote to John Sasser and Bruce Edmonds that he intended to create a showcase example of how budget and long-range planning should be done. This would include planning for such projects as the Seeb-Sohar corridor, forming a natural gas company, selling gas to the UAE, refinery expansion and a dozen other projects for the future.

[19] Ibid., Tetra Tech International Inc., *Industrial Gas Utilization, Policy and Pricing*, March 1978.
[20] Ibid., Tetra Tech International, Inc., *Recommendations for the Second Five Year Plan for the Ministry of Petroleum and Minerals*, May 1980.

The final TTI report that went to the ministry in May 1980 was very extensive.[20] It covered costs for continued development of oil, natural gas and minerals and specific recommendations that the government might ask PDO to address. It proposed that reservoir studies be undertaken on the nine major producing fields, with onsite supervision by the ministry. It included an expanded program for secondary recovery projects. With the aim of reducing flaring of associated gas, it proposed projects collecting and shipping the gas by pipeline to the coast. The report essentially covered every subject that advisors, going back to the pre-TTI days of Stribling Snodgrass, had at one time or another proposed.

At this point in time, there were seven oil concessions in Oman, but the PDO concession was the only one that required direct government investment. The others were production-sharing agreements in which operating expenses were paid by the companies and recovered from eventual sales of crude oil.[21]

Cost estimates also were included in the plan, should the government decide it wanted to either nationalize PDO or take the lesser step of nationalizing the PDO pipeline system and operating it as a common carrier pipeline for all companies producing oil in Oman. This proposal came about over the issue of permitting Elf to send its high-value crude from the tiny Salmah field into the PDO pipeline system. PDO wanted to place an unreasonably high tariff on this. If they persisted, the Oman government would have a difficult time enticing companies other than PDO to get involved in exploration. Ultimately, PDO responded with a lower and more reasonable tariff.

With regards to natural gas, no economically feasible export project had been identified. Should gas projects become feasible, the government was advised that it would avoid financial risk by going only for production-sharing agreements. The government could continually reassess its position to accommodate changes in gas export technology, gas pricing and natural gas discoveries as a result of oil exploration.

The report further recommended that studies be done on the desirability of building a national gas grid on the rectangle Yibal-Buraimi-Sohar-Muscat and, if gas became available in the Marmul area, extending

[21] Ibid. In 1980, companies with production sharing agreements in Oman were PDO, Elf-Sumitomo, which would be producing oil beginning in 1981, Amoco, BP-Deminex, Elf-Aquitaine, Gulf/Quintana, and Cluff.

a gas pipeline to Salalah. Gas discoveries offshore in the Musandam area had created interest in the possibility of developing a system not only for Musandam but for the UAE region as well.

When more gas became available as a substitute for diesel fuel in electrical power generation, such as at the Gubrah power station in the Greater Capital Area, extension of pipelines to other population centers needed to be considered. The timing of the switch to gas at Gubrah could not have been better. The government realized huge financial savings in substituting gas for diesel oil when crude oil prices soared as high as $40 per barrel.

As for the minerals program, the report recommended that the Oman Mining Company (OMC) become an operating arm of the ministry. The OMC-ministry relationship could resemble that which existed between the ministry and PDO. The ministry would assume program control through a joint management committee but would leave day-to-day operating decisions to the mining company.

On staffing, the report, taking note of the ministry's plan for reorganization, estimated there would be a need for additional direct hires. It was well known that the ministry determined the level of foreign consultants it wished to keep on staff at any one time. In order to lessen this dependence on foreign technical advisors, the report recommended that the ministry adopt a policy of sending a select number of college graduates overseas each year for advance training in the technical disciplines it required.

While not every "i" was dotted nor every "t" crossed, TTI had given the ministry a comprehensive document from which to develop its five-year plan. During the summer of 1980, Arthur Rypinski, the architect of the report, made his first trip to Oman.

The sultan approved the Five Year Plan 1981-1985 in December 1980. Qais Al-Zawawi, in his role as deputy chairman of the Development Council, forwarded the final project figures to the ministry. The totals were considerably less than those in the TTI submission, but, interestingly, important recommendations, such the much touted oil reservoir studies, were to be funded. Also, there was a line item for "long term planning for energy," which brought a certain sense of satisfaction to Jim Critchfield. Perhaps his messages were getting across.

PART III

CRITICAL DEVELOPMENTS IN OMAN 1980 – 1990

Ten years ago, when we set out on that long road together, we had little but our faith in our destiny to sustain us. We were poor in everything except in the strength of our Omani traditions and in our determination to succeed in spite of all obstacles….the powerful aid of modern science and technology has been harnessed to our needs….our economy has been placed on a sound and viable footing….our people enjoy the fullest freedom to lead their lives as they wish….abroad, we have earned ourselves a place in the international community of respect and trust.

Sultan Qaboos bin Said
10th National Day
November 18, 1980

16

1980 – LOOKING BACK, LOOKING FORWARD

As the Sultanate of Oman prepared for its tenth-anniversary celebration on November 17, 1980, Sultan Qaboos could look back with considerable pride at what the nation had accomplished under his leadership. He could also be thankful for the changing circumstances that resulted in world oil prices first quadrupling and then consistently rising each year.

Oman crude oil, along with world crude prices, was at an all-time high. In April 1979, OPEC had priced Saudi marker crude at $14.56 per barrel. Saudi Arabia raised this price to $24 per barrel in December 1979 and to $28 in April 1980. By December 1980, world oil prices were $32-36 per barrel. While not a member of OPEC, Oman oil sold for similar prices.

Since 1970, Oman, in a kind of modern miracle, had developed an impressive infrastructure. This would not have been the case in a world of $10 barrels of oil. The economy was booming almost to the point of overheating. New houses and office buildings were going up on all sides. Rents and lease costs had doubled. The hotels were full. Imports of automobiles and consumer goods were up. Working as a civil servant with security and status while being an entrepreneur on the side was ever more in fashion.

The additional income Oman gained from higher oil prices was staggering. In 1978, Oman's oil revenues were OR458 million ($1.32 billion). In 1980, Oman oil sold for around $32 per barrel, bringing OR770 million ($2.23 billion) to the Oman treasury. In addition, the south Oman oil fields would be brought on stream in 1981, adding to production for export. Budget planners predicted there could be an additional OR1 billion ($2.89 billion) in revenues. Economic growth in the 1980s looked assured. All this good news made for a happy National Day.

But money does not buy security or stability, particularly when your neighbors become embroiled in conflict. The dramatic increase in oil prices, while of great benefit to Oman, was a direct result of the tensions in the area. The Iranian Revolution took 2.5 million bpd of oil off the world market, resulting in an immediate price rise. The United States was brought into the fray when, on November 4, 1979, extremist Iranian students took over the American Embassy in Iran and held its employees hostage for 444 days. A hostage rescue mission in April 1980 failed, and in July, the United States broke diplomatic relations with Iran.

When Iraq invaded Iran in September 1980, breaking its 1975 treaty and proclaiming sovereignty over the Shatt Al Arab waterway, the oil market reacted immediately with further price increases. In November 1980, Iraq captured the southern Iranian port of Khorramshahr. These events produced a dark foreboding over the Arabian Peninsula and Oman. This battlefield was too close for comfort. There was concern that the war could spread –particularly that Saddam Hussein, who had quite skillfully improved his ties with the other Arab states in the region, might extend his attacks on Iran to the lower Gulf. Fortunately, the much publicized reinforcement and disposition of the U.S. Navy Sixth Fleet at the Gulf's entrance and the deployment of four American AWACs to Saudi Arabia reduced the danger.

During this time, and no doubt influenced by revolutionary changes in Iran and stepped-up Soviet military activities in South Yemen, Sultan Qaboos and his advisors began to review foreign policy issues and Oman's own national security. They thought it was time to open a more active dialogue with the United States. While relations with the U.S. government had always been good, they had been somewhat aloof, and the United States had not had any significant military dealings with Oman.

Oman relied on the United Kingdom for most of its arms and military manpower and paid a high price for it. Some elements in the United Kingdom had always seen this thinly camouflaged British military presence in Oman as a strategically important vestige of British manpower in the Indian Ocean. As time passed, the Omanis and even some Britons believed that the limits of the old formula had been reached.

In January 1979, American officials and some non-official American visitors, such as David Rockefeller and Steve Bechtel Jr., were advising Oman not to be too optimistic about either direct support from the

United States or about its exerting an effective influence in the region on their behalf. This had a sobering impact on key Omanis. Omani-Saudi relations were good enough to support an active dialogue, but not good enough to produce significant results without Oman making concessions on the border issues still outstanding between the two countries. Also, Saudi Arabia looked somewhat askance at Oman's support of the pro-Egyptian line on the Camp David initiative. On the other hand, Oman's support of U.S. peace initiatives that resulted in Egypt and Israel signing the Camp David Accords in 1979 tended to strengthen Oman-U.S. relations.

Prior to 1980, Oman's security policy had been one of self-reliance, but the government continued to be worried over threats from a Soviet-influenced South Yemen. It was concerned, as well, about security in the Strait of Hormuz. Action on either of these fronts would require from outside. In the final analysis, what the Omanis would want, as the 1980s unfolded, was more U.S. involvement and support for improved security in both the Dhofar region and the Musandam Peninsula. The best of all worlds would be some form of Saudi/U.S. participation in a coordinated security plan for the Arabian Peninsula to fill the gaps made by Iran's withdrawal, something like a Saudi/U.S. agreement to deploy Saudi air defense capabilities in Oman in times of crisis.

These ideas were informally communicated over time. Jim Critchfield never lost an opportunity to convey his views to U.S. officials. He used his appointment to the Chief of Naval Operations Executive Panel to make his views known. He also communicated with Harold H. Saunders, a trusted contact in Washington with whom he had worked when Saunders was on the National Security Council under President Nixon and who was at the time the Assistant Secretary of State for Near Eastern and South Asian Affairs. Having been on the ground in Oman for five years, Critchfield felt confident in passing on to Saunders and others what he perceived to be current Omani thinking.[1]

Chester Nagle, military advisor to Sultan Qaboos, also acted as key liaison between the Palace and the White House and delivered various communications to and from the sultan. Nagle recalls giving Alexander Haig a letter from Sultan Qaboos as Haig was getting dressed for President Reagan's inaugural ball. Nagle also introduced Tim Landon to General Haig and national security advisor Richard Allen before they

[1] James H. Critchfield, *Oman Papers, 1968-1991*, personal writings of J. H. Critchfield.

took office. Allen, as a private citizen, was given a tour of Oman and flown over the Strait of Hormuz. Nagle also spent time on Capitol Hill seeking legislation to grant Oman with significant funds to upgrade their military facilities, particularly runway construction, engine overhauls and related projects.[2]

Following the fall of the Shah of Iran, the United States reinforced its interest in regional security in the Arabian Gulf. U.S. influence in Oman widened with the signing of a facilities access agreement in June 1980 (renewed in 1990) providing the U.S. military access to Omani bases under specified conditions. This was part of a larger regional strategy that also included facilities in Somalia and Kenya. The air bases at Seeb and Thamrit and on Masirah (the latter abandoned by the British in 1977) were upgraded with American assistance.

The U.S. Army baulked at providing the hundred TOW missiles and ten launchers Oman had requested. However, when Sultan Qaboos met privately with President Reagan in April 1983, the sultan's second official visit to Washington, the issue of the TOW missiles was raised. Reagan turned to his chief of staff and said, "That shouldn't be a problem, should it General?"[3]

The Joint United States–Oman Commission was established in 1980 with the mandate to fund and administer economic assistance programs in the country. This opened the door for the U.S. Agency for International Development (USAID) to fund and participate in a number of such programs. Activities funded through the commission reflected sectoral priorities and included school construction, scholarship and training, fisheries development and a water resources project.

Until that time, American participation in the economic life of Oman had been through private companies. TTI, which had been advising the government since 1975, acted only on the government side of the table. The company was unique in that it was there at the pleasure and the expense of the Oman government. TTI welcomed the news that USAID would be working in Oman.

At the November 17 National Day celebrations, Critchfield noted a mixed Carter-Reagan delegation was observable in a sea of British uniforms, a somewhat ill-at-ease group given the recent U.S. elections, but nevertheless they were there. It was a sign of the times.

[2] Interview with Chester Nagle, October 2006.
[3] Ibid.

The British/American Game in the Arabian Gulf

The British were worried that the United States was secretly trying to usurp its dominant position in Oman. Therefore, the arrival of U.S. military negotiators, contractors and arms merchants in the UAE and Oman in the early 1980s created first concern and then anxiety within the British community. It vigorously reasserted its commercial influence, led by the rallying cries of Prime Minister Thatcher herself. The results were quite remarkable. Concerted pressures were applied in Oman and the Gulf from the highest political levels to every remote corner of the British community. This effort was crowned in the summer of 1981 by the delivery to Oman of a completely packaged staff for a Unified Command of the Sultanate's Armed Forces to help with the Dhofar War.

The chief of staff of the Unified Command was General Sir Timothy Creasy, a veteran of the "Irish Problem" and a highly decorated officer. General Creasy was not happy about the American military presence, but he did accept with equanimity the U.S. facilities agreement. He was actually present at the White House celebration of the event in 1983.

Although sharing a common heritage and an alliance that has survived two world wars and formed the backbone of NATO, the British and Americans have, more often than not, been at odds in Arabia. This deeply competitive game between the British and the Americans on the turf of the Arabian Peninsula remained an obstacle in the 1980s to development of complementary, if not common, strategies in the region.

There has also existed a historical conflict between the rising House of Saud, with its puritanical Wahhabi influence, and the Arabs of the lower Gulf and Oman, whose attitudes and lifestyles were shaped more by association with the British Empire and the patterns of trade and commerce in the Western Indian Ocean than by Wahhabi interpretations of Islam. This conflict had its origins in tribal, religious, cultural and territorial conflicts that symbolically centered on the Buraimi Oasis and Saudi efforts to extend influence east of the Rub Al Khali. Twice in the years since World War II, the British resorted to armed force to turn back Saudi intrusion into what is now Abu Dhabi and Oman territories.

In 1982, Shell remained the dominant foreign oil company in Abu Dhabi and Oman; the four American oil companies that built Aramco continued to exercise dramatic advantages in the world oil market because of almost half a century of total control over the world's richest oil deposits in Saudi Arabia. While the nationalization of foreign oil companies, the influence of OPEC and the proliferation of independent oil companies of every political hue lessened the intensity of these oil rivalries in the peninsula, old antagonisms and suspicions persisted.

In a sense, the British and Americans were now on the outside looking in. No self-respecting Arab regime would acknowledge that it was within the sphere of influence of either. Both the British and Americans were now attempting to define what their new role was to be. Their respective goals were not well defined; indeed, they were often apparently in conflict. The American interest – Aramco aside – was weighted heavily on the side of strategic responsibilities, with a secondary interest in commercial gains, while the British placed commercial interests above all else, although they also were genuinely concerned about the strategic security of the region. The United States attached little importance to whether American companies gained a significant advantage in the markets of the Gulf and Oman. For the British, continuing domination of these markets was a deadly serious matter. The Gulf states and Oman had been a closed British market for decades. Only in recent years did American companies, largely on their own and with no encouragement or assistance from the U.S. government, go after lower Gulf and Oman contracts.

In the Gulf region as a whole, the U.S. policy objective was to deny the USSR control of the Gulf, or, stated more positively, to ensure the continued freedom and stability of the Gulf nations. It began by quietly encouraging the new Gulf Cooperation Council (GCC) to evolve into something that might produce a political environment more favorable to a U.S. military presence in the region. In Oman, the United States had two well-defined military aims: First, it hoped that Oman would play an active and influential role in the regional air defense system that seemed to be gaining acceptance in the GCC. Second, it. hoped that Oman would, within realistic and financial limitations, become an extension of the operating realm of the U.S. fleet in the Indian Ocean.

On its side of the table, Oman had three separate sets of military relationships: its regional ties and roles within the GCC; its national security forces that had been traditionally entrusted to British leadership and suppliers; and its special relationship with the United States, which over the long term could contribute directly to the ability of the U.S.

fleet to operate in the western Indian Ocean supported by land-based facilities in the Arabian Peninsula. The British aim was clearly to retain an exclusive position in Oman's national security forces and to have British systems included in the GCC air defense structure. The United Kingdom was also trying to play a broker role in U.S./Oman bilateral military relations.[4]

Non-Military Questions for Sultan Qaboos

In looking back over the past ten years, Critchfield continued to be positive about the pace at which Oman was developing, but he thought there were critical questions that needed to be addressed. The first question was how much Oman could put into national defense and still maintain a viable development program. It was still allotting a major portion of its budget – 30 percent in 1980 – to military expenditures. Should military security be a national or a regional problem? What was Oman's formula for national security?

The second question addressed the attention given to economic and social development projects in the outlying population centers. Were they sufficient to slow down and even halt the flow of population to the Greater Capital Area? Critchfield wondered if enough genuine, long-term productive projects were being pursued that could survive a decline in oil revenues. So far, oil production dominated the economic scene.

And finally, he asked the question (rhetorically) whether too much of the population was being drawn into an unproductive civil service rather than being taught long-term productive skills that would be needed in the private sector when oil revenues declined. Critchfield believed that there was almost no issue of domestic or international policy facing the sultanate in 1980 that was not relevant to these three questions.[5]

Status of Tetra Tech International

At the end of his visit to Oman to attend the National Day festivities, Critchfield told Kirk Agon that he thought it was time to batten down the hatches in Oman and concentrate on performance within the framework of TTI's current contracts. Any additional responsibilities

[4]Ibid.
[5]Ibid.

should be based exclusively on clear-cut requests from the Oman government. Critchfield felt that TTI's profile in Oman was perhaps already too high. He also believed that top performance was critical for the company to remain there, but he knew that everyone was stretched too thin, despite efforts to augment the personnel roster.

TTI's contract with the Ministry of Petroleum and Minerals was going into its sixth year. There were seven resident advisors, and the annual contract fee was $1.25 million. Oddly enough, staffing problems were the most critical in this area. The oil industry in Oman was larger and more complex than it had been five years before. Qualified geophysicists and petroleum engineers were in high demand worldwide and were therefore hard to find. Minister Said Al-Shanfari was unhappy with TTI's inability to meet his demands immediately. Showing some frustration, he indicated he was thinking of hiring two or three of TTI's advisors directly and turning the rest of the work over to Shell. Critchfield did not take this comment lightly. He knew that Al-Shanfari had also been looking at the British and French markets for talent, but, thus far, he had not made any decisions to add to his foreign advisory staff in the ministry.

The Musandam Development Committee (MDC) contract, which covered the period 1980-83 for a $6 million fee, needed both better staffing and better support from the government in facilitating the movement of material and people into and out of the Musandam Peninsula. Agon was looking locally in Oman and the Gulf area for staff. One British civil engineer, Peter Rowland, was locally hired, and John Sasser arrived in January 1980 to give Kirk Agon much welcomed assistance. Critchfield felt that if TTI could get through the first year of working in this remote area, the project would be successful.

The TTI contract for the Public Authority for Water Resources (PAWR), which was created by royal decree on December 4, 1979, became effective on April 1, 1980. It provided for staffing by TTI of the technical secretariat in the amount of $2,151,950 for the first year and a 10 percent increase for the following two years up to December 31, 1982.[6] Even before the contract was signed, TTI personnel were establishing themselves in the PAWR district offices and work was under way to locate and develop these scarce but critical water resources.

---

[6] Ibid. From TTI contract files.

The road from Khasab to Bukha carved into the edges
of the fjords of the Musandam Peninsula – 1979

Flaring off associated gas as seen by Stribling Snodgrass
on his early visits to Oman – 1972

Traditional agriculture in the Musandam Peninsula. The cultivated area
is within the stone walls at the center and in the foreground.

Yousuf bin Alawi, in the dark jacket, inspecting
a newly drilled water well in the desert – 1977

The port of Khasab on the Musandam Peninsula – 1977

Only accessible by boat, Kumzar is an isolated village
strategically located on the Strait of Hormuz.

A father and his children in Kumzar. The village has been inhabited for approximately 500 years.

A water boat leaves Kumzar – 1979

Josee Sasser amid Omani schoolboys at Kumzar – 2006. The tower of the desalination plant is visible in the background.

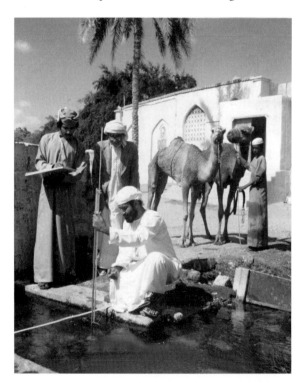

Omani technicians monitoring the water flow of a traditional *aflaj* irrigation system as part of a regional water survey for the PAWR

Above: John Sasser at Mahada *falaj*

Above left: Nga and Kirk Agon at the TTI office in Muscat – 1979

Left: Arthur Rypinski

Below: Sam Patterson on the sea wall at the port of Mutra

The zigzag road to the port development at Khawr Naid – 1980

The refinery at Mina Al-Fahal – 1983

17

THE REGIONAL DEVELOPMENT COMMITTEE

Known as the Z Project, the Regional Development Committee (RDC) began in the spring of 1981 when Sultan Qaboos told Critchfield that he was considering applying the lessons learned in the Musandam Development Committee (MDC) to the Buraimi-Dhahirah region.[1] Together the two regions constituted all of Oman's border area with the United Arab Emirates except for the Batinah plain border north of Sohar.

The historic Buraimi Oasis occupies an important role in the history of the southeastern corner of the Arabian Peninsula. For hundreds of years, the oasis was at the center of dynasty and tribal conflicts, which had both religious and economic overtones. In the post World War II period, the oasis was an object of unresolved conflict, with Britain, Oman and Abu Dhabi more or less united on one side, and Saudi Arabia, with Aramco and low-key U.S. support, on the other. Oil and water were the underlying causes of the conflict. Shell and Aramco were in the background advocating and hoping for a resolution to these problems. Only in very recent years was a degree of political stability achieved. Oil revenues made this possible, but the UAE seized the advantage early and began development of the border region before Oman.

By 1981, a single but divided city had been catapulted into the modern era. Roughly one quarter of the city was in Oman; this part was called Buraimi. The rest, in the UAE, was called Al Ain. The UAE policy for developing Al Ain created circumstances that would heavily influence Oman's development of its own Buraimi area. The creation of modern Al Ain was not based on careful scientific research. It had been built by mining the waters of the historic Buraimi Oasis at a rate that exceeded

[1] James H. Critchfield, *Oman Papers, 1968-1991,* from a Tetra Tech International interoffice memo dated April 18, 1981, regarding Buraimi development.

recharge by a factor of ten. It should not be overlooked that Al Ain was the birthplace and home of the ruler Sheikh Zayid bin Sultan Al-Nahyan, who clearly wished to see the development of the region where he had been born. Sheikh Zayid, who succeeded his brother as ruler of Abu Dhabi in 1966, became president of the UAE in 1971.

From the beginning of his rule, Sheikh Zayid began to transform the UAE into a leading destination for business and tourism and a gateway to the Middle East for much of Europe, Asia and the United States. Dubai, in particular, became a central stop for travelers between Europe and Asia.

Abu Dhabi's oil wealth allowed for the development of a beautiful garden city where the ancient Buraimi Oasis had existed. It can be reached from the Arabian Gulf by a 78-mile divided highway that is an unending display of green trees and floral extravagance fed daily by miles of drip irrigation and large water trucks.

Rapid development of Al Ain contrasted sharply with the backwardness of Buraimi, which was characterized by miles of refuse scattered along the "western gateway to Oman" and cheap and ugly shops and garages along the central Buraimi road. Buraimi residents lived without electricity on the summer's hottest days, without piped water supplies, without telephone service in most residential areas and without organized agricultural assistance. Hidden within the family homes lurked one of the most serious problems: sons without residential plots to house their growing families. Living conditions were even harsher in the small, outlying villages of the region.

The Buraimi Oasis was a natural phenomenon that resulted from rainfall on the Omani Hajar mountain range 93 miles to the east. For centuries, the rainwater has migrated through underground channels to collect in a permanent, natural, underground storage area or aquifer. The runoff was sufficient to keep the aquifer filled, with a lens of fresh, sweet water lying on the top, where it was easily accessible to the tribes of the desert, who came and went from the oasis.

By the time the era of oil brought sweeping changes to the Arabian Peninsula, nine villages had sprung up and were more or less permanently occupied. Three of these made up the town of Buraimi; six were clustered at the foot of Jebel Hafit on the Abu Dhabi side of the border. The aquifer, even during periods of periodic drought, had remained more or less in balance for centuries. Wells, dug to a depth of about 50 feet, originally fed the Buraimi villages. The wells increased in depth to 500 feet, and in the early 1980s, Al Ain authorities pushed them to 1,500 feet. At that time, Abu Dhabi began laying a large diameter pipeline from the Umm Al Nar desalination plant 78 miles uphill to Al Ain to bring 15 million gallons of water a day to the rapidly expanding city that would soon be served by an international airport. The dimensions of the aquifer underlying Al Ain and Buraimi had not been scientifically explored or studied by any party. Virtually no effort had been made to control well drilling and extraction. It was estimated that the water table was dropping by three feet a year and the quality in some parts of the aquifer was deteriorating.

More and deeper wells were drilled in Al Ain without any consideration for maintaining a balance in the ancient aquifers. For Oman, this development had serious consequences. The huge aquifer under Al Ain was also the source of water pumped from wells in Buraimi. Destruction of the aquifer would eventually do equal damage to both towns.

Gradually, Buraimi began to take on a greater importance for the sultanate. In the early 1980s, the Public Authority for Water Resources (PAWR) took initial steps to determine how much water was available in the Oman watershed and what was happening as a result of the dramatically dropping water table under Al Ain.

Critchfield had long felt and communicated to top Omani officials that water would eventually be the most disputed resource shared by Oman and the UAE. Groundwater that accumulated in Oman moved into many areas along the border. The issue would almost certainly become acute in the Buraimi area. The planned development of Al Ain into a city of 165,000 by 1990 (it was about 130,000 in 1981) would increase the demand for Oman water. Sheikh Zayid had spent several billion petrodollars in developing his version of an American Palm Springs in an area that had been a palm tree and thatched-roof village of 4,000 people only a few decades before. Wedged into this plush town was the comparatively poor and certainly neglected Omani village of Buraimi. TTI's criticism of the neglect of Buraimi probably played some role in the sultan's decision to accelerate its development. He gave TTI the task without as much as a word of discussion.

Sometime in early April 1981, Qais Al-Zawawi, in his capacity as Deputy Chairman of the Development Council, called a meeting at his home without telling any of the participants in advance what it was about. Attending were Minister of Electricity and Water Hamoud Al-Harithi, Minister of Communications Salim bin Nasser, Minister of Land Affairs and Municipalities Ahmed Al-Ghazali, and Minister of Interior Sayyid Badr bin Saud bin Hareb. The topic of the meeting turned out to be Buraimi; Sultan Qaboos wanted action to be taken to develop it, using the Musandam Peninsula as a guide.

Al-Zawawi told the group that Sultan Qaboos was very pleased with the results of the MDC and he wanted development in the Buraimi region to be handled the same way – i.e., that the responsibilities of the various ministries be turned over to a new development committee operating as an executive body. Al-Zawawi indicated that Minister Sayyid Badr bin Saud bin Hareb would probably be made chairman of the new group. Al-Harithi, as a member of the committee, would be expected to provide guidance based on his experiences as head of the MDC. The group presented for consideration some ideas for Buraimi, such as agriculture potential, construction of a gas pipeline to Buraimi with the possible sale of gas to Al Ain, construction of roads, and border demarcation.

A week later and after a meeting with the sultan, Al-Zawawi stated that the committee would be formed.[2] The sultan added two additional members: Director of the Palace Office General Ali Majid, and Minister of Agriculture and Fisheries Abdul Hafidh Al-Rajab. A royal decree would be issued soon, but it would not be publicized. For the time being, the existence and activities of the committee would be treated as confidential. Al-Zawawi indicated that the scope of activities of this committee would be significantly larger than the MDC and it would have more or less "unlimited access to funds." This was a statement that would later be challenged. Essentially, the region was envisioned as residential with pockets of small-scale agriculture and light industry. In addition to the obvious agriculture, water resources, and electricity development, the program would include an extensive road system and the establishment of settlements in the vicinity of the border. That was probably why Qais Al-Zawawi advised that the activities of the committee be treated as confidential.

There were differences between the areas of the MDC and the Buraimi region. Buraimi was the main land gateway to Oman. The

[2] Ibid.

Musandam, a vital strategic region, had very limited capacity for long-term economic and social development, unless local industries supporting oil and gas production were to become a factor. Militarily, Musandam would become more important. In contrast, the region around Buraimi had the potential to develop into an attractive population center with resources, agriculture and industry capable of sustaining a much expanded community. Water was the key. While the Buraimi project would be modeled on the MDC, the differences between the two regions would become more evident as time went on.

On May 2, the committee met under the chairmanship of Minister of Interior Sayyid Badr, who reiterated the concerns of Sultan Qaboos about the welfare of the citizens in the Dhahirah region. He said that TTI would be asked to launch the project along the same lines as the MDC. Kirk Agon was charged with drafting the royal decree. TTI was given 90 days to put the project together; 30 days after that, staff was expected to be in place. Once again, the company was faced with taking over hundreds of government employees and current operations. In effect, it would be building a duplicate of the MDC.

The Z Project came along at a time when oil revenues were declining and 1982 budget figures for current projects were being reexamined. Agon estimated that if the Z Project were to be funded along the lines of the MDC, it would effectively mean committing at least $100 million in capital over the next five years. He personally questioned whether a project of this magnitude was really necessary. He wrote to Critchfield in Rosslyn that perhaps it was a mistake for the government to push too hard on development at this time. But the fact remained that Buraimi was right next to Al Ain, a jewel in Abu Dhabi's crown. The contrast between the sister cities was just too stark. Also, Sultan Qaboos did not want the development committee to focus only on Buraimi, but on the Dhahirah region as a whole. Although Buraimi might be ahead of other villages in the region, it was backward compared to Al Ain. This could become a political problem as interaction with other Gulf states began to mature.

Critchfield viewed the Z Project as a major development and a remarkable opportunity to undertake a large and important activity. TTI was pleased with this evidence of the government's continued confidence in the company. But at the same time, Critchfield greeted this development with mixed feelings. The decision by the sultan further consolidated TTI's quasi-official position as an institution that worked only on the government's side of the table.

However, Critchfield knew that TTI was already stretched thin in attempting to provide the administrators, engineers and technicians to do the MDC job. And there were several major vacancies in the TTI staff at the Ministry of Petroleum and Minerals. "Our major problem is recruiting," he acknowledged in a letter to Tetra Tech Pasadena, which he had been pressing to help fill the gaps. He clearly felt that things were moving too fast, and he did not want to get TTI into a situation in which it would be unable to perform. His experience with the Development Council and the Water Resources Council was that they were fine for integrating broad policies but were sure death for tasks requiring action. Furthermore, he thought that a committee of seven ministers to deal with Buraimi was a situation that would ensure failure. Ministers have to put their prestige on the line in decision making; it was far more productive to run the committee by undersecretaries and work out agreements that could then be stamped by the ministers. That would have been his preference.[3]

In July 1981, Kay Heilig, a project officer for a telecommunications company in Africa, was hired to be the site manager for Project Z in Buraimi. He would report to Kirk Agon in Muscat. Critchfield anticipated that they would have to borrow some personnel from the PAWR to handle water issues. While the committee would be modeled on the MDC, the differences between the two regions would inevitably become more evident as TTI proceeded with getting organized.

As the first order of business, Kirk Agon drafted the royal decree announcing the formation of the development committee. It still did not have a name. The ministers did not want to call it the Buraimi Development Committee, as it was intended to have a broader scope of responsibility than just Buraimi. It continued to be referred to as Project Z.

Critchfield need not have been concerned about the pace with which Project Z was proceeding. As of January 1982, TTI had not yet gotten its contract through bureaucratic channels. He was reminded of Qais Al-Zawawi's statement that anyone who spent money without a contract in Oman was a fool. Given the high-level decisions yet to be made on the project, Critchfield said he would move aggressively only when he

[3] Ibid., letter from Critchfield to Agon, April 21, 1981.

had it directly from Sultan Qaboos that he wanted him to move, or when TTI had a contract signed by Al-Zawawi and Sayyid Badr.

Nevertheless, pressure was on for the TTI staff to produce a development plan. Work got under way without the formal contract, but TTI did obtain interim financing to cover costs. Project Z was given the ambiguous name of Regional Development Committee (RDC). In May 1982, the royal decree for the creation of the RDC was made public.[4] TTI then had to play catch-up and put together the budget proposal. It hoped to do that by July, along with the MDC and PAWR budgets.

Working under the direction of the new chairman, Minister of Interior Sayyid Badr, who had given his full personal support, Agon began to develop a plan for the Buraimi area and its environs. Drawing on assistance from John Sasser, Arthur Rypinski, Heilig and his newly acquired small staff, the team worked out a basic development plan. The committee, like the MDC, was charged with accelerated development of this important area of the sultanate. The mandate given the development committee specifically for Buraimi was to accomplish four tasks: clean up Buraimi and organize refuse collection; relieve the public water supply problem; upgrade the appearance along the main carriageway through Buraimi; and award new residential plots in the town.

Development was to be financed solely with funds previously allocated under the second Five Year Plan (1980-85) to the various ministries for works in Buraimi. No new funds were appropriated, despite Qais Al-Zawawi's initial promises. The funds provided were no greater on a per capita basis than development funds appropriated throughout the country. This should have been a warning sign, but everyone was anxious to see the project get off the ground and they were not thinking long term.

For the region as a whole, the development plan outlined programs for building basic infrastructure to include electricity, water, roads, agriculture, municipalities and lands, and telecommunications.[5] The administrative structure was not too different from that of the MDC. The principal operating staff would be the secretariat, which TTI would provide. The Muscat office would have a support staff of 33 personnel;

---

[4] Ibid. Middle East Economic Digest, *New Regional Organization Created,* May 28, 1982.

[5] Ibid. Regional Development Committee, *Development Plan,* July 16, 1982.

the Buraimi office would have 15 professionals and 17 support staff. The secretariat would supervise all development projects and report their progress directly to the chairman. At the same time, the secretariat would undertake the training and development of Omani staff as managers, technicians and engineers to take over these responsibilities when appropriate.

Forty percent of the funds went immediately to rectifying the electrical supply problem. Demand for electricity had grown rapidly throughout the sultanate, and the cost of diesel power generation was becoming prohibitive. In its initial development plan, which went first to the RDC and ultimately to Sultan Qaboos, TTI stated that if growth in electricity consumption was to be sustained, it was essential to convert to gas-fired electricity generation using large central stations.

The first project was to construct a power transmission line from the Sohar power station to Buraimi using gas from Sohar as fuel. Once that was completed it would be extended to Mahdah, the second largest town in the region. When Buraimi itself expanded, there would be a continuing requirement to double the capacity of the line. The cost forecast for accomplishing these tasks in 1983-85 totaled OR10 million ($29 million).

With regard to water, there was a pressing need to identify and design a system to develop water sources adequate to provide for the growth of Buraimi through the end of the century. Safe piped water was also needed for the expanding population outside of Buraimi. In 1980, the PAWR had discovered a highly productive aquifer located about 20 kilometers east of Buraimi capable of producing water of excellent quality. Designing a delivery system to bring this to Buraimi would be the next step. At that time, there was no provision for house water connections, and this needed to be addressed. Outlying areas, such as Mahdah and beyond, needed water brought to them. Also, in the mountain villages, the *aflaj* damaged by storms needed to be repaired. The cost forecast for water projects was OR3.7 million ($11 million).

The roads program had three objectives: to design a system of graded roads to provide access to all the towns in the region but with a shorter distance than the existing roads system; to improve the quality of the roads system; and to provide paved streets in Buraimi and Mahdah. The cost of doing this was enormous. It was estimated at somewhere on the order of OR80 million ($232 million).

The first order of business in the agricultural sector would be to construct a new extension center, with full veterinary facilities, in Buraimi. The center would provide advice and technical assistance to the farmers, including information on agricultural equipment. Smaller sub-centers would be constructed at Mahdah and Ajran. A water appraisal program would be carried out to determine whether irrigation systems could be built for agricultural use. The plan was to do a study first in the vicinity of the Oman-UAE border to determine the type of crops that could be grown and the irrigation technology required to get a program under way. To start a program would require substantial land reclamation, an additional cost to the government. Estimates for these projects over three years were placed at OR4 million ($12 million).

Town planning projects would have to begin with an effective system of land registration and allocation, good maps, a demographic survey, a land survey and the appropriate siting for development of the infrastructure. Existing services would have to be upgraded, including house water connections and sewage treatment facilities. It was estimated that these survey projects would cost OR2 million ($6 million). Upgrading the existing telephone service and adding service in Buraimi, Mahdah and other outlying areas was estimated to be OR2.8 million ($8 million).

Before getting started, there were employees to be housed, vehicles to be maintained, and office space to be identified. Buraimi itself was comparatively rich in facilities and it was possible to rent accommodations and office space for most of the planned activities. However, this was not the case in the more remote areas of the Buraimi region. There was only one gasoline station in the entire area, and it was run by a UAE company. Stations would have to be constructed in Buraimi, Mahdah and elsewhere. Although the main purpose would be to provide fuel to government vehicles, they would also be open to the public, thus rendering an important service to the locals. These public works projects were estimated to cost about OR600,000 ($1.7 million).

These projects represented an outlay of almost $300 million for 1983-85. That was three times what Kirk Agon envisioned before the RDC was even organized.

As events unfolded, a basic philosophical question was beginning to surface. Since the early days of the development of the sultanate, emphasis had been on improving the services of the nation and the lifestyle of its citizens. This quite naturally began in the Greater Capital Area. As a result, the sultanate began seeing a significant shift in population from the rural towns and villages to Muscat and its environs. Rural residents were awed by the difference between the quality of life they perceived being offered in the capital area as compared to their home villages, and they had a natural tendency to gravitate toward the Greater Capital Area. As a consequence, the rural areas were becoming depopulated, and the government was having difficulty expanding its infrastructure to cope with the influx of new residents. One result was a huge backlog of applications for plots of land. It was becoming even more critical to improve the quality of life in selected rural towns and villages.

Town planning in the Buraimi area, therefore, would become a priority. Buraimi would likely continue to be a residence for citizens who worked in the UAE. Other villages in the region would be largely devoted to agriculture. If rapid development of infrastructure was achieved, the pressure would be taken off the Greater Capital Area. The group working in Buraimi could perhaps become a suitable vehicle to organize rural town development in other areas in Oman. It could at the very least be considered a model for change. But first, the RDC had to show results in Buraimi and its environs.

Kay Heilig, together with a newly hired on-site manager by the name of Harry Harvey, an engineer with broad experience in the Middle East, opened an office in Buraimi. They set up RDC transient quarters – a walled-in complex that was clean, almost austere in style, but adequate. One of the rooms was furnished as a small lounge, with comfortable chairs, a large coffee table and no other amenities. Another room served as a kitchen that could provide breakfast for transients. There was no regular food service of any kind. For restaurants and shopping centers, they would have to go to Al Ain.

It was not until July 1983, when Critchfield was in Oman, that the two-year negotiation of the RDC contract was concluded. The effective date was April 1, 1983. It was a three-year contract valued at $9 million. Sayyid Badr, the RDC chairman, complained mildly to Critchfield when they met in November about the lack of progress in cleaning up the Buraimi mess. When asked when he had last inspected it, he replied, "in September, I think." Critchfield reminded him that the ink on the contract was hardly dry by then. But the pressure was on to perform.

Critchfield would make an inspection in December and report to both Badr and Sultan Qaboos.

One of the early actions of the RDC was to address town planning. A town planning team from Shankland Cox, the British firm with whom TTI had worked in Musandam province, began working on the problem in December. Craig White, TTI's Arabic-speaking liaison with the local Omani tribal and government authorities, shared with Shankland Cox some of the complex issues that he had encountered in land use planning and administration. For example, the Omani official responsible for land use grants in the region had refused to turn files over to the RDC office. They had to bump this problem up to the chairman, Sayyid Badr, and basically could do nothing until it was resolved. Land grants were the number-one political issue.

Dr. Fred Turner, a senior TTI agricultural consultant, arrived in Buraimi and would spend several weeks developing an assessment and proposals for agricultural development of the region. He was assisted by Nick Saines, a PAWR hydrogeologist. TTI water experts had been working in the area before the RDC was formed and had acquired an absolutely unique understanding of the water system that created the inland desert oasis.

It was Critchfield's view, and he so advised Sayyid Badr, that Oman should unilaterally proceed with plans to identify and develop aquifers to the east of Buraimi, which could be put into production and expand towns and communities in the Dhahirah without drawing water directly from the Al Ain-Buraimi aquifer. At the same time, he thought it prudent that Oman proceed with a full study of the international water laws applicable to Buraimi and begin to prepare for litigation of a dispute that seemed almost inevitable. TTI would examine this legal issue and make it part of its recommendations to the RDC.

Some time later, a PAWR hydrogeologist, Don Davison, discovered that as a result of pumping rates on the UAE side for many years, the gradient had steepened sharply near the border and the decline in the water table in Buraimi was alarming. The Oman groundwater flow rates were still sufficiently slower than the UAE extraction rates. This meant that the UAE would dewater its side to bedrock before disastrous damage was noted on the Oman side.

This technical fact entirely altered the complexion of the situation. The water experts recommended that a plan be implemented to allow groundwater flows to the UAE equal to but not more than the historical norms that existed prior to the introduction of wasteful UAE extraction policies. The RDC, in conjunction with the PAWR, would undertake a water resource project plan right away and a report would be produced for Critchfield to brief Sultan Qaboos on his next trip. Critchfield wrote to Sayyid Badr that after two years into the program for accelerated development of the Dhahirah region, water remained the principal constraint. The success of every RDC project would depend on resolving the region's water problems.

18

THE LONG TERM ENERGY PLAN

Soon after Sultan Qaboos approved the Five Year Plan 1981-1985, the Petroleum Ministry's technical director, Khalifa Al-Hinai, asked TTI to give him a list of consultants qualified to draw up a long-range energy plan for the ministry. Critchfield's immediate response was that he thought the ministry could do the job with its existing staff, i.e., TTI. He mentioned that firms such as Bechtel and Booz Allen Hamilton did that type of work, but suggested that TTI could start immediately. Then, if the ministry felt the need to retain an additional consultant, it could do so at a later phase. In January 1981, Arthur Rypinski was assigned to the Muscat office to assist Al-Hinai on this project. Rypinski told Critchfield that he felt quite capable of undertaking such an exercise. And in this way, the Long Term Energy Plan (LTEP) for Oman was born.

The LTEP came at a time when oil revenues were at their highest. The Finance Council and Development Council chose to plow these windfall profits back into the economy at a very rapid pace, and before long the economy became overheated. There were Omanis in key positions in government who were clearly concerned about this. One senior official put the blame squarely on the shoulders of his government, which was trying to push money into the economy faster than it could efficiently absorb it. Critchfield made three trips to Muscat between May and October of 1981 and described the Omanis as being in a euphoric state of mind. He commented that these huge profits from oil had suddenly become an inalienable birthright.

The LTEP fell within the framework of TTI's current advisory role with the ministry. Team 1 in both Rosslyn and Muscat would contribute, as would Brad Dismukes from Texas. The finished product would cover a wide range of subjects, such as assessment of future supply, demand for revenue, production schedules for light, medium and heavy crudes, enhanced recovery, gas supply and demand, electric power generation, energy conservation and alternatives for electric power. Critchfield hoped the effort would contribute something to a prudent and well-planned exploitation of Oman's energy resources and a planned approach to meeting Oman's energy needs. This would be a major effort that would cover the period 1983-2022.

Undersecretary Salem Shabaan, in a letter dated January 1983, acknowledged this undertaking. "We should like here to say briefly that we are appreciative of Tetra Tech's continuing efforts over the years to carry out long term studies of this kind on our behalf. We value such work highly. The Department of Planning and Legal Affairs will be the ministry's coordinator on this program and we look forward to reviewing the items to be included in your effort." The letter also noted that this work would be done without additional payment.[1]

Now that he had a mandate from the government to do long-term planning, Critchfield was in his element. He had been spending most of his spare time on this subject. It concerned him that the policy of PDO and Shell consistently was to maximize production while not looking to the future. Although PDO did an increasingly impressive job of management, planning and presentation of the data, it was his impression that the good news of today was highlighted and the bad news of tomorrow skillfully and consciously obfuscated. It was Critchfield's view that Shell was aware of this but believed, with considerable encouragement, that they were telling the 60-percent shareholder what he wanted to hear. Critchfield felt that TTI had a very serious responsibility to ensure that both the good and bad news were put before the client. He predicted that at the turn of the century, the year 2000, the client might conclude that neither PDO nor the advisors told it quite like it was.

It was possible, of course, that a lot of the future production from Lekhwair, Marmul, Nimr and a number of smaller fields would fill the gaps, but this could not be reliably predicted until various enhanced oil recovery pilot programs had been run and decisions made on long-term production. In the short term, the easiest course of action was to produce the light crudes from north and central Oman. These were easier to

---

[1] Ibid., MPM/USO/15-02/06/83, *Long Term Energy Plan for Oman*, letter from Undersecretary Salem Shabaan to James H. Critchfield, January 26, 1983.

forecast than were the fields in the south Oman area, where enhanced oil recovery techniques were in the early phase of testing.

One could not miss the point that much of the production that was being planned for the 1990s was dependent on a favorable outcome of further exploratory drilling or, more often, on increased reliance on significantly enhanced recovery operations. This would result in a major increase in capital and operating costs as the more cheaply produced light crudes in the north and central regions were gradually depleted. The TTI production forecast for 1988-93 would leave Yibal, the workhorse of the Oman producers, with 342 million barrels of reserves, or 42 percent of its current reserves.[2] For Oman's future as an oil exporter, everything depended on how much new oil would be found each year from 1980 until 2000, what the quality of the oil would be, and what ultimate recovery could be achieved with and without enhanced oil recovery. Critchfield hoped to have the LTEP, which would address these issues, completed and in the hands of the clients by the end of 1983. Arthur Rypinski returned to Washington permanently in September 1983 and would devote most of his time to this project.

Dismukes Philosophizes on Long-Range Energy Planning

As work began on the LTEP, Critchfield asked Dismukes for his thoughts on long-range energy planning for Oman. In his engineer-like manner, his response cut straight to the core of the subject.

- The wealth of Oman springs from petroleum.

- PDO produces 96 percent of Oman's crude oil and is a major consumer of energy.

- Energy supply and demand studies need to be coordinated by PDO and the government. Annual estimates to cover the next twenty years are desirable. Spot peeks for each five years thereafter, up to fifty years, also should be included.

- On the supply side, the operators' annual reserve estimates of oil and gas plus their estimates of potential oil recovery improvement should be employed. Estimates of undiscovered resources are also needed.

- Other energy sources, such as solar and wind power, deserve attention, particularly for the outlying areas.

[2] Ibid., Tetra Tech International Inc., *Long Term Energy Plan of the Sultanate of Oman 1983-2022*, July 1, 1984.

- Energy conservation among major producers inside Oman is worthy of consideration. PDO needs to embark on an energy conservation program.

- A study of oil operations might reduce field losses, such as spills and weathering.

- While gas flaring has already received attention, a renewed effort could be profitable.

- The use of LPG (liquid petroleum gas) as vehicular fuel in the fields needs to be considered for PDO. No doubt Shell Marketing expects to continue profiting from fuel sales to the oil fields and would oppose the use of LPG.

- Even closer monitoring of PDO to learn its objectives and motives is needed. These may or may not become apparent as the budgets and programs are submitted to the board for approval. Early knowledge will help to defend government interests. Also, PDO's operational efficiency and cost effectiveness will be made clearer. This points up the need for representation within PDO and possibly other operators later.

- The Ministry of Petroleum and Minerals has a tendency to look to PDO for guidance rather than to its own technical advisors. If the question of government interests or Shell interests comes into play, there is no doubt Shell's interests will prevail. This would be most evident if Shell, as purchaser, desires a product or price different from that offered by the government.[3]

Yibal Set for a Detailed Reservoir Study

From the beginning, Brad Dismukes had played a significant role in advising Oman on its oil policy. The petroleum ministry, acting on his urging, decided to undertake a major effort on the Yibal field.[4] It asked Dismukes to find the right company to do the work. After reviewing several bids, he settled on Scientific Software Corporation. Scientific Software Corporation was a Denver-based company that had extensive experience in computer model analyses of reservoirs worldwide. They had developed reservoir simulation programs for the petroleum industry and had state-of-the-art enhanced oil recovery technology. Its clients ranged from giant companies, including Exxon, Mobil and Shell, to smaller companies operating in Libya, Iraq and Abu Dhabi.

[3] Ibid., Dismukes Memorandum to Critchfield, October 23, 1982.

On March 7, 1981, Minister Al-Shanfari formally contracted with the company to provide the ministry with a statement of recoverable hydrocarbon reserves in Yibal's Shuaiba reservoir and to submit a specific plan for the recovery of reserves that would yield the highest economic return. The conclusions of these findings were to be coordinated and agreed upon by PDO. PDO was initially reluctant to have this outside intrusion, but the technical staff in The Hague and the expanding reservoir engineering staff in Oman gradually became full participants in the effort.

PDO, in the meantime, moved ahead with its plans for exploration and enhanced oil recovery. PDO's target was to add to the reserves at least the same volume as was produced each year. And it would continue to collect the necessary data for comprehensive reservoir and enhanced oil recovery studies, "with advisory assistance from abroad as necessary," to achieve its objectives.

Brad Dismukes continued to work from Dallas, but it was not long before he notified Critchfield that he would not renew his contract. "Developing my lateral earth boring system has progressed to a stage where most of my working time is required. I plan to build and test a prototype drilling tool this year." Brad did say he would complete his assignment on the long-term energy plan. He added that his five years of association with TTI had meant a great deal to him both personally and professionally.

Dismukes stayed in touch on the Scientific Software Yibal project. This effort was the culmination of everything he had pushed hard for. Not everyone had supported the heavy-handed tactics he had used with PDO over the years. Some accused him of using a two-by-four approach when dealing with Shell. But the key player in the ministry, Khalifa Al-Hinai, never called a halt to Dismukes's methods, indicating that he at least felt Dismukes was working in the interests of Oman.

TTI Staffing at the Ministry of Petroleum

In July 1981, the Ministry of Petroleum and Minerals renewed TTI's contract for $6 million for three years. Bruce Edmonds and Dr. Ernie Murany did not renew. Two new advisors, Don Bowtell and Don Parker, both experienced in oil exploration, joined Ken Bodine in the ministry. A few months later, Stan Thurber, a reservoir engineer who had been with Gulf Oil, joined the group. Critchfield had been looking for a qualified resident reservoir engineer for more than four years. Thurber was spotted by Tom Barger through an old Aramco contact. By the time Thurber arrived, the ministry had made a decision to go on a two-track program: (1) pushing PDO to do more in-house studies, with the ministry advisors playing a monitoring role, and (2) selectively doing outside studies under direct contract of the ministry. On the latter point, PDO was still reluctant to cooperate, but it was getting better.

In December 1981, Tom Fitz rounded out the team of advisors. As facilities engineer, his job was to represent the ministry in its relationships with the various concessionaires in the planning and execution of capital production facilities projects. He would monitor both the expansion of field installations and pipelines. In practice, Fitz spent a big chunk of his time monitoring the construction of the new oil refinery.

By this time, Tetra Tech Houston was playing less of a role. Minister Al-Shanfari wanted his advisors to be physically in the ministry. Compared to the early days of 1975, Houston's role had faded to almost nothing. Having the TTI advisors within the ministry, however, did not mean that they worked as a team. Each one sat in a separate office and reported individually to a specific ministry official, such as Undersecretary Salem Shabaan, director of technical affairs; Khalifa Al-Hinai, director of planning and legal affairs; Ali Al-Battashi; and even Al-Shanfari himself. Critchfield tried to strengthen the institutional function of TTI within the ministry, but it did not work. There was never a team leader, as in TTI Rosslyn, and none of the advisors was in charge of the other. This was the way the ministry wanted it, and they were paying the bills.

TTI Acquired by Honeywell Corporation

In May 1982, Tetra Tech Inc. was acquired by the Minneapolis-based company Honeywell Inc. As a result, Honeywell found it owned a small international company known as Tetra Tech International doing business in a small nation in the Arabian Gulf. Ownership of TTI was somewhat of a surprise for corporate executives in Minneapolis. They were frying bigger fish.

Once acquired by Honeywell, TTI Rosslyn began a public relations effort to inform the Honeywell management that there was business to be done in the Arabian Gulf along the same lines as it was doing in

Oman. A visit to Oman was set up for selected Honeywell executives to see for themselves. Critchfield saw that TTI's future rested on its ability not only to continue to perform well in Oman, but also to develop new business for Honeywell in the Gulf.

The clients in Oman took little notice of the Honeywell acquisition. As far as they were concerned, TTI and Critchfield were synonymous. TTI's position in Oman was good. It had four principal contracts dealing with the Ministry of Petroleum and Minerals, the Public Authority for Water Resources, the Musandam Development Committee and the Regional Development Committee that would carry them until December 1985. The staff in Muscat was strong, with John Sasser, who dealt mainly with the MDC; Arthur Rypinski, a man for all seasons and who dealt across the board with various economic and development ministries; the addition of Robert Zunzer, who arrived in Oman in July 1982 to manage the growing administrative infrastructure of the company; and the very competent staff of Omani and expatriate personnel. Zunzer, a retired government administrator whom Critchfield had known in Germany in the 1950s, agreed to a full-time assignment to Muscat. He had been on contract there the previous year doing a survey of the company. Like so many before him, his visit to Oman was captivating enough for him to say "yes" to a permanent assignment.

19

TTI AND LONG RANGE PLANNING: CRACKS APPEAR

For the first time since the era of oil in Oman began in the 1960s, Oman had most of the information it needed to confidently project in quite specific terms its options for the next forty years. In Critchfield's view, the decisions made in the next ten years would largely determine the economic circumstances of Oman through the first decades of the twenty-first century.

In a letter dated September 1, 1983, Critchfield reported to the undersecretary to the Ministry of Petroleum and Minerals, Salem Shabaan, on the progress of TTI's work on the Long Term Energy Plan (LTEP). He was confident that it could now be estimated how much oil Oman would be able to produce in the next forty years, how production policy could be manipulated to move production forward and back within this period of four decades, what influence could be exerted by the ministry on scheduling the production of lighter and heavier crudes, what the cost of production of various reservoirs would be, and what the government's take would be as a result of these factors. There was a significant risk in having reserves run too low. There was also risk in relying on heavy crudes, when exporters with larger reserves could still produce a greater proportion of lighter crudes. This would be particularly true in a market that might have a surplus of supply over demand well into the 1990s.

At some point, it would be possible to pass the cost of production by enhanced oil recovery on to the consumer, but not until this higher-cost crude found a market. An exporter that sells all of its light crude and becomes primarily a producer of heavy oil could be in trouble. The practice in Oman over the past ten years of finding and producing as much of Oman's oil as rapidly as possible had given priority to the crudes that were less costly to produce. The current practice of producing as much as 380,000 bpd of predominantly light crudes and striving to increase capacity to 450,000 later in the 1980s was, in Critchfield's view, either poor or short-sighted national oil policy – or, more likely, a result of an absence of long-term national planning. But he understood that the forces that determined production were the demands for ever-increasing oil revenues, and this was largely beyond the domain of the ministry.

Over the years, as the ministry well knew, TTI attempted to present the case for conservation, both in oil field practices and in the broader terms of planning the use of a non-renewable resource. Brad Dismukes had expressed the view that while the battle over "oil field practices" had been won through concerted efforts within the ministry and PDO, they had made no progress at all in making the case for long-term planning,. In his opinion, it was getting quite late in the game to address the subject.

Dismukes wrote: "If it were my decision to make, I would advise His Majesty that prudent policy would be to cut the pattern of future spending to fit a production of 300,000-320,000 bpd through the year 2000. I would shut in 75,000 bpd of light oil until we have in hand very solid results on the technical feasibility and the cost factors of enhanced oil recovery projects. At the same time, the economics of giving high priority to a large exploration program through the next ten years are clearly persuasive." All of this, Dismukes mused, would have a certain shock impact on the leaders in the sultanate, but that shock would be milder and more easily accommodated than the series of shocks that would come if a longer view were not taken.[1]

TTI Presence in Oman

By June 1983, TTI had a team of eight full-time senior professionals fully engaged in providing services to MPM: Ken Bodine, Tom Fitz, Patrick McCullough, Don Bowtell, Don Parker, John Shute, Stan Thurber and Ted Wilkerson. McCullough had recently joined the staff as TTI's new senior petroleum engineer. The final advisor to join the staff was Warren Carlson in 1985. He had been in Oman from 1979-1981 supervising the construction of the Sohar gas pipeline for Shell and had worked closely with Khalifa Al-Hinai. In his current capacity,

[1] James H. Critchfield, *Oman Papers, 1968-1991*, letter marked Confidential from Critchfield to Undersecretary Salem Shabaan, September 1, 1983.

he acted as an advisor on pipelines and refineries.

In a November 1983 meeting with Minister Al-Shanfari, Critchfield fired the opening round on renegotiating the TTI contract, which would expire on June 30, 1984. He pointed out that TTI's role in the petroleum ministry had been to provide the technical staff for what was now a $4 billion operation. Oman had no national oil company; the ministry was serving in this capacity. In pushing the role of TTI, Critchfield pointed out that theirs was a substantive and highly technical role concentrating on both short- and long-term policies. It had become more complicated year by year. Al-Shanfari listened, but made no move.

In December 1983, TTI contracted with Frank Reiber to become a ministry advisor for four months. Reiber, who had been in the UAE working on oil facilities development, had previously done some consulting work for TTI Rosslyn. Oman was now putting huge resources into rapidly expanding field facilities and would be doing more in the years ahead as the geography of PDO fields expanded, more pipelines were built, and enhanced oil recovery installations became increasingly important. Reiber was asked to take an overview of the oil facilities, both existing and projected. He would study all reservoir management programs, those existing and those programmed for early installation.

Before Reiber left Rosslyn for Oman, Critchfield reviewed with him the course of events in TTI's relationship with the ministry since 1975. The early work on pricing had been done by Ken Bodine and Critchfield, then Tom Barger isolated and emphasized the importance of the ministry's getting into reservoir engineering and developing an independent view from PDO. In Barger's view this was the single most important objective of the ministry and would have an impact ranging in the billions of dollars for the nation. Brad Dismukes's efforts were the tangible results of this. Reservoir engineering was now an integrated function within the ministry.

TTI's efforts were also effective in getting the ministry and the government to act on gas utilization and the move toward replacing the wasteful use of ever more costly diesel for electric power generation.

If there was a single area in which Sam Patterson and the team of TTI geologists and geophysicists excelled, it was in keeping pressure on PDO to increase the exploration effort. Tom Fitz brought the ministry into its first exploration adventure under a systematic cost-control effort. This led to the addition of Ted Wilkerson to the staff. For several years,

TTI had intermittently focused on the subject of massive (for Oman) investment in field oil and gas facilities. Reiber's presence would now give the ministry the capability of asserting its own influence on the many hundreds of millions of dollars that would be spent on field facilities in the next two decades.[2]

Fallout from the Ashland Oil Refinery Contract

After completion of Oman's first oil refinery, Ashland provided the staff to operate it. Circumstances outside Oman, however, caused the company to lose its contract. Regrettably, its president, Orin Atkins, became involved in less than ethical business dealings outside of Oman with his friend and business partner Yehia Omar, a close advisor to Sultan Qaboos. There are many versions of the business ventures of Atkins and Omar during the same time Ashland was building and then operating the Oman refinery. This caused the Ashland staff dealing with the refinery construction a great deal of anguish and frustration. The story as told here was pieced together from Security Exchange Commission records, the press and TTI internal documents. After reviewing it, a former Ashland executive commented that the events were accurate to the best of his recollection.

The Orin Atkins–Yehia Omar story goes back to the days in Libya before Qadhafi took over and in some ways takes on the character of a story of two men and two families: Orin and Yehia and their attempts to organize things for their next generation. As president of Ashland, Orin Atkins on many different occasions put before the board proposals for business ventures with Yehia Omar. One of these was that Ashland acquire an interest in a chromium mining operation in Rhodesia owned by Tim Landon. The mine had relatively little value, but presumably the seller could influence purchases of oil from Oman. Another scheme was that Ashland invest in a sausage casing process, a process that was untested and highly speculative. There was also a proposal that the board authorize payments to an Abu Dhabi official to secure oil.[3] Whereas the relationship between Atkins and Omar could have produced any number of business projects that might or might not enhance their

---

[2] Ibid., *Report on Facilities and Operations Review of Oman's Oil and Gas Production Operations,* Frank Rieber, March 20, 1984.

[3] Taken from a shareholders lawsuit against Orin Atkins dated August 13, 1986.

personal wealth, their involving the Ashland Oil Company is where it all came apart.

This is also a classic case of a clash of cultures. Given the nature of Yehia Omar, he was socially incapable of understanding the U.S. Foreign Corrupt Practices Act, saw it as not affecting him and obviously was very successful at manipulating Orin Atkins.

In 1981, the Ashland board decided it was time to take a close look at these activities. On May 21, the board of directors of Ashland Oil retained outside counsel to review all transactions between Ashland and the Sultanate of Oman from January 1, 1978, to May 20, 1981, to determine whether any actions were in violation of the Foreign Corrupt Practices Act. The firm of Kirkpatrick, Lockhart, Johnson & Hutchison of Pittsburgh, PA, completed an 800-page report and sent it to the board on October 26, 1981. The firm's opinion, after conducting dozens of interviews and examining hundreds of documents, was that Ashland Oil Co. had not violated either the provisions of the Foreign Corrupt Practices Act or any other applicable U.S. criminal statutes.

In May 1983, Jeff Gerth of the *New York Times* broke a story that the SEC was being taken to task by the U.S. Congress for not investigating questionable payments by Ashland to Oman government officials for crude oil, implying that the company might have violated the 1977 Foreign Corrupt Practices Act.[4] Wheels started turning. The fact is, there were political undercurrents to this story. Both of the congressional committees critical of the SEC's performance were headed by Democrats. The top officials of the SEC were Reagan appointees. And both sides knew that Ashland Oil Company had been conducting its own internal investigation related to Oman.

In 1983, two Ashland executives, one of whom was Bill McKay, blew the proverbial whistle and a SEC investigation began. The Ashland board of directors turned over its report by the independent counsel to the congressional committees and the SEC. Much of the investigation had centered on whether Tim Landon and Yehia Omar were officials of the Oman government. If it was determined they were official representatives of the government, then Ashland's business dealings with them would be in violation of the Foreign Corrupt Practices Act.

[4] Jeff Gerth, "SEC Is Said to Face Inquiry in Ashland Role," *New York Times*, May 12, 1983.

Informally, it was learned by sources close to the investigation that the SEC had decided that Landon and Omar, while acknowledged as being personal advisors to the sultan, did not make good "foreign officials" after all. The SEC investigation continued at a slow pace until July 8, 1986, when it issued a complaint against Ashland. It was never tried; it terminated in a consent decree. No further action was taken. The SEC decided that the enforcement division did not have a case, thus making the Ashland-Oman affair a dead issue.

That summer, Tim Landon told Critchfield that he had discussed Ashland with Sultan Qaboos at length since Yehia Omar first came up with the idea of selling Atkins the chromium mine. His understanding was that while Omar would participate in the Ashland transaction on the mine, he would not be involved in any way in Oman crude sales to Ashland. That would mean no commissions related to sale of Oman oil or in Ashland's efforts to establish itself as a major U.S. presence in Oman. Omar was to be hands-off in any activities related to the refinery contract or other initiatives.

The sultan regarded the excitement as another typical example of the press trying to sensationalize the world of Arab oil sellers. Having sold them the chrome mine, Tim said, his main interest in Ashland was to get them off his back with regard to their internal problems between members of the board and their then chairman. He did regret the unnecessary publicity but had warned Sultan Qaboos that Omar was heading in this direction. It did not appear to worry him very much. Nevertheless, Yehia Omar's star in Oman was beginning to fade.

Critchfield told Landon that he thought the entire story was beginning to lose some of its appeal. Some journalists were trying to find plots and conspiracies and trying to revive the intelligence angles.[5] It was unpleasant but probably not fatal.

Critchfield advised the Omanis not to stonewall the issue but to make a statement along these lines: "The government is aware of the SEC case, but views it as an internal U.S. affair involving complex domestic political matters involving U.S. official agencies and a U.S. company. It is not aware of any involvement of Oman citizens or other Oman interests. The fact that Ashland purchased crude oil from the Ministry of Petroleum in late 1980 and early 1981 is acknowledged,

---

[5] Here Critchfield was referring to the never-ending efforts to link Tetra Tech with the American CIA.

231

but it was a transaction that had been handled routinely within the ministry."[6] Critchfield later learned that Minister Al-Shanfari was asked about the Ashland contract. His response was: "As far as the Ashland refinery project was concerned, the ministry negotiated the contract for Ashland to operate the refinery and there was no outside involvement."

This situation did cause pain for Ashland refinery operators in Oman and indirectly for TTI, as it had recommended Ashland to Al-Shanfari and the petroleum ministry. But after six years of inquiry, the record did show that neither Critchfield nor his company were in any way involved with the events that caused embarrassment to the Oman government. Nonetheless, the perception remained that TTI was somehow mixed up in it, and this did affect its relations in Oman.

Unfortunately, Yehia Omar blamed Critchfield for his deteriorating relationship with Sultan Qaboos, Tim Landon and others in the Inner Circle, when in fact it was Omar himself who caused the fractures. Had he and his good friend Orin Atkins not involved the Ashland Oil Company in projects it should never have pursued, everyone on all sides would have avoided the internal Ashland investigation, the SEC investigation and the embarrassment to the Oman government that all this caused. Ashland might still be operating the refinery in Oman instead of Shell, which assumed the role when Ashland's contract ran out December 31, 1990. The management and operating services agreement between Ashland and the Oman Refining Company was ended after nine and a half years. At that time, John Hall, Ashland's president and CEO, wrote the following letter to Minister Al-Shanfari.[7]

> I want to take this opportunity to thank you and your associates in the Sultanate of Oman for giving Ashland this opportunity to work with you. We hope our efforts were satisfactory and that our personnel were able to do a professional job for you. During our period of service, the refinery was started up, reached full capacity, and was subsequently expanded. Many Omani citizens were trained to operate and

[6] James H. Critchfield, *Oman Papers, 1968-1991*, Critchfield letter to Tim Landon, June 10, 1983.

[7] Ibid., letter from Chairman and CEO of Ashland Oil, Inc., to Minister Said Al-Shanfari, January 7, 1991.

maintain the refinery and to function in staff and support areas. Ashland employees who were assigned to this project and lived in Oman enjoyed their stay in your lovely country and appreciate the friendliness with which they were received. We wish you continued success and hope that at some time in the future we will have other opportunities to work with you and your associates.

Best wishes for a peaceful and successful 1991.

Sincerely yours,

John Hall

A sad postscript to this story was found in a letter Critchfield sent to Omar on June 20, 1988: "I do regret that the Ashland affair seemed to damage our long association and friendship. Eventually the lawyers and the press came to the conclusion that I had really played no role in the entire affair although the damage had been done. However, I'm not sure to this day that you understand this."[8] Yehia Omar never responded. He died in Geneva in September 2002 after a long illness.

To the director of the Palace Office, Major General Ali Majid, Critchfield wrote on June 30, 1988: "I think the Ashland affair has about run its course. It should never have happened in the first place. Quite a few people did Oman and His Majesty a disservice in causing the whole episode. I hope we have heard the last of it. The publicity was also damaging to my company and me. The record is now clear that neither I nor my company were in any way involved in these controversial issues."[9]

TTI Criticized for the LTEP

When he was in Oman in February 1983, Critchfield met privately with Minister Al-Shanfari and discussed oil policy for the new five-year plan. In essence, he summarized the LTEP, which was still in draft form. Al-Shanfari told Critchfield he did not believe the data used in the LTEP was an accurate reflection of the facts. He expressed confidence that the real reserves far exceeded what PDO showed in its annual program. His own estimate was that Oman could produce from 500,000 to 1,000,000

[8] Ibid., letter to Yehia Omar, June 20, 1988.
[9] Ibid., letter to General Ali Majid, Palace Office, June 30, 1988.

bpd in the early years after 2000. The LTEP, in contrast, cautioned the government to have a production ceiling at 380,000 bpd and a target of 320,000 bpd. At the same time, the LTEP recommended that the government insist upon the development of an accelerated exploration program that would yield better data on reserves and could be used in long-term planning. As a matter of policy, the LTEP advised the government to avoid increasing production when oil prices were depressed. Such action was not sustainable in the context of long-term planning. These words had the familiar ring of those of Brad Dismukes the year before.

Al-Shanfari instructed Critchfield not to show these early LTEP drafts to anyone. Once finished, he wanted TTI to give him one copy, with no other distribution.

Following this visit, Critchfield heard that Sultan Qaboos asked Said Al-Shanfari to press Shell for a new projection. Shell came back with a more conservative projection than the 1983 program data. Coincidentally, Qais Al-Zawawi also asked Al-Shanfari for a firm projection on price and production through the next five-year plan, 1986-90. Al-Shanfari turned to task over to TTI, which make it a part of the LTEP process.

Brad Dismukes, who was never shy about expressing his opinion, summed up his views in a letter to Critchfield in April 1984.[10] He said, "Oman has never had any substantial volume of undeveloped light oil reserves. It had only reserves of heavy (lower than 25 degrees API) oil, which neither the government nor the private shareholders wanted to produce except in time of a worldwide crude shortage. However, the heavy oil reserves are the only solid base available for long-term planning. The undiscovered reserves are highly speculative."

According to Dismukes, PDO has made an intentionally pessimistic forecast of future oil discoveries. In its presentations, exploration results are halved every five years. The methodology appears to be quite arbitrary while possibly giving some appearance of having a solid basis. One plausible explanation of the pessimistic forecast lies in the fact that the private shareholder investment in petroleum development in Oman had become relatively unrewarding. Shell could purchase all the crude it needed at an equal or lower price without making any investment. Shell's

---

[10] Ibid., Dismukes letter to Critchfield, April 1984. Although Dismukes was no longer active in Oman, he was continuing to assist TTI Rosslyn in its wrap-up of the LTEP.

reasoning might be: if I make an optimistic exploration forecast, the government will press me to find the oil and having found it, to develop it. Then I will have to make an unprofitable investment. In these days of crude surplus, the private shareholder wants to invest in Oman only with the capital necessary to protect his vested interests. The expressed PDO objective is to find each year as much recoverable oil as was produced the previous year.

Critchfield Comes under Fire

In early 1984, Undersecretary Salem Shabaan told Kirk Agon that Minister Al-Shanfari had heard Critchfield was sharing information from the LTEP with third parties in Oman. He was threatening to renew TTI's contract for only one year. He was definitely angry.

Agon assured Shabaan that the LTEP had not been shared with anyone and tried to differentiate between the LTEP and long-term planning per se. Critchfield immediately wrote to both Shabaan and Said Al-Shanfari, assuring them that none of the LTEP was shared with anyone outside the ministry with the exception of His Majesty. He also urged Shabaan to renew the contract for three years, as had been done in the past. To revert to a one-year contract would be the equivalent of asking Shell to staff the PDO operation on the basis of a year-to-year agreement.

In a letter to Salem Shabaan, Critchfield wrote,

> It is with deep personal concern that I read Your Excellency's letter of March 15 charging that confidential information relating to the LTEP had found its way to third parties. I wish to assure you that neither the LTEP nor any part of it has found its way to third parties through our hands. You are to the best of my knowledge and belief the only Omani official who has actually physically examined the draft study. The minister was briefed on the status of the study at a meeting on March 19. The only other discussions I have had in Oman were on March 20 with the president of the Palace Office and with His Majesty on February 26. Since these discussions conformed to the pattern of periodic audiences for the past

decade, I assume these were not the cause of Your Excellency's letter. To the best of my knowledge and belief there has been no violation of this obligation whether related to the preparation of the LTEP or any other undertaking on behalf of the government.[11]

Critchfield hoped that the matter of confidentiality had been put to rest. However, in a separate letter to Al-Shanfari, Critchfield explained that he had a lengthy discussion on the LTEP at his February 26 meeting with Sultan Qaboos and defended his right to speak candidly with him. For almost a decade, he had openly expressed to the sultan his opinions on the impact of long-term oil development on the future of the sultanate. Extending long-term planning forty years into the future was of vital importance and was not being given the attention it needed. He told the sultan he thought that PDO forecasts on future discoveries were too conservative, and that significant additional amounts of oil would be discovered by PDO exploration. He thought Said Al-Shanfari, Oman's most famous optimist, shared this view. Sultan Qaboos smiled and said that he too tended to be an optimist. He recalled the dismal prediction made to him on declining oil production and revenues at the time of the financial crisis in early 1975. Those forecasts were proven to be wrong.

Completion of the LTEP

Ken Bodine delivered the long-awaited *Long Term Energy Plan of the Sultanate of Oman, 1983 – 2022,* dated July 1, 1984, to Said Al-Shanfari in his office. It was bound in an orange notebook with bold black lettering. According to the cover letter to the minister, only one copy was delivered and no other distribution was made.[12] The report went into the minister's safe and, to Bodine's knowledge, no further distribution within the ministry was made.

On the character and requirement for long-term energy planning, the LTEP clearly stated that the mid 1980s was obviously a time to pause, review the history of Oman as an oil exporting nation and assess the future in terms of resources and national goals. The LTEP planning

[11] Ibid., letter to Undersecretary Salem Shabaan, March 21, 1984
[12] Ibid., letter to Minister Said Al-Shanfari, July 1, 1984.

horizon was two generations, or forty years. This planning, the report urged, must be done within the realities of Oman's geopolitical setting and against a constantly updated forecast of the world energy supply and demand that would ultimately determine the real price of oil and gas as well as alternative sources of energy.

The LTEP pointed out that the practice of PDO each year was to focus on a 1-5-20–year horizon. There was no comparable planning effort in the ministry. Central planning in the government was done in the form of a five-year plan, a device that lacked continuity. The LTEP urged the ministry to adopt a forty-year planning horizon and outlined recommendations on how to proceed. It also recommended that the government limit production of oil by conventional oil recovery methods to 300,000 bpd through 1992 and 320,000 bpd through 2002. These should be adjusted upward only after new discoveries or improvements in enhanced oil recovery techniques. There is no question that the LTEP was a cautious and conservative document.

While no one knew if any or all of the LTEP had been circulated in or outside the ministry, inside TTI, it was the bible. It was constantly being reviewed in the context of new information. Critchfield admonished his staff to keep the LTEP, Arthur Rypinski's Public Finance report, and the Five Year Plan forecasts consistent. TTI had to be sure it was speaking with one voice.

Critchfield was also concerned about the lack of communications with the clients. A lot of work came close to being "deliverables" but had not been completed for distribution outside the ministry. Daily contact and memos were not enough. He asked Team 1 Muscat to pause every six months, look at the LTEP and attempt to measure whether changes to the estimate needed to be made.

Despite Minister Al-Shanfari's threats, the July 1984 TTI contract with the ministry was renewed, not for one but three years. In May 1984, Kirk Agon, who had been on the front line in Oman for almost a decade, transferred to TTI's Rosslyn office, where he began to establish a team to develop new business in the Arabian Gulf. John Sasser moved from the MDC secretary's job to replace Agon. Josee Sasser replaced Nga. Fortunately, the clients knew and liked Sasser, so it was a smooth transition.

20

THE PUBLIC AUTHORITY FOR WATER
RESOURCES IN THE 1980s

Shortly after it was organized, the Public Authority for Water Resources (PAWR) began its work in all five districts around the country.[1] The greatest attention, however, went to the Batinah and the Greater Capital Area districts. In the Batinah, the increasing population and agricultural activity had significantly impacted the region. When the district office opened in Sohar in 1980, the first order of business was data collection. The staff needed to determine the areas where saline intrusion had or might become a problem, to identify areas where water could be pumped and to select sites suitable for dams and infiltration ponds. A staff of six hydrologists would be working full time at the Sohar and Muscat district offices on this project.

The water for the Batinah still came from shallow wells near the coast. These were no longer operated by hand or by animals, but by diesel pumps. The team's first effort was to identify wells where over-pumping was causing sea water intrusion into the aquifer. About 350 wells located between the coastal gardens and the ocean were sampled. The main aquifer along the Batinah coastline contained fresh water inland and salt water seaward. As water levels from the inland part of the aquifer were lowered by the pumping of wells, the aquifer began to draw in saline water. This water was unfit for most uses. Inland migration of the saltwater/freshwater interface was experienced along much of the Batinah coast. As a result, a number of wells and some agricultural tracts had been abandoned.

By February 1983, the situation had become so critical that the PAWR recommended a well-drilling moratorium be declared for three separate areas along the coast extending from Seeb airport northward. There was also a need for regulations to restrict the rates of pumping

[1] See Chapter Twelve.

from wells based on the uses of the water, types of crops grown and historical patterns of water use. There was, however, no enforcement agency within the government to control water use, so the wells continued to be pumped.

Wadi Al Khawd

Most of the technical advisors to the PAWR recognized that Oman needed dams to enhance the natural recharge of aquifers. Unfortunately, much time had been lost to bureaucratic wrangling over where the dams were to be built.

One of the first initiatives, known as the Wadi Al Khawd project, was in the Seeb watershed area. This was to be a pilot project that, if successful, would be a model for development elsewhere. Initially, it was planned that the PAWR would see the project through to final construction. However, before completion, the Development Council interceded and assigned the project to the U.S. Corps of Engineers. Months later, after two rounds of redesigning the project and to the chagrin of Dr. Bob Dale and his team, the U.S. Corps of Engineers produced a plan that in character, scope and purpose was not significantly different from the PAWR plan. At that point, the U.S./Oman Joint Commission took over the project and assigned it to the Ministry of Agriculture. From that time on, Hamoud Al-Harithi, the PAWR chairman, and Bob Dale, in a state of frustration, disclaimed any further responsibility for the project, although in practice they were both required to monitor it as members of the Water Resources Council.

TTI under Pressure

PAWR, having been finessed out of the Wadi Al Khawd project, did no more work in this area, turning its attention instead to exploring possibilities for aquifer recharge in the watershed between the Greater Capital Area and Quriyat. It concentrated on identifying, drilling and testing aquifers, and even designed a plan to build dams to enhance recharge of these aquifers. But in May 1982, this work was suspended. It was becoming obvious that PAWR was being made the scapegoat for the growing anxiety and concern that was prevalent at higher government levels as evidence surfaced of a mounting water problem in the Seeb-

Batinah area. Everyone seemed to be going around in circles, and PAWR along with TTI seemed the easiest to blame.

Critchfield and TTI were asked why nothing was being done to address the threatening ecological disaster in the Batinah area. After all, they were the ones who alerted the highest levels of government to the problem. Top Omani officials were beginning to quietly question whether the PAWR was the proper vehicle for managing water resources. A campaign was under way to attack the PAWR as an institution, Hamoud Al-Harithi as chairman, and the PAWR technical staff, which was managed by TTI. The attack originated in the Ministry of Agriculture, but other ministers with scores to settle soon joined the fray.

In discussions with his staff, Critchfield commented:

> We are not as well prepared as we might be to cope with this attack. I am convinced our 20 experienced PAWR water engineers are a high performance team. Since exploration drilling has been our main effort in Oman, performance must be measured on the record of results. We must put together a definitive report on this. Other things we have done – establishing district offices and establishing a data collection system – will in the future serve Oman well. But whatever our real achievements have been, the preparation and distribution of reports has been a dismal performance. Key officials have repeatedly called this to our attention. Our public relations work with Hamoud Al-Harithi and all members of the government has been poor. I asked His Majesty in 1980 for three years to get the PAWR launched and into business. I said that I would get back to him in early 1983 with a personal report on what had been accomplished and where we stand. I am now faced with this task.[2]

In June 1983, Hamoud Al-Harithi announced that he was reducing the TTI staff by 50 percent by the end of 1984.[3] It was no secret within TTI that the PAWR operation had been plagued by management, planning, administrative and organizational problems. There had been intermittent personnel crises that resulted in abrupt and badly handled

[2] James H. Critchfield, *Oman Papers, 1968-1991*, TTI Interoffice Memo, Critchfield report on *Status of the PAWR*, July 7, 1983.

dismissals of several PAWR staff members. Critchfield's immediate response to Al-Harithi was that this action was contrary to Oman's interests and he opposed a premature cut. Al-Harithi countered that he planned to cut the staff from twenty to thirteen advisors. His decision was firm. Later, he added, the staff would be reduced to ten.

In an unsatisfactory meeting with Al-Harithi, Critchfield had trouble convincing him that this was not the time to make budget cuts. Al-Harithi explained that it was he and TTI that were under attack, not the PAWR. There were elements in Oman that were trying to gain a dominant role in water. The deterioration of water quality on the Batinah coast had become a major issue, and he was being criticized for not fixing the problem. He had to take action. Critchfield said, "TTI does its work well and at a reasonably cheap rate. It compares favorably with PDO expatriate professional costs, which are something over $300,000 each."

However flawed the performance, Critchfield noted to his staff, TTI had put a basic structure into place in Oman for the management of Oman's water resources. If TTI were to lose its position and influence in water affairs, the Omanis were quite capable of destroying the PAWR and losing much of the gain that had been made.

Critchfield told Al-Harithi that Oman's long-term interest was in the PAWR's water program. It was a multi-disciplined and highly technical operation that was attempting to force the pace of technological transfer into a society that was not ready to cope with it. Critchfield saw that the water program was in deep trouble for a number of reasons: a lapse in communications with the sultan on the subject, too much emphasis on TTI's own technical work, neglect of effective reporting techniques to educate the clients, and, probably most serious of all, being caught in the middle of a cabinet conflict on the issue of water. If TTI survived this, its salvation would be that a lot of very solid work had been done. TTI was at the point where it could speak comprehensively about the totality of Oman's water resources and what long-term plans and actions were required through the year 2000.[4]

In mid-summer 1983, Critchfield decided to make some changes at the top. Dr. Robert Dale was transferred to the Rosslyn office to work on a historical review of the Oman water program. Dr. William W. Doyel, a PAWR hydrologist who had been on the staff since its inception, replaced Dale. Doyel, a graduate of the University of Texas,

[4] Ibid., informal memo on water resources by Critchfield, December 1983.

had a long career as a hydrologist with the USGS. He had worked previously in Egypt, Libya and Chile. His deputy would be Barghash Ghalib Khalid Al-Said, a member of the royal family. In preparation for this position, Barghash spent July and August 1983 attending a training program in Denver sponsored by USGS. He visited sites of retard structures in the San Francisco area, including the San Francisco Bay model that was managed by Tetra Tech Inc. He also visited the USGS headquarters in Washington and the Earth Satellite Corporation to survey its imagery program.

By the end of the year, Hamoud Al-Harithi was replaced as Minister of Eectricity and Water and PAWR chairman by Khalfan bin Nasser Al-Wahaibi. The appointment of Al-Wahaibi introduced a new element into the equation. At their initial meeting, Critchfield expressed his personal thoughts on the state of the national water program. He said the sultanate had renewable water resources that, if well managed, should meet its future national requirements for consumption by people and livestock, for commercial and industrial needs and for agriculture. It was axiomatic that the supply of water for human consumption in populated areas would receive top priority. In many areas, however, there was an adequate supply of water for all vital purposes. Nevertheless, the current national water program was deficient on many counts, and significant changes needed to be made. The problems, Critchfield emphasized, went far beyond the PAWR.

The PAWR represented the beginning, a good beginning, of a highly professional national technical service with a unique knowledge of Oman's water situation. It represented a national asset of great value. But it needed more staffing. Cutting the staff from twenty to thirteen and then to ten was incomprehensible. The savings were insignificant when compared to the need for water resources data. It was not in the national interest. Recurring water crises would be avoidable only through an improved national water program.

Under the terms of the Five Year Plan, the PAWR had completed 30 percent of its drilling programs and had spent about 15 percent of the available funds. Critchfield had authorized extra well sitters and approved temporary assistance into 1984 to compensate for the reduced staffing. He told the minister he would not share in the irresponsibility

[5]Ibid., aide memoire, *The Status of the Sultanate's National Water Resources Programs*, December 13, 1983.

of gutting the water program and TTI would finance this staffing itself, even if this resulted in a lower profit margin.[5] Critchfield decided to keep his staff of twenty specialists on the job for the first few months of 1984 at TTI's expense rather than leave tasks half-finished. In his opinion, a severe cut in the water program was one of the last economies the government should make.

Critchfield had an audience with Sultan Qaboos in Salalah on February 26, 1984, and briefed him on water issues:

> The sultanate has sufficient water to meet its critical needs for the indefinite future provided there is efficient management of the limited supplies. Management of water is in the long term as important as the management of oil and gas. The future supply of water for human consumption, particularly in areas of dense population, should receive clear priority over all other demands. In 1979, His Majesty's decisions on water led to the establishment of a new Water Resources Council and PAWR. Unfortunately, many of the management objectives have not been met. Functions and responsibilities are poorly defined and promulgation of water codes and laws still do not exist.
>
> There is neither an effective regulatory agency for water nor any effective arrangement for the enforcement of water laws and policies. Use of water for agriculture, the main consumer of water, in most cases is geographically located near supplies of water, but that was not true in all cases, such as the Greater Capital Area, where water for human consumption has clear priority. The government needs to accelerate the development of extensive civil engineering works to recharge aquifers capable of supplying water to users. This program deserves an effort comparative to that of the exploration and production of oil and gas. It cannot be dealt with piecemeal. This program will require clearly assigned responsibilities, continuity of effort over the next 20 years, the application of high technology, the availability of sophisticated engineering experience and the allocation of considerable financial resources.[6]

[6] Ibid., Critchfield report of his meeting with Sultan Qaboos, February 26, 1984.

It was Critchfield's impression that Sultan Qaboos understood the urgency and importance of going forward with a national program, but he did not think all the key government officials shared this understanding. Looking back, Critchfield concluded that TTI basically failed to offer evidence that a solid program was being developed, and the government simply lost confidence in the PAWR and by extension in TTI. In his opinion, the PAWR's lack of communication from beginning to end had been TTI's greatest failure in Oman. It was essentially one of managerial lapse shared by Dale, Agon and Critchfield himself.

In 1985, during a meeting with Qais Al-Zawawi, the deputy chairman of the Development Council, Critchfield said he had heard from the PAWR chairman that there would be a mid-1985 review of TTI's role in Oman as part of planning for the Five Year Plan 1986-1990. Critchfield expressed the view that Oman had gotten its money's worth out of TTI in the past ten years. He hoped wisdom would prevail. The deputy chairman hastily assured Critchfield that he did not think any basic changes would be made. The discussion of a review was to focus mainly on the PAWR contract. Both let the subject drop at that.[7]

The planned cuts in the TTI staff at the PAWR, however, would very nearly leave TTI out of the loop. The message from Critchfield to the TTI team in Muscat was, "The existing water resources effort is not accomplishing the job and cannot without an overhaul. If the TTI staff is allowed to run down, our days in Oman in the water business are numbered." He instructed the team to communicate with PAWR chairman Khalfan bin Nasser only through Bill Doyel. Everyone should avoid multiple uncoordinated contacts during this critical period.

Having done this, Critchfield noted that Doyel, quite unexpectedly, went the next step and almost cut out TTI completely. He started bypassing John Sasser and the Muscat office and sending his correspondence directly to Critchfield in the Rosslyn office. He was also hiring professionals without informing or consulting the company. Obviously irritated and somewhat fed up with bureaucratic jockeying inside his own company, Critchfield sent Doyel a terse reminder to deliver all messages to him via the Muscat office.

By 1985, the PAWR was basically operating on its own. The Water Resources Council and Khalfan bin Nasser had assumed control. The PAWR had been "discovered" by other sectors of the government and by

[7] Ibid., Critchfield report of his meeting with Qais Al-Zawawi, April 1985.

consulting engineering companies seeking water data and information for water development and management activities around the country. The government kept the TTI presence at thirteen, including Bill Doyel, but the key position of contract officer was now filled by a Britisher from the firm of Dames and Moore.

The PAWR began a crash exercise of hiring forty-seven new professionals, including drilling inspectors, field geologists, a librarian and a chemist. These would come from Canada, the United Kingdom and the Philippines. This was in addition to the Indians, Pakistanis and Sri Lankans already on board. Six months remained on TTI's contract, but Critchfield considered TTI's influence in the PAWR to be minimal at best. The joint U.S./Oman Commission Washington office prepared a report in 1985 that came closer to being a de facto water plan than anything done thus far. It dealt fairly with TTI's work, including that in the PAWR, but no action was taken on this report.

In January 1986, Brigadier Tim Landon wrote to Critchfield that he had heard unofficially that Bill Doyel and his deputy Bargash were in despair with regard to the current and future use of water resources in Oman. They were particularly concerned about the Batinah, where excessive drilling had caused saline water to travel farther inland, causing damage that they believed would take fifty years to remedy. They also pointed to problems in the Jebal Akhdar, Nizwa and on the Salalah plain. No one who had access to Sultan Qaboos wanted to be the bearer of bad news in the current mood of national euphoria. Also, there were too many people in high places whose own interests would be jeopardized were they to bring this matter to his attention. Landon wrote to Critchfield, explaining that he has been asked to speak with the sultan.[8]

Critchfield was pleased to hear that someone had plucked up the courage to do something about this issue. He had been a lone voice on the situation in the Batinah for several years. In response to Landon's letter, he promised that this would be his last effort to lobby him on what Oman needed to do about its water resources. He said that a handful of Sultan Qaboos's ministers bore responsibility for too much neglect and too many conscious moves to undermine a sensible water program to serve their own narrow interests. At the height of Oman's reaping a $7 billion windfall profit from the second oil shock, game playing among a few ministers and unnecessary cost cutting had produced

[8] Ibid., letter from Brigadier Tim Landon to Critchfield, January 16, 1986.

a 50 percent reduction in the PAWR staff, basically bringing TTI's activities to a crawl.

Sultan Qaboos needed a water czar. The management of water resources thus far had been a failure. Critchfield noted that his influence had come to an end. He had been effectively shut off from contact with the sultan for some months. Sultan Qaboos, he continued, was surrounded either by people who were so devoted that they wanted him to hear only good news or by people whose economic interests were served by his taking action they know to be ill advised or not in the public interest. He cited two examples: Salalah and the Batinah. The PAWR had gradually developed systems for collecting data and had repeatedly reported excessive use and damage to the aquifers.

In Salalah, the Palace Office called for new wells near His Majesty's stables that needed an additional three million gallons of water a day. This had undoubtedly been presented to the sultan in positive terms of added beautification. The current amount of water taken out of the Salalah central aquifer was four million gallons a day. Water quality was declining; salt water was slowly migrating inward and upward. To proceed with the new field would be the equivalent of sabotaging the Salalah water system. Critchfield did not know where avarice, making points with His Majesty, or plain ignorance began and ended. PAWR and the *wali's* water expert, an experienced and qualified Omani, were opposing the project and suggesting alternatives that involved trying to locate wells in the far western rim of the plan and piping the water into Salalah. Critchfield hoped common sense would prevail.

The abuse of resources and deterioration in the Batinah was, of course, an old story by now. Occasionally, the Water Resources Council announced plans for vigorous measures to control drilling in the Batinah, but the next month there were new drilling rigs evident from Seeb to Sohar. The solution of last resort was recourse to another desalination plant. There were many who saw this as a solution to the Batinah problem. A 25- or 50-million-gallon-a-day plant at Barka was on the drawing board for 1987.

Critchfield thought that Khalfan bin Nasser should take a hard look at the cost of the incremental gallon of water in the Batinah and the Greater Capital Area. Then he should make all the users pay for it, whether it came from a desalination plant or a well with a big diesel on the farms and estates that had been developed along the Seeb-Sohar highway. This would be a shortcut to sanity in water management in the Batinah.

Critchfield had nothing but praise for Khalfan bin Nasser. He was serving both the ministry and PAWR well. He thought the ministers involved with agriculture and oil, the two main users of water, had too much control of water resources policy. Furthermore, PDO steadfastly refused to share data on their water drilling and production, so no one really knew how much water they had found and what they did with it. Khalfan bin Nasser had been trying to solve that problem. While water was a scarce resource in Oman, it was basically a renewable one. Oil and gas were not. There needed to be better management of both.[9]

A Major Change in the Organization of Water Resources Management

In September 1986, His Highness Sayyid Shabib bin Taimur Al-Said, the minister of the newly organized Ministry of Environment and Water Resources (MEWR) and deputy chairman of the Water Resources Council, became the new water czar. Sayyid Shabib was a cousin of Sultan Qaboos and a trusted advisor. The Water Resources Council was renamed the Council for Conservation of Environment and Water Resources (CCEWR). Criticism of the work of the PAWR continued; its survival seemed likely to be in Sayyid Shabib's hands.

A formal letter signed by Sayyid Shabib to Critchfield on September 29 informed him that the council had decided that the Sultanate of Oman would not be renewing the TTI contract. The contract would terminate in three months. But there was another paragraph. The council would like to continue its established relationship and requested that negotiations begin for drawing up a separate and new agreement![10]

John Sasser, by now a TTI vice president, was given the task of sorting out all of this. The PAWR in its various parts would be integrated into either the CCEWR or the ministry.

Sasser met with Sayyid Shabib on October 19 to discuss what was to go where. Shabib told Sasser that he believed the restructuring was

---

[9] Ibid., Critchfield letter to Brigadier Landon, January 24, 1986, marked Private and Confidential.

[10] Ibid., letter from Shabib bin Taimur, Minister of Environment and Water Resources, to Tetra Tech International, Inc., CCEWR/2-4/17/1986, September 29, 1986.

consistent with the other council-ministry relationships in Oman. He realized it would take some time, particularly since his ministry was in its infancy. Although the trend in government was toward the use of direct-hire employees, he wished to continue a relationship with TTI. He admitted he had little knowledge of the company and its activities in Oman. He had asked Sultan Qaboos whether any special relationship existed with TTI that would preclude him from changing the character of the association. The sultan responded that there was no such relationship, but that he was aware that Critchfield had used his company funds to support the PAWR effort. He wanted an amiable settlement.

In further meetings with John Sasser, Sayyid Shabib asked what TTI's position would be with respect to the direct hiring of some of TTI's professional staff. He said that as a businessman he could well understand if TTI was not prepared to relinquish its employees, although this would mean losing the benefit of those staff members who had accumulated so much knowledge. He was aware that a great deal of research had already been lost because of the failure of the Water Resources Council to act on PAWR studies. Another loss of this institutional memory would simply be considered part of the investment cost of putting water affairs in order. He specifically wished to hire Bill Doyel to become the technical advisor to the new CCEWR.

Sasser told the minister that the government could negotiate directly with TTI personnel, but that TTI as an organization still had much to contribute that transcended simply a commitment to supply staff. In particular, he suggested the work TTI had done in the development of the national water resources information system, which went beyond contractual requirements and was done because the company felt it was necessary.

The lack of a national water plan was a frustration that went back many years and had not yet been addressed. No one was blameless on this account. As an example, Sasser showed Sayyid Shabib the draft water management plan prepared by the Regional Development Committee. He agreed this was the type of activity that he hoped his ministry would pursue.

Sasser's impression of Sayyid Shabib was that he was a strong individual in command of his opinions. He seemed to have the full authority of Sultan Qaboos to do whatever he believed was required to sort out the water problems. He had firm ideas on what the correct structure should be and intended to move forward with creating the ministry to handle the function. Sasser told Critchfield that, given the big American salaries and the reduced financial resources, he expected TTI would be phased out of the water research function.

Sayyid Shabib had been hiring a number of young British personnel on the environment side of the ministry at less cost. Sasser thought that TTI's best opportunity for maintaining a future presence was to target the very highly skilled technical functions, which would justify the additional expense of American expertise. Bill Doyel, an unabashed supporter of American technical superiority over the British in the field of hydrology, might be able to convince Sayyid Shabib that access to such American talent was necessary.

On October 29, Critchfield met with Sayyid Shabib in Oman; on the 30th, he sent a letter telling him that Bill Doyel was available for direct hire. He proposed that the TTI contract, which was to expire on December 31, be extended for three months to provide time to develop a new organization and to arrange required staffing. He recommended that the new contract cover five district office heads and five professional staff in the central office.

Lest Sayyid Shabib not be fully aware of the history of PAWR and TTI's work in Oman, Critchfield prepared an aide memoire for his background:

> The PAWR was created in 1980 to evaluate the water resources of Oman. The major contributions over the past six years have been:
>
> 1. Discovery of 13 significant groundwater aquifers in the sultanate.
>
> 2. Preparation of a map of the sultanate depicting the relative likelihood of groundwater discoveries by size and water quality based on the results of 560 exploration bore holes, geophysical surveys, geological reconnaissance, analysis of satellite images and aerial photography and isotope studies.
>
> 3. Development of a hydrologic data collection network managed by permanent staff for four district offices that monitor:
>> - 1,350 observation wells and *aflaj* for water level and quality data

- 110 surface water (*wadi*) gauges
- 20 recording precipitation gauges
- 250 non-recording precipitation gauges
- 8,550 well inventories

4. Detailed delineation of the groundwater resources of the Batinah coast and the submission of recommendations for drilling and pumping in areas of salt-water intrusion.

5. Mathematical modeling of the groundwater resources on the Salalah Plain and the delineation of salt-water intrusion culminating in the submission of recommendations regarding further agricultural development on the Salalah Plain.

6. Appraisal of the recharge potential of the Greater Capital Area and development of general conclusions regarding the types of recharge schemes likely to be successful in Oman.

7. Development of an algorithm to determine approximate values for flood peak, discharges based upon the envelope curve approach. These values are used to design flood control and protection measures.

8. Recommendations regarding a flood protection scheme for the city of Salalah.

9. Establishment of a highly efficient water quality laboratory.

10. Development of the National Water Resources Information Center which incorporates computerized data bases of ground water, surface water, water quality and meteorology.

11. Submission of a draft water code that addresses regulatory control of water use and priorities among competing demands.

12. Creation of a government-wide forum for the expression and exchange of ideas regarding the planning of water resources use.

13. Organization of an in-house training and specialist workshop and sponsorship of overseas training of PAWR Omani staff.[11]

The aide memoire did not do the trick. In November 1986, Critchfield wrote to Sayyid Shabib, "I regret to inform Your Highness that as a result of the termination of the TTI contract with the PAWR

[11] Ibid., aide memoire, *Primary Contributions of the PAWR*, September 13, 1986.
[12] Ibid., letter from Critchfield to Brigadier Landon, November 17, 1986

and, in the absence of any new agreement, all TTI staff assigned to PAWR will be departing the sultanate on or about the 31ˢᵗ of December."

Critchfield wrote to Tim Landon shortly thereafter, commenting that he found the water situation in total disarray. The PAWR had been gradually eliminated, and what remained of the program was to be absorbed into the CCEWR and then into the ministry itself. Critchfield reiterated that he thought the current exercise was not in the interest of the sultanate.[12] The next day the *Oman Observer* carried a photograph on its front page of the British ambassador meeting with Sayyid Shabib to offer him "at no cost to the sultanate the service of His Majesty's Government in providing master water resources planning for the Sultanate."

Critchfield did not know until December what that meant. On December 24, he wrote to Landon:

> That lovable rogue Doctor Omar Al-Zawawi finally won. I must concede to him. When I gave my senior PAWR employees notice on December 1, the next thing I knew they had been hired by Hydro Technica, represented in Oman by Dr. Al-Zawawi's company OMZEST, which contracted for their services. The data that the good doctor is presenting to Sayyid Shabib as a gift is of course all the data collected under the PAWR contract and long integrated into the PAWR data base. But what does it matter. It was a good show. As a consolation prize we were at the eleventh hour given a contract to maintain a man in each of the five district PAWR (now CCEWR) offices with no central role. I will present my sword in humble defeat when I next see the Doctor.[13]

Critchfield added that whatever faults it still had, the PAWR was almost certainly the best water resources program in the Arab world.

Postscript

In April 1989, the Public Authority for Water Resources was resurrected, and Sultan Qaboos appointed Critchfield's friend Brigadier

---

[13] Ibid., letter from Critchfield to Brigadier Landon, December 24, 1986.

Al-Mutasim bin Hamoud Al-Busaidi as acting president. Critchfield wrote to him, stating:

> The decree reestablishing the PAWR is very good news. Permitting PAWR to simply run down and disappear two years ago with no study of the consequences was not in the interests of the sultanate. I hope the data and continuity have been preserved. When it happened, TTI was simply pushed aside and we were not informed of disposition of vital data. Our files covering the entire history of the Water Resources Council and the PAWR were intact. Computerized technical data on all wells, stream flows, rainfall etc. were also there when PAWR was absorbed by the Council for the Conservation of the Environment and Water Resources. I assume all of this reverts to the new PAWR. I am preparing for you a summary of my views and description of Oman water records we have here in Rosslyn. Because water becomes valuable only when it is not available, management of water resources is a difficult task. I wish you well.[14]

On May 11, 1989, Critchfield forwarded to Al-Mutasim the July 1, 1985, paper TTI had done on water resources, stating he would not change a word of it.[15] He reviewed for the new acting president TTI's philosophy on the water program in Oman. He said that the PAWR he recommended to His Majesty, which was approved by him, would one day be judged one of the success stories in the Arabian Peninsula by anyone who really looked at the record. The concept was that water resources development in Oman must be based on management of water in the individual basins. There was no other way. Within a basin, there might be both populated areas (towns and cities) and less densely populated areas. Most basins would be subdivided for water planning and management. PAWR had defined these basins and sub-areas in detail. It was important for senior officials to think of water resources in terms of the geographical basins.

The Batinah was the first area TTI identified as requiring priority attention. It did not get it. Too many private interests opposed water

[14] Ibid., letter from Critchfield to Brigadier Al Mutasim.
[15] Ibid., *The Management of Oman's Water Resources*, July 1, 1985.

management. Water management in the Batinah must give priority to human consumption. Much of the Batinah should by now be in water mains run by a public utility. The PAWR had done some very detailed work on the Batinah. There was room for both agriculture and suburbia. What was needed was policy – that and the authority and resoluteness to make it stick. This was not easy when water was at stake.

In any basin where water was already or would soon be in short supply, the PAWR must make an early basic decision: supply water centrally through a government-owned, government-controlled system (water mains, *aflaj* or whatever) or decentralized to individual wells. In most cases these decisions were made late or not at all. But management and enforcement must rest wholly with responsible Oman officials. In a basin where there was a high demand and limited water, it was urgent that the government establish its ownership of the water and its responsibility to distribute it as early as possible. Users should be charged a fee for each unit of water. Once a citizen actually gains control of a well, it would be almost impossible politically for the government to get it back and integrate it into a water system. In the Musandam capital of Khasab, TTI established the supply and the transport system of water mains fairly early.

In Buraimi, TTI began its basic exploration and study but lost early control to individual farmers who moved in, got control of water from TTI's exploration wells and then started farms. Eventually, TTI got better control, and by the time it left Buraimi had established a modern water-supply system with mains going into all the new housing. Supply was by pipeline to controlled well fields some miles above Buraimi. The old aquifer of the Buraimi Oasis had basically been destroyed 10-15 years before.[16]

The Batinah and the Greater Capital Area should still get high priority. These heavily populated areas should be in a central water main system, with all supply belonging to the government. In parts of the Batinah, the value of water was, as in Muscat, equal to the cost of desalination. Whether the government could ever regain control of the water situation in the Batinah was questionable. But the effort had to be made. Oman had a great abundance of water for human consumption. It is for other purposes that demand exceeded supply.

[16] The Buraimi/Al Ain water situation is further explored in Chapter Twenty One.
[17] Ibid., Critchfield letter to Brigadier Al-Mutasim, May 11, 1989.

Critchfield said that when he left Oman, the government was headed for additional expensive desalination in the Greater Capital Area and the Batinah. Simply adding desalination capacity at great expense was not good water policy for Oman. He suggested to Al-Mutasim that it might be useful to identify those places where there is a good water situation and then make sure that development of farming and industry take place there. Too many Omanis had left villages with good water potential and migrated to the Greater Capital Area, adding even more consumers of desalinated water.[17]

The resurrection of the PAWR was short lived. After less than six months, the management of water resources was transferred to a newly created Ministry of Water Resources, thereby separating it from environmental affairs. In 2001, the Ministry of Water Resources was disbanded, and the responsibility for water went to a new ministry called the Ministry of Municipalities, Environment and Water Resources. Water conservation and management were once again coupled with environmental issues, and both were to be dealt with not only nationally but regionally as well. In September 2007, Sultan Qaboos brought back the public authority, this time creating the Public Authority for Electricity and Water (PAEW). As of 2009, the PAEW remains the regulatory agency for water resources. The concept appears to have come of age.

21

REGIONAL DEVELOPMENT
IN MUSANDAM AND BURAIMI

The MDC Comes of Age

The work of the Musandam Development Committee (MDC) had been conceptualized and carried out by TTI staff since 1975.[1] One of the harshest environments and most inaccessible areas of the Arabian Peninsula made the early years of this project a period of uninterrupted crises. Beginning in 1982, however, the MDC proceeded rather smoothly. The main components of the programs it had launched were generally conceded to be successful, which led directly to TTI's being handed the task of repeating the performance in the regions of northwest Oman, including the Buraimi Oasis.

In the early 1980s, there were twenty-five TTI professionals on duty with the MDC. Hamoud Al-Harithi had been the MDC chairman since 1978. In 1982, Jim Critchfield expressed the view to Al-Harithi and the deputy chairman of the Development Council, Qais Al-Zawawi, that the MDC effort had reached a level where the government should begin planning to replace the TTI secretariat with Omanis, probably by the end of 1985. That was the year the TTI three-year contract was due to expire.

Early in 1982, Brigadier Al-Mutasim bin Hamoud Al-Busaidi took over the chairmanship of the MDC. At the time, he was minister of regional municipalities affairs. Hamoud Al-Harithi retained his posts of Minister of Eectricity and Water and chairman of the Public Authority for Water Resources. Al-Mutasim made an eleven-day camping trip to the Musandam Peninsula and visited all of the major and most of the minor centers in the region. Following this visit, he called for speeding

[1] See Chapter Thirteen.

up the development program in order to finish the infrastructure before the end of 1985. He recommended that Sultan Qaboos replace the MDC and put in place a new administration for the Governorate of Musandam. He hoped that by then the clamor of the people for land and basic services would end. He later told Agon and Sasser that the sultan agreed with the target date of 1985 to complete the project. TTI's role would, for all intents and purposes, come to an end at that time. Al-Mutasim made it clear, however, that he would not consider moving ahead with an accelerated development plan for Musandam without TTI involvement.

Great strides had been made in the Governorate of Musandam. The completed road connection from Khasab through Bukha to the UAE had fundamentally changed the historic reliance on the sea for access to Musandam's traditional markets and suppliers. Moreover, it had enabled the MDC to extend basic services to the area's numerous small coastal villages, thereby reducing migration to the larger villages. The results were impressive. Easy road access was eliminating imports by sea and as a consequence was reducing prices in the Musandam markets while expanding dramatically the quantity, quality and mix of goods available. The road also enabled Musandam residents with employment in the UAE to commute daily or on weekends. Fishermen no longer wasted valuable fishing time sailing to the UAE markets; the market could come to the Khasab port, where middlemen purchased the fish and hauled them by truck to retail outlets in the Gulf.

The road connection through the mountains from Khasab to Bayah had a similar stabilizing effect on the inland region. Because access to these villages was easier, water deliveries were possible to the mountain settlements bordering this road, and there was now a viable system for water storage. This slowed down population migration to the larger villages. Even the annual summer migration to the coastal villages, very much present during the 1970s, was declining.

The MDC's Cold Store in Khasab also brought fundamental change. Despite once being viewed as a market of last resort, it now guaranteed the fishermen an outlet for their catch. The Cold Store was leased by the MDC to a private company, Musandam Fisheries. This company had made remarkable and surprising progress in gaining the confidence of the Musandam fishermen. The company adopted a policy that guaranteed a fixed year-round price, a price that was less than the UAE market highs in the low-catch season but substantially higher than the UAE lows in the high-catch season. On average, fishermen earned more from selling to the Cold Store than they did on the market. In turn, the Cold Store made a marginal profit from Gulf wholesalers interested in the fixed monthly volumes that the Cold Store could guarantee.

This system was totally foreign to the traditional marketing mentality of the local fishermen. Through exceedingly careful and skillful management, the company earned the trust of the fishermen and proved to them that economic gains would result from dealing with the Cold Store. By the mid-1980s, over 50 percent of the fish caught in northern Musandam was sold to the Khasab Cold Store.[2]

Some of the projects that had not been in the original plan but which Brigadier Al-Mutasim wanted to see completed were paving the streets in the major villages, hard surfacing the gravel road connecting the Ras Al Khaimah border through Bukha to Khasab and developing residential subdivisions complete with all services to support 500-600 new residential plots. This would require an additional OR15 million ($43 million) to be worked into the budget.

In September 1984, William Rockey arrived in Muscat to join TTI Team 3 and act as deputy to John Sasser; Sasser had replaced Agon as MDC chairman. Rockey, a retired U.S. marine officer, was a U.S. Naval Academy graduate. Bill and his wife Anna joined the happy group of expatriates living in the Muscat community. Rockey's principal job was to supervise the completion of the many projects under way in Khasab and elsewhere in the province.

By the end of 1985, the economic situation was good and people were enjoying the improved standard of living brought by the services of the MDC as well as the military build-up of the area. But as projects came to an end and contractors demobilized, it would become necessary to develop alternative income sources to maintain the population base and to satisfy the raised expectations that had been a byproduct of the MDC and military programs. The TTI team went to work on this problem.

In 1986, a TTI report for Al-Mutasim, called *An Economic Review of the Musandam Peninsula,* was handed over for his use in an upcoming meeting with Sultan Qaboos. John Sasser reported back to Arlington

[2] James H. Critchfield, *Oman Papers, 1968-1991,* Musandam Development Committee *1980-1981 Report to His Majesty Sultan Qaboos,* March 1, 1982.

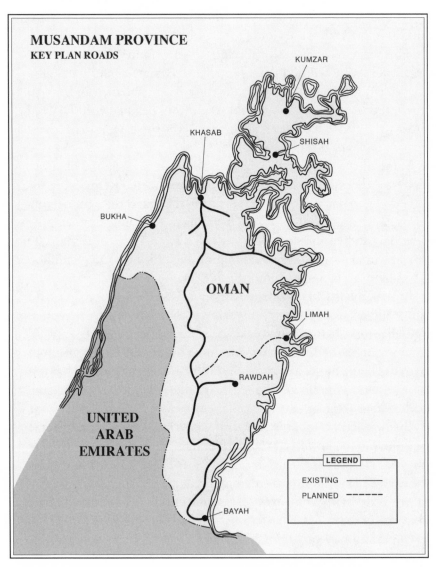

Existing and Planned Roads in the Musandam Peninsula

that Al-Mutasim was extremely pleased with the effort. Eventually, thirty copies of the report were printed in Arabic and English for distribution among the ministries. This would be TTI's final written report prior to the completion of its contract with the MDC.

TTI recognized that, economically speaking the Musandam Peninsula had very few comparative advantages; nevertheless, there were some opportunities ahead in the fields of fishing, aquaculture, small cargo transshipment to Iran, support to the oil and gas industry, support to military facilities, tourism and agriculture. These were outlined in some detail in the report.

Twenty percent of the adult male population in the region were fishermen. They were currently bringing in a catch worth about OR1.2 million ($3.5 million) per year. With the success of the Khasab Cold Store, there were opportunities to increase exports beyond the traditional markets in the UAE and Qatar. The Oman National Fisheries had offered to purchase the Cold Store's frozen fish stocks at a reasonable price. This opened the way for direct discussions with Iranian authorities in Bandar Abbas and Qesh Island about the possibilities for both fresh and frozen fish sales. The report recommended that fish trade missions be sponsored to Kuwait and Saudi Arabia to search for additional markets.

To further assist the fishermen, TTI's report suggested that commercial fishing studies be carried out to include exploratory fishing, inshore reef inventory, algae resources and crayfish resources. Further development of the fisheries infrastructure was recommended. The report also recommended that a second Cold Store be opened in Bayah; ice plants be constructed in Kumzar, Limah and Bukha; a mobile engine repair team be formed; and remote village fish landing points be established.

If the resource base was found to be adequate to introduce commercial fishing operations into Musandam, then various downstream fish processing opportunities existed. It was felt that the Iranian market would be more than sufficient to absorb the increased volumes of whole fish caught by commercial operators. Fish not sold could be processed for fishmeal or other products. Moreover, future opportunities of high value could be added, such as the processing of smoked fish and fish canning.

The report took note of and endorsed a study, commissioned at an earlier date by the Ministry of Agriculture and Fisheries, of the aquaculture potential of the sultanate. The conclusion was that there was high potential in the Musandam for aquaculture activities, particularly those involving aquatic algae, edible oysters and clams. There was a good global market at the time for aquatic plants.

By 1985, total exports and imports to and from Iran, documented by the Royal Oman Police customs declarations, had increased dramatically. However, exports, mainly fish and clothing, were still less than a third of imports. Khasab now had the infrastructure to be a transshipment point for selling more goods to Iran. It could not compete with Dubai, where the larger trading dhows came from India, Pakistan and Iran, but it might be able to attract some of the traffic away from Dubai. Khasab was closer than Dubai to all three trading countries, and there might be some financial incentives arising from the shorter haul distances. More important, many of the Khasab Omani merchants were of Iranian tribal origin and had filial ties with family members across the Strait of Hormuz. This could encourage dhows bearing goods for ultimate import to Iran to use Khasab as their transshipment point. If the Oman government were to make a public statement asserting its desire to strengthen trade with Iran, it might embolden the Musandam merchants to seek out such opportunities there.

Earlier exploration for oil and gas offshore had been disappointing. Elf-Aquitaine had drilled the Henjam-1 structure that led to the discovery of gas condensate, but it abandoned the project because only a third of it was in Oman territory. Furthermore, the gas/oil ratio was such that production to gain the oil would involve the flaring of a massive volume of natural gas. A second gas condensate reservoir was discovered offshore near Bukha but was abandoned due to insufficient volumes. However, this acreage was being reinterpreted. Should these projects see the light of day, there would be increased opportunities in both Bukha and Khasab to provide support.

Location of government and military training centers in the Musandam would produce spin-off economic benefits to the local community. Khasab, Bukha and Bayah all had sufficient land and services to accommodate such institutions.

The potential of tourism in the Musandam had not yet been explored. In striking contrast to the featureless beaches and endless desert of the UAE, the Musandam Peninsula offered the type of dramatic mountain, fjord, and cove beaches constantly being sought by well-traveled adventurers from Europe and elsewhere. Socially, the Musandam lifestyle, although changing with the accelerated development brought by the MDC, had still not lost its character or charm. The area remained rich in heritage, tradition and history. Visitors seeking traditional Arab culture and geographic beauty would not be disappointed.

Recognizing Musandam's rugged beauty, the MDC had commissioned a feasibility study for a resort hotel complex located at one of the scenic beach sites. Up to this time, the Oman government had not encouraged tourism, and all tourists who visited Oman were privileged guests. Quantam Associates, a consulting company specializing in tourism, completed a study and concluded that a modest resort hotel complex with full amenities and constructed to international standards could become a major component of a viable domestic travel industry. Musandam's proximity to the UAE, which boasted three international airports, provided access for future regional and international tourism.

The development of a small resort hotel facility in Musandam would clearly be a pioneering project. Over the long term, however, tourism in the Sultanate of Oman could become a significant source of revenue. It would require relaxation of some current immigration regulations for GCC nationals to encourage visits from the UAE by road. Paving the shoreline road from Khasab to the UAE border would facilitate traffic and enhance prospects for a tourist hotel. The Seeb-Khasab airfare could be structured to make flights to the facility enticing. It could also be included in tour packages of other spots such as Muscat, Salalah and Dubai. A government grant or loan might be required to stimulate private investment in such a venture.

Major development of Musandam's agriculture was constrained by limited arable land and sparse water supplies. Nonetheless, the MDC had been encouraging the development of small agricultural holdings to make use of what resources did exist. The MDC conducted a pilot project in Bayah aimed at stimulating small-scale development to help local small farmers via an MDC agricultural extension agent. While it was recognized that agriculture would probably never play a dominant role in Musandam economics, it could enable small farmers to capitalize on the economies of scale usually available only to the larger farmer.

The MDC report had some interesting thoughts on matters of political interest. While it noted that the government's first priority should be to interest Musandam residents in investing and working in

Musandam, employment opportunities within the UAE should not to be discouraged. Commuting daily or weekly to the UAE from Musandam was certainly practical and offered a good source of income and foreign exchange. The report further recommended that the government should establish all of Musandam as a free zone and eliminate all import and export duties. Taxing Musandam residents in this manner would only reduce their already meager disposable incomes.[3]

The year 1986 was to become a turning point for TTI. The MDC contract expired on December 31, 1985. The plan was to renew it in some form until the MDC itself was disbanded. A contract was currently under review at the Directorate of Finance. The original MDC contract was priced in 1980, when the British pound was $2.43; in January 1985 it was $1.10. This alone, Critchfield knew, would be a powerful incentive for the Oman government to turn to Europeans to replace TTI when the contracts ran out.

Status of the Regional Development Committee

By 1983, TTI activities in support of the Regional Development Committee (RDC) were moving forward at a rapid pace.[4] The TTI staff continued to work out of a building in the town that doubled as an office and sleeping quarters. During the fall of 1984, Kay Heilig moved on and Critchfield put John Sasser in charge of both the MDC and the RDC. Teams working on a myriad of projects involving electrification, roads, housing and town planning moved in and out of Buraimi.

While work on building a new Buraimi continued at a steady pace, everyone was aware that the water problems in the region were far from solved. There was no government legislation regarding the use of groundwater in the region. Local use was governed by custom and Islamic law. Even more critical was the lack of any international agreement covering the use of water between Buraimi and Al Ain in the UAE. Generally speaking, the rule was that the owner of the water source had first call on all he could use and then the neighbors could use whatever they needed "without wasting any."[5] That phrase could be a key in any Omani claim that Al Ain was dangerously drawing down water from

---

[4] See Chapter Fifteen.
[5] D. A. Caponera, UNDP/FAO Report to the Government of Oman on Water Legislation and Administration, Rome, August 1975.

Buraimi for use on unnecessary projects, such as landscaping irrigation. In September 1984, Critchfield asked the TTI Rosslyn staff to research water laws in other Islamic countries and precedents for water sharing. Chairman Badr approved this approach and asked for a recommended plan of action.

Meanwhile back in Oman, John Sasser had unofficially obtained a study done by Shankland Cox, which also was working in the UAE on a master development plan for Al Ain. Shankland Cox had previously done work for the MDC and was currently working with the RDC in town planning. The information and conclusions in the study that related to the Al Ain water supply were, in Sasser's view, dramatic and even explosive. It provided documentation that clearly described the magnitude of the water-supply problem facing the Buraimi–Al Ain area. It was evident that the current agricultural and landscaping policies in Al Ain would lead quickly to elimination of all storage in the regional aquifers and result in fundamental changes in local agricultural development, even in the absence of development on Oman's side of the border.[6] It was also clear to Sasser that competition would develop between Buraimi and Al Ain users for the little fresh water that remained.

While the numbers could be disputed, a major problem existed that Oman and the UAE could not ignore for very long. Sasser thought that cross-border dialogues should be opened in the very near future. Needless to say, the UAE authorities would be extremely upset if they knew the document was in TTI's possession. But, because the conclusions reached in the document were extremely important to Oman's development of a regional strategy, Sasser urged that on his next scheduled visit Critchfield brief the RDC and the Palace Office on the policy options for Oman. Sasser gave the Shankland Cox report to the Public Authority for Water Resources (PAWR) for analysis.

PAWR hydrologist Bob Dingman completed his analysis on September 29, 1984. His report confirmed that the use of groundwater in Al Ain had important implications for the future of water resources in the Buraimi area. There was a serious decline in the level of the water table in Al Ain proper. The catchments located on the western side of the Oman mountains were the sole source of recharge to the groundwater

[6] James H. Critchfield, *Oman Papers, 1968-1991*, Shankland Cox International, *The Master Plan and Traffic Transportation Study of Al Ain Survey, Volume 1: Planning Studies,* 1984.

system in Al Ain. In Oman, the water level decline had been relatively small, but the inflow towards Al Ain had been extremely high. The uncontrolled mining of groundwater in Al Ain had reached the point that most of the dug wells in the village of Buraimi were going dry and three of the nine *aflaj*, which were the traditional water sources for the Buraimi Oasis, had failed.

At least fifteen UAE water-drilling rigs were actively working along the Oman border in early August 1984. As pumping increased on the Oman side, the water taken would be that which had previously moved on to the UAE. Dingman's report recommended a comprehensive water resources development plan for the entire Buraimi area. He noted that the water moving to the UAE could be intercepted if that were decided to be in the best interests of Oman. It would require drilling numerous wells and extensive pumping that could be very expensive and wasteful unless there was careful long-term planning for such use of this water. If not, many million cubic meters per year could be wasted.[7]

Dingman's report was sent to Rosslyn to be combined with the legal study of water rights being done there. Sasser reminded the Rosslyn office that the Water Resources Council and the RDC were expecting this report in late October. Most of the TTI staff agreed that there was probably no hope of cross-border cooperation at this point, but felt, nevertheless, that Critchfield should recommend this when he briefed the Omani principals.

When Critchfield briefed the Omanis in October 1984, he laid out in some detail the status of water resources in the Al Ain–Buraimi border region. He told them that Oman and Abu Dhabi were on a collision course in their respective plans for development. Oman had been slow and conservative in developing Buraimi. Abu Dhabi had been profligate and hasty in developing Al Ain. There was no question that water conflicts among nations had caused bitter legal battles over the years, even wars. He recommended that Oman and Abu Dhabi, both of whom were members of the Gulf Cooperation Council and nations with a long common history, consider the creation of some kind of joint water commission to ascertain the facts and seek an accord on what rights each party would have to the total water available in the Al Ain–Buraimi region. He also recommended that Oman proceed with

[7] Ibid., PAWR report by Robert Dingman, *Effects of Groundwater Development in Al Ain on the Water Resources of the Buraimi Area,* September 29, 1984.

plans to identify and develop aquifers to the east of Buraimi that could be put into production and expand towns and communities in the Dhahirah that need not draw water directly from the Al Ain–Buraimi aquifer. He further recommended that growth in the center of Buraimi be constrained, but he warned that Buraimi would almost certainly encounter water problems before the year 2000.[8]

Critchfield came away from these discussions with the feeling that much more work needed to be done by both the RDC and the PAWR on both the technical and the legal aspects of this issue. He wrote to Sayyid Badr on December 1, 1984, that obtaining factual data to confirm the impact of Abu Dhabi's excessive water use on future water supply in the Dhahirah should be considered a high-priority task in the RDC program. In order to do this, PAWR would establish a district office in Buraimi and begin preparing an estimate of groundwater availability, which would include computer models of the principal aquifers. Then the RDC would be in a better position to provide the sultanate with options for its development of the region that would reflect a realistic water program.

John Sasser agreed that the water resources issue in Buraimi lacked definition. After getting together with Bill Doyel of the PAWR, he drafted a detailed work plan that, when completed, would predict both the short-term decline and the long-term yields of the aquifers in the region. Out of this would come a master plan for 1986-2000 for operating the municipal water system and the agricultural areas and for the preservation of the Buraimi Oasis.

By the end of 1985, the RDC presented Sultan Qaboos its 1985 Annual Report, a publication of considerable beauty, written in both Arabic and English, and containing extensive photography of the entire region, town planning maps and detailed discussion of all the projects that had been undertaken. The investment in the infrastructure – roads, electricity, municipal water delivery systems, agricultural stations, residential and commercial buildings – had indeed brought a higher standard of living to this region. These new services were also stimulating local private investment. But the report cautioned that growth had to be carefully controlled in order not to put undue strain on the infrastructure. The rate at which the infrastructure could be completed,

[8] Ibid., Critchfield paper, *Preliminary Thoughts on the Buraimi Problem*, October 1, 1984.

the report pointedly stated, would depend on the level of funding appropriated to the RDC during the Third Five Year Plan (1986-1990). Despite earlier hopes, this funding was no more or no less than received by the other outlying regions in the sultanate.[9]

The RDC had moved ahead and solved many basic problems. There were reliable supplies of electricity for the foreseeable future, and electricity had been extended to all of the major rural villages. A new water resource for Buraimi was located and developed. Reservoir and pipeline construction were under way. A water supply system was established to serve all rural villages that did not have adequate drinking water. Telephone service was extended throughout Buraimi and introduced into Mahdah. A graded road system was established throughout the region, reaching virtually all of the smallest rural villages and enabling these residents to take advantage of the work opportunities and the goods and services located in the larger villages. Progress was made in planning and designing other major infrastructure development projects to be implemented when funds became available. The Buraimi dual carriageway was fully redesigned to incorporate the new town plan. Detailed designs were completed for a sewer system within Buraimi, but implementation had not yet been funded. As a result, the shallow aquifer beneath Buraimi was being increasingly polluted, although this would be a matter of more concern to Al Ain than to Buraimi.

John Sasser believed that the RDC's greatest contribution might well have been its organization of land affairs. The land award and registration system RDC inherited could be charitably described as chaotic. Land grabbing and development without building permits were rampant. Many plots were issued by the local *wali* (governor), but he frequently awarded land without survey plans or even basic descriptions of plot size or location. The Ministry of Housing, recognizing the problem, refused for more than a year to give the land registration registers to the RDC, and it continued to award plots without regard to RDC plans or policies. This became a severe handicap.

Finally, the RDC got organized. It took back land from those who had failed to develop their plots. It fined those who had illegally developed their land. It prepared comprehensive town plans. It designed, surveyed and awarded major new residential subdivisions. As a result of these efforts, town plans existed for each of the major villages in the region,

[9] Ibid., RDC, *1985 Annual Report to His Majesty Sultan Qaboos bin Said.*

and sufficient residential plots were made available to meet demand into the 1990s.

The town of Buraimi grew dramatically during the RDC's tenure, but the growth was controlled and consistent with the long-range development plans. Services kept pace with growth. Because of financial constraints, plans to redevelop the town center and beautify the commercial corridors along Buraimi's main thoroughfares would have to be postponed. Buraimi's new economic vitality continued to be derived primarily from the employment, business opportunities and agricultural produce markets provided by its sister city Al Ain. It was likely to remain so for the foreseeable future.

Still, Buraimi was a vibrant place. Its markets were always active and crowded. While the village lacked the landscaped beauty of Al Ain, it more than made up for it in character. Buraimi was thought to be more traditional, more comfortable. People liked to live there. Another aspect of Buraimi's comfort was its housing. Residential subdivisions were close to the town center where residents could easily shop and take advantage of public facilities. There was a feeling of community there.

In his reporting to the RDC, Sasser attempted to persuade the various ministers that he felt a wonderful opportunity existed to preserve and promote the beauty and heritage of the Buraimi Oasis. The gardens were filled with date palms, orange and lime trees, and alfalfa patches that provided a view of *aflaj* irrigation and how effective it was, even in modern times. The oasis was flanked by the commanding presence of the history-rich Hisn Al Khandaq and Fort Al Sudairi. Hisn Al Khandaq had recently been restored and was being used by the *wali* for his monthly local council meetings. In developing a concept for a major area attraction, Sasser and his colleagues envisioned brick-paved pathways through the Buraimi Oasis leading to Hisn Al Khandaq, Fort Al Sudairi, the Hamassa ruins, a revitalized vegetable market area, and a carefully crafted new commercial area to replace the rundown nest of houses between the forts. Tours providing history and cultural information would surely bring in busloads of people from the emirates.

Sultan Qaboos, on his way to the UAE in early January 1987, had been heard to comment that while Buraimi looked cleaner, it still appeared much the same every time he drove through, and when was the RDC going to get rid of the unsightly plywood shacks that served as shops along the roads? The sultan was reminded that the development that had gone on thus far had all been underground and consequently invisible and that the project that would change Buraimi's appearance dramatically – the dual carriageway – had been held up for nineteen months due to lack of funding. After hearing this criticism, Sayyid Badr met with Sultan Qaboos and presented him with a detailed report on projects completed and projects delayed due to lack of funds. In the meantime, they went to work to get rid of the plywood shacks.

But Sayyid Badr had become very frustrated by the lack of support he had been getting from Muscat. The final straw seems to be an isolated incident in which Qais Al-Zawawi opposed funding for a small project to redo the main street and town center in Buraimi. Irritated with criticism from the local sheikhs, Sayyid Badr, apparently without discussing it with anyone, went to Sultan Qaboos and recommended dissolution of the RDC. On December 26, 1987, Sayyid Badr sent Critchfield an official notice that TTI's contract would not be renewed.[10]

The RDC was dissolved shortly thereafter and all projects were transferred to the appropriate ministries. Upon his return to the United States, John Sasser prepared a final report summarizing the situation in the Buraimi area. On April 11, 1989, it was sent to Sayyid Badr and General Ali Majid for presentation to Sultan Qaboos.[11] Interestingly enough, the dual carriageway was funded shortly thereafter and built precisely to TTI's specifications for the Buraimi town plan.

---

[10] Ibid., letter from Sayyid Badr to Tetra Tech International, Inc., MU/4/3/532, December 26, 1987.

[11] Ibid., John Sasser, final report to His Majesty Sultan Qaboos bin Said, *Future Challenges of the Buraimi Area*, April 1989.

22

BACK TO THE BEGINNING: OIL

In 1985, on the fifteenth anniversary of Sultan Qaboos's successful reign, Oman was still "all about oil." Times were good, very good, but there were warning signs about a worldwide fall in the price of oil. Most knew it was coming, and everyone had their own views. Back in 1982, Jim Critchfield reviewed the situation in a report he circulated to his clients in Muscat:

> Up until 1973, the major oil companies controlled prices and production. Then OPEC took over in October 1973 and pushed prices as far as they could through 1981. The sharp upturn in prices in 1973-4 and again in 1980-81 was largely artificial in market terms. Following the outbreak of the Iran/Iraq war, Saudi Petroleum Minister Ahmed Zaki Yamani even said that OPEC was wrong in raising the prices three fold. He repeatedly warned other members of OPEC that high prices would lead to a reduction in demand. But no one listened.
>
> The situation looked different to the man on the street, depending on where he was. The man in Topeka would describe the increased oil prices as a time of conservation and economic adjustments that cut into his life style. The man in Muscat in the same period witnessed dramatic expansion in development activity as money flowed into the Oman economy. Inflated land and building costs became a reality when large amounts of money trickled through to a large number of people. In Topeka, the period after 1979 brought the beginning of a recession that by 1982 had set in with a vengeance. The changes in the economic environment for the man in Topeka were

almost as dramatic as the changes to the Omani in Muscat, but in opposite directions.

Now, in 1982, the concern is, when and how far would prices drop. The bottom price of oil will be determined by three factors: (1) the cost of oil produced, (2) supply and demand and (3) the intervention of powers, whether governments, OPEC, big oil or force majeure. The power in the oil industry has shifted from the oil companies and the industrialized countries to OPEC governments and their developing national oil companies. But before prices slide to cost levels, a coalition of powers would almost certainly intervene. But this has not happened. No one has the force necessary to fix a firm bottom. It is still a free for all with thousands of economic and political forces coming into play in the spot market. Buyers and sellers are moving away from long term contracts into the free market. If this situation grows, the spot market could be renamed the free market.[1]

Over the years, Oman had been pursuing a policy of matching oil price declines with production increases in order to maintain revenues and support the economic boom. Oman's oil situation in January 1985 could be described simply: It had produced 2 billion barrels of oil; it planned to produce about 3.2 to 3.3 billion barrels in the next twenty years and could expect, using known data, to have something like 1 billion barrels left to produce after 2005. This would all come from conventional oil recovery methods. Beyond this, a less well-defined program of enhanced oil recovery would produce as much as 60,000 bpd toward the end of the period 1985-2005 and would then carry on for a longer period of time, producing something like 100,000 bpd.

The pattern for 1985 was the same as for prior years. The bulk of reserves growth came from extensions to already discovered fields, particularly the old fields in north Oman, while reserves growth from new discoveries increasingly lagged production. This pattern lent support to Brad Dismukes's argument that increased production should be accompanied by increased exploration. While improved reservoir management was resulting in a steady but not spectacular upgrading of

[1] James H. Critchfield, *Oman Papers, 1968-1991*, Tetra Tech International, Inc., *Analysis of the World Oil Market*, 1982.

reserve estimates on some reservoirs, Yibal being the most dramatic example, more exploration was imperative.

At one time, the PDO fields had the capacity to produce 450-500,000 bpd over a decade, but this was no longer possible. There were professionals, but they were in the minority, who believed that increased exploration drilling would add to the proven reserves to either allow raising production higher than 500,000 bpd or stretch out production for longer periods.[2]

TTI's recommendation to the Ministry of Petroleum was to establish a 450,000 bpd capacity, producing through 1990 at 380,000 bpd and expanding exploration over the next ten years for the sole purpose of acquiring more competent data on reserves available for later production. Hope and optimism on more oil being discovered did not justify a policy of sustained production at the 450-500,000 bpd level; this would only result in a rapid rundown in the late 1990s.

Critchfield discussed the TTI forecast in detail during his critical meeting with Sultan Qaboos on January 12, 1985.[3] The sultan responded that in the past he had agreed with Critchfield's analyses, but he was now somewhere between TTI's conservative position and Said Al-Shanfari's always present optimism. Critchfield returned several times to his production forecast (2 billion to 3.3 billion to 1 billion) as hard reality – all taken from PDO production planning figures. He told the sultan that TTI was working on long-term energy planning to 2022, but he had found few users or clients for this work. The government was not overly enthusiastic about long-term planning. The majority of ministers wanted to see plans for their ministries only and were opposed to any planning that crossed ministerial lines.

Turning to the subject of money, Critchfield recalled that the first effort at a public finance study had been the Morgan Grenfell 1975 report.[4] In more recent years, TTI's economist Arthur Rypinski had built a computer model in which he kept up-to-date public finance data. This had been an "in-house" activity and had not yet been shared with the government. The most recent computer run had been made in

---

[2] The government pursued a strategy of applying EOR techniques and exploration into the 1980s and 1990s, but the number of fields discovered that held large reserves during that decade was declining. Oman oil production peaked in 1999.

[3] See Prologue.

[4] See Chapter Five.

early January and produced results that he found sufficiently disturbing to compel him to discuss them with the sultan before taking any other action. He then went over Rypinski's January 1985 report, "Public Finance in the Sultanate of Oman."[5]

As way of introduction, the report stated that the Oman government had made two economic decisions: oil production would be raised to 500,000 bpd no later than 1987, and development spending would increase 28.6 percent in 1984, with the most spectacular growth coming in the fourth quarter. The trend would continue into 1985. Projects then under way – the Bustan Hotel, the Sultan Qaboos University and residential development in the Seeb-Ghubrah area – would require additional investment in water, electricity, gas and sewage. Electricity and water demand in the Greater Capital Area alone would triple by 1990. It would be necessary to triple annual development spending for water, electricity, gas and sewage in the next Five Year Plan to OR180 million ($522 million). This increased spending was clearly not sustainable. Critchfield showed the sultan the accompanying array of dizzying charts and graphs.

Shocked and also skeptical, Sultan Qaboos asked Critchfield for his recommendation. His reply was succinct, "Since oil prices are beyond our control and oil production is approaching its limit, there are only two choices – cut costs or increase debt

After the audience, Critchfield commented to his staff that he had the feeling that Sultan Qaboos was no more interested in hearing the kind of bad news that came out of Arthur Rypinski's Public Finance model than did President Reagan on the subject of the deficit and all that flows from it. There was a great deal in common between Oman's attitude on its economy and that of the United States in those days. President Reagan simply dispensed with his Council on Economic Advisors, because they were always bearers of bad news, and Critchfield had the feeling that TTI was quite capable of presenting oil and financial data to the Oman clients that might produce the same fate.

In its way, Oman was as captive to interest groups that represented social services and defense spending as was the United States. Unlike the United States, however, Oman as a modern state and society was new and its elite was made up of young men whose experience at governing

[5]James H. Critchfield, *Oman Papers, 1968-1991,* Tetra Tech International, Inc., "Public Finance in the Sultanate of Oman," April 1985.

had been almost entirely in the era of the petrodollar flood in their part of the world. It was not at all clear how they would cope with the financial and economic problems that could hit them in the near future because of lower oil prices and the more serious problems they would face a decade or two ahead from less oil and more expensive production.

Critchfield felt uneasy. He was apprehensive that the Omanis would react strongly and irrationally as they became more conscious of the developing financial pressures. The economic impact of reduced oil revenues would manifest itself similarly throughout the Middle East. From 1982 to 1985, OPEC had attempted to set production quotas low enough to stabilize prices. However, various members of OPEC continued to produce beyond their quotas. As a counterbalance, Saudi Arabia cut its production to stop prices from falling.

At the time of Critchfield's meeting with Sultan Qaboos, the benchmark Saudi light price was $28 per barrel. The Iran-Iraq war continued to rage, with Iran taking the offensive. There was heavy bombing from both sides and mounting casualties. On the oil scene, OPEC was losing customers to cheaper North Sea oil, and by August 1985 the Saudis were linking their price to the spot market while at the same time raising production. As Zaki Yamani predicted, demand was in the driver's seat.

Critchfield estimated this would put Oman oil at about $28 a barrel. Based on this analysis, he advised the Omanis to get prepared and adjust their budget accordingly. He advised them to postpone major capital expenditures by one or two years and prepare the Oman population for a period of some austerity. He felt confident that the long-term prospect was for a price increase at a rate several points higher than inflation.

In August of 1985, the Saudis, who were steadily losing market share, linked their oil prices to the spot market. Saudi production increased by three million bpd and crude oil prices collapsed. Rumor mills were predicting that oil would go below $5 a barrel. In a panic, OPEC went back to the drawing board. Some insisted that Saudi Arabia resume its swing role, to which Yamani replied, "Not on your life. We all swing together or not at all. On this point I am as stubborn as Mrs. Thatcher."[6]

[6]Daniel Yergin, *The Prize*, New York, Simon and Schuster, 1991, p. 760.

Tensions were high among the staff of the Ministry of Petroleum and Minerals as well. On November 10, 1985, Stan Thurber, TTI's resident reservoir engineer in the ministry, exchanged views with Ken Bodine on the subject of increased exploration drilling, which TTI Rosslyn and Team 1 in Muscat were promoting. Bodine, in turn, forwarded Thurber's views to Critchfield in Rosslyn. Thurber prefaced his remarks with the comment that his memo "is terribly caustic and may give you indigestion; either I'm crazy or the rest of you are blind, either is bad." Thurber wrote:

> There is no one in Rosslyn charged with keeping track of what goes on in PDO on a day-to-day basis. What we have are a group of "experts" who occasionally meet to "brainstorm."
>
> Having said that, let's attack the question of whether we should have a greater exploration effort. PDO does not believe there is sufficient undiscovered oil to support our presently envisioned plateau rate infinitum. They have, in fact, forecast a severe under discovery rate beginning in 1984. However, in 1984 and 1985, they have managed to overcome their pessimism and more than replaced production over the two year period. What will the future hold? Undoubtedly, PDO's estimates are pessimistic and more oil is to be found, but how much? From technical and resource planning points of view, it would definitely be good to have a better handle on this. A two year or more program of accelerated exploration effort would help resolve this quandary; thus, technically, I support the idea in some form.
>
> However, now we come to the crux of the matter. To talk of long term conservation and resource planning in Oman is [expletive deleted]. The government has over the last three years shown a complete disregard for any planning. Critchfield admits that all TTI-recommend reduced plateaus have been ignored in favor of a policy of all-out production.
>
> While we are not committing any major sins from a reservoir management point of view, we certainly are doing many things inefficiently in our mad-dog rush to raise the production level. A good example is the Nimr [southern Oman heavy oil] field. PDO Technical Director Mike Pink and

Minister Al-Shanfari were already discussing 600-650,000 bpd with Al-Shanfari asserting his intent to push PDO up to a production of 1 million bpd.

Now given the fact that the government is dedicated to all-out production, it appears that an intensified exploration program, if it were successful, would only give the government more oil to produce. Does that sound like long range conservation and resource planning? No, that sound like "rape and run", the very thing for which we have castigated PDO, and I, for one, will have no part of it.

For as surely as PDO was playing with Oman's resources in the mid to late 1970s, an increase in discoveries, as a result of our recommended increase in exploration activities, would be rapidly exploited by the government. This would put us in a position of allowing the government to play that game itself.[7]

Thurber supported the proposed expanded exploration proposal of two to four rigs on technical grounds, but on moral grounds he was opposed. While his memo was not circulated within the ministry, Critchfield did review the letter he had sent to Undersecretary Salem Shabaan the month before regarding exploration drilling. He was satisfied that TTI's position was clear. Any increase in drilling made it more urgent than ever to determine just how much total oil Oman had, both in place and recoverable, in order to develop a long-term oil production plan sooner rather than later.

At year's end, Critchfield prepared an analysis for the ministry with his views on where the oil market stood worldwide and in Oman.

The price of oil, for the first time in history, is being determined almost entirely by market forces. This situation was reached in late 1984 and was recognized by OPEC actions in early 1985. The market is, however, in a correcting phase reacting to the 1979-1982 behavior of the oil industry and the world economy when oil prices soared to roughly twice the real value of oil. During the next two or three years, the price of oil may fall below the trend line and one cannot totally rule

[7] James H. Critchfield, *Oman Papers, 1968-1991,* memo from Thurber to Bodine, *Increase in Exploration Drilling,* November 10, 1985.

out the free fall below $20. The world will almost certainly be moving into an energy crisis during the decade of 1995-2005.

The Company Undergoes a Change

In the midst of all this turmoil, Critchfield found himself in the surprising position of becoming sole owner of TTI. Honeywell Inc. simply could not find a fit for this small subsidiary, fascinating as it was. Several Honeywell executives had visited Oman and explored all its nooks and crannies. So, Honeywell put TTI on the market, for sale to anyone who might have need for a small engineering company with experience dealing in the Middle East. Science Applications International Inc. participated in serious negotiations for the acquisition of TTI, but its board eventually backed out. Honeywell then offered the opportunity for Critchfield to do a personal buyout. On August 15, 1985, a deal was struck and James Critchfield became TTI's new owner.

In order to buy TTI, Critchfield formed Gulf Futures Inc. It would become the umbrella for TTI Oman and all business projects outside Oman. The selection of the name Gulf Futures reflected the intent of this new company to concentrate its efforts on the Arabian Gulf region in recognition that this region alone would be the source of significant oil reserves early in the twenty-first century. The aim of Gulf Futures would be to develop knowledge, understanding and sound planning assumptions on the future of this critical area of the world. Critchfield planned to produce a newsletter on developments in the region for sale to prospective clients. In August, he informed his Omani clients that he was now not only president of TTI but also its owner. This made little difference to the clients. The presence of Honeywell had little or no impact on their activities.

1986 – The Oil Bubble Bursts

In 1986, world oil prices dropped 50 percent. Saudi oil had flooded the markets, triggering a price war. The price of OPEC oil fell to $10-15 a barrel. The Iran-Iraq war continued, and OPEC production-cut talks failed. For the next thirteen years or so, world oil prices would remain under $20 a barrel, except for a brief period at the beginning of the Gulf War in 1991. It would be 1999 before the price tide turned, tripling the price to $34 a barrel.

As world oil prices crashed, Oman was in the midst of continuing major development projects. The government now needed to reorder its priorities. Oman crude oil went from its high of $41 in early 1981 to a low of $6.80 in 1986. Fortunately, it quickly recovered to about $14. But that was half the price it had been during the past three years. It was an oil shock in reverse.

Nevertheless, the agenda for the scheduled January 26 PDO board meeting, which the Technical Director Mike Pink sent to the ministry, still called for the proposed production levels at 550,000 bpd for 1986 and 1987. Pink attached a cover letter to this package, noting that because this topic had high political and strategic significance for Oman's future, he would like to meet with ministry officials prior to the meeting to discuss the future production levels and depletion rates with a view, presumably, of making some changes in the program.[8] However, no immediate changes were made.

Early into 1986, Critchfield called Brad Dismukes back from Carrolton, Texas, to do an economic analysis of petroleum exploration and production operations. He was in Oman for thirty days under the sponsorship of the petroleum ministry. Because PDO produced more than 98 percent of the sultanate's crude oil, only its operations were examined. Dismukes spent two days in south Oman and three full days in The Hague, with the remaining days spent in the ministry and at PDO offices. While in the field, he examined four operations that were using enhanced oil recovery techniques at Yibal, Nimr, Lehkwair and Marmul.

His immediate recommendation was that the profitability of all these projects be re-examined. They were approved when crude was selling for $28 a barrel, and it was now bringing in only half that. Also, some of these projects would have several years of negative cash flow despite being profitable over the long term. The government might wish to defer starting some of these investments until oil prices rose.

PDO told Dismukes, however, that the 1986 PDO budget was still intact and, until notified otherwise, it interpreted this as a green light to proceed with all projects. On the other hand, he was aware from

---

[8] Ibid., PDO letter from Technical Director Pink to Khalifa Al-Hina, *Objectives and Guidelines for the 1987 Programme*, December 17, 1985.

his conversations at the ministry that the government expected PDO not to carry out unprofitable projects. This produced somewhat of a Catch-22. The decline in oil prices had been so rapid that most of the ongoing projects had not been reviewed. Prudent policy would indicate the urgent need for a thorough review of the economics of all proposals, both those approved and those pending.

Dismukes listed in his report various projects from the 1986 Production Program Book he felt should be examined right away. He also noted that one alternative investment opportunity for Oman was to increase the exploration effort using some of the funds designated for enhanced oil recovery. The average technical cost of producing new fields was less than the cost of enhanced oil recovery projects. Also, oil from new fields was more easily and cheaply produced. Dismukes felt that the combination of plentiful wildcat prospects justified careful examination of this alternative investment opportunity.

In general, Dismukes commented, the world was unprepared for the precipitous decline in crude oil prices. Reductions in oil-related budgets and other retrenchments had been both deep and wide in the United States. Exxon, for example, postponed a $300 million research facility. Texaco closed some 1,600 wells in California and canceled some new steam flood projects in the same area. Mexico, Venezuela and even Saudi Arabia were postponing announcement of their 1986 annual budgets. He mentioned these items simply to emphasize the urgency of reviewing production programming in Oman. PDO had the experience and the computer facilities available to do this work. He thought it was preferable that PDO, rather than the ministry, do it, because PDO held most of the specific information needed. But first the government had to tell PDO that it wanted such a review done.

In his final remarks, Dismukes warned that to accelerate oil production during times of abnormally low prices would be totally uneconomic. He recommended that all accelerated projects be postponed, at least until the price of crude oil recovered. Dismukes completed his report in March 1986, when the price of crude oil was bottoming. It was under $10, and there was no assurance that it was going to go back up anytime soon.[9]

[9] Ibid., N. D. Dismukes, *Review of Petroleum Operations in Oman, prepared for Tetra Tech International,* March, April and June 1986.

Something close to panic set in during July 1986 when Oman hit the bottom: it was selling oil costing almost $6 to produce at $6.80 barrel of oil. Fortunately, the price did recover somewhat. The ministry's undersecretary, Salem Shabaan, notified PDO that it was to reduce production cost to $4 per barrel. PDO asked for clarification. "Was it to undertake a planning exercise or actually execute the reduction?" Shabaan said his instructions were to reduce production costs to $4 per barrel and "if that meant staff reductions, then that meant staff reductions."

The biggest issue was whether PDO would postpone exploration to alleviate the government's immediate cash flow problems. John Sasser reported back to TTI Rosslyn that he was virtually certain that gas exploration would be deferred and the bulk of the oil exploration program would probably be postponed as well. TTI advisor Don Parker, assisting the ministry in this analysis, used a zero-based approach to budgeting. He was working from the bottom up to determine what the minimum obtainable production cost could be conceptually. Sasser thought that perhaps Shabaan's $4 target cut PDO down to where it should be, but then again it might not. Without this analysis, the best the ministry could hope to do was keep reducing the target until PDO screamed so loudly that the government knew it had hit the bone.

By December 1986, Oman's oil production reached 558,000 bpd and was selling for $15 per barrel. The deficit was RO700 million ($1.8 billion), or 28 percent of GDP. At this time, Oman had numerous multiyear contractual commitments that required funding. The Omani government couldn't possibly cut spending as rapidly as oil revenues were declining and, to his credit, Sultan Qaboos realized that defaulting on existing contracts would be disastrous. So, the government did several things. It devalued the Omani riyal so that the dollar-denominated oil revenues went further. It drew reserves from the Contingency Fund that had accumulated in previous years. And it turned to the commercial market. The government obtained a $500 million syndicated Euroloan, the major sponsors of which were the Gulf International Bank and the Chase Investment Bank. The ministries were all given across-the-board spending cut requirements, but these cuts would not be felt for some time.

Omanization – Ministry Style

When Critchfield preached to anyone who would listen that it was in Oman's best interests to cut costs and reorder priorities, he knew it could come back to his front door, and he was all too aware that market forces were against him. For years, he had been talking with his friend Qais Al-Zawawi about long-range planning. He considered the Long Term Energy Plan, done for the Ministry of Petroleum and Minerals, and to his knowledge still sitting in the minister's safe, to have been a pilot project to get them interested in long-term planning.

His admonition had not entirely fallen on deaf ears. During a visit to London in October 1985, he met Ray Christopherson from Systems Engineering and Technology Company (SETCO), a London-based engineering company. Christopherson told him that SETCO was undertaking oil and gas long-term planning for the Oman government, specifically for Deputy Prime Minister Qais Al-Zawawi and Said Al-Shanfari. The question SETCO had was whether it should associate with TTI. Since the government had informed TTI of this development, Critchfield said he would discuss it when he returned to Oman in December. In the meantime, he wrote to Salem Shabaan asking him for guidance. From what Christopherson told him, SETCO's plan would follow the general outline of the LTEP.

By January 1986, the situation with SETCO was beginning to unsettle not only those in the ministry, but also TTI. Critchfield had only recently made a proposal to Qais Al-Zawawi for a TTI role in developing a database for his new Center for Economic Planning. Qais was clearly uncertain what role he wanted TTI to play, and the Ministry of Petroleum, it appears, was reluctant to give up much turf to Al-Zawawi and SETCO. That was the last TTI ever heard of the SETCO project in Oman. Apparently the deal fell through. Shortly after that, Arthur Rypinski was seconded to the Ministry of Finance to install and operate the Oman Public Finance model to work out budget calculations in the face of falling oil prices. He had both Qais Al-Zawawi and the Undersecretary for Finance, Muhammad Musa, looking over his shoulder, but he returned to Arlington feeling that the project had been a great success. The work had all been done at no extra charge.

On March 10, 1986, John Sasser telephoned Rosslyn with the news that Minister Said Al-Shanfari has just advised him that he planned to cut the TTI staff in the ministry by 50 percent. There were no further details. Critchfield would be leaving for Muscat on March 27, but in the interim he wrote to Al-Shanfari.

> I will remain in Oman for whatever period is required to clarify the numerous problems that have developed as a result of the rapid decline in oil prices. I am surprised at the severity of the reduction reflected in your recent decision. Oil prices have been up and down during the years we have served as advisors and are, in 1986 dollars, at roughly the level they were in late 1973. I fully expect them to rise to the level of 1978, which in 1986 dollars would be about $22 a barrel. I assume, therefore, that your decision to make a deep cut in our position reflects in some degree your dissatisfaction with our performance. It is my opinion that we have served the interests of the sultanate professionally and well in our role as advisors. The impact of our efforts has in the past been translated into hundreds of millions of dollars of added oil revenue. I must admit that I was surprised and disappointed to learn of what was described to me as your firm decision.[10]

Critchfield met with Shanfari on March 31. Al-Shanfari was adamant that the sole reason for the cuts was the need to economize; there was no dissatisfaction with TTI's performance. Critchfield responded tersely and made little effort to hide his disagreement with the decision. He reminded Al-Shanfari that the mission of Tetra Tech since 1975 was to provide professional and experienced advisors capable of advising the ministry on matters related to the technical and economic management of the sultanate's oil and gas resources.

By separate agreement with the Palace Office, TTI was precluded from having any agent or partner and from participating in any business in Oman except providing advisory services to His Majesty and the Oman government. TTI was excluded from bidding on any competitive tenders of any kind. This agreement was to ensure that Tetra Tech would have no conflicts of interest. TTI had abided meticulously by this agreement and believed Al -Shanfari and the ministry was not dealing fairly with TTI.

[10] Ibid., letter from Critchfield to Minister Al-Shanfari, March 13, 1986.

Critchfield pointed out that TTI's advice to the ministry over the years had significantly influenced the way in which the ministry had participated in the management of its major oil activity, the PDO. TTI advisors also participated in the ministry's supervision of the activities of other foreign companies engaged in energy-related activities in the sultanate. Critchfield said he was personally concerned that the professional management of technical and economic activities of the sultanate's most significant source of revenue was being neglected in these difficult times.

Critchfield felt that the minister had at times been uncomfortable with TTI's constructive adversarial role with PDO and judgments of a technical character concerning the exploitation of the oil and gas resources in the PDO areas. But, in his view, the government must be represented in its relations with all foreign oil companies in Oman by an organization with professional oil experts whose loyalties were only to the government. Royal Dutch Shell was, as Tom Barger pointed out in his report in 1977, one of the world's finest and most experienced oil companies. However, its interests and corporate objectives did not always coincide with those of the government. Shell, like any large oil company, must be given independent scrutiny if the full interests of the sultanate were to be protected.

The ministry's day-to-day participation in the PDO operation had resulted in many positive outcomes that would otherwise not have happened. The period 1986-90 was a time when technical and economic planning related to the future development of Oman's oil and gas resources would require more, not less, professional attention. But since the minister's decision regarding TTI was considered to be final, Critchfield said he would reluctantly proceed with the actions needed to achieve the necessary reductions. It was a very tough session. He returned to the United States and saw little of Minister Al-Shanfari during the coming months.

Whenever Critchfield perceived dark clouds looming on the horizon, he turned to Tim Landon. This time, in a letter dated September 1986, he wrote:

> I fully realize that I sound like a broken record on the need for planning for the future, but I have long since lost Said Al-Shanfari's interest and attention. Ever since the foreign

shareholders in PDO shifted virtually all exploration and development costs to the government in 1977, they have had a free ride as production almost doubled and prices soared to a high plateau that lasted for almost four years and only collapsed in 1986. I simply reject the assertion that the interests of Oman and the foreign shareholders have been identical in these years. But since the bonanza of the second oil shock was so good to everyone, no one seems interested in keeping score. The legitimate argument was made that it is in Oman's interest to maximize production in the years of very high oil prices and that Shell, as the operator, did so much for Oman that it deserved every bit of profit it made. Ever since I recommended in 1983 that a ceiling of 380,000 bpd be the basis for planning the current five year plan budget, my views have become increasingly unpopular. At the time, I thought that oil would level off at about $25, which I consider still to be its real value. I never envisaged that Saudi Arabia would dump oil on the market in a strong reaction to all the other producers, OPEC and non-OPEC, taking away barrel by barrel what the Saudis view as their just share of the market.

The basis for my 380,000 bpd recommendation was that there were too many question marks stretching out ahead to go beyond that. There could well be a case made for higher production. Production topping 625,000 bpd was certainly a long way from the dark days of late 1976 when it was predicted to decline to as low as 250,000 bpd. The concept of the ministry doing any independent long-term planning has no more support now than it had in 1983. I have become silent on this whole subject (except for periodically expressing my remaining concerns to you). From recent reports I have had from Oman, I will be quite surprised if Said Al-Shanfari does not, when I ask about his intentions for 1987, suggest a phasing out of our remaining advisors. If so, I will disengage with dignity. It will still have been a great experience and I will depart with the satisfaction that we really did quite a lot of good.[11]

---

[11] Ibid., letter from Critchfield to Brigadier Tim Landon, September 18, 1986.

In late 1986, when Al-Shanfari was dealing with TTI Muscat on cuts to its staff, he made a direct hire of a personal economic advisor who would sit in his ministry. The advisor was Herman Franssen, a former chief economist at International Energy Agency in Paris. Franssen had been introduced to Al-Shanfari by the Dutch oil trader John Deuss, who had since 1985 been doing substantial business in Oman and had skillfully kept Oman's incremental oil production moving in a competitive market. Franssen overlapped with Ken Bodine for about six months.

Did their jobs conflict? The answer to this question is not clear. Bodine had a friendly relationship with Franssen, as well as with John Deuss, with whom he played tennis on many occasions. Indirectly, however, the answer is probably yes.

Back in December 1985, Landon asked Critchfield what he thought of John Deuss. Critchfield had not met him, but he was aware that he helped sell a lot of Oman's oil and was apparently a bright fellow. It appeared to him, however, that Said Al- Shanfari, who had demonstrated that he was a good oil trader, was deferring more and more to Shell and John Deuss. They were the ones he turned to when other buyers were not cooperating. Deuss was in and out of Oman regularly in his private jet and maintained contacts at the highest levels of the Oman government.

Ken Bodine and others who knew him described John Deuss as brilliant, dynamic and skilled as a trader and oil entrepreneur. But Critchfield suspected that Deuss wanted to bring in his own team of advisors, and the cutting of TTI staff was a propitious time to make such a move.[12]

Early in 1987, Minister Al-Shanfari met with Critchfield in Muscat and told him he wanted all remaining TTI staff in the ministry to become direct hires as of July 1, 1987. However, he also wanted Critchfield to remain as a personal consultant. Critchfield countered with an alternative of cutting TTI's fee to $800,000 for the remaining nine employees. Al-Shanfari stuck to his offer. They agreed to disagree. Critchfield said he would give his employees ninety days' notice, and they and the ministry would both be free to negotiate any future relationship.

[12] Efforts by the author to interview Deuss in Bermuda in June 2004 failed. His office responded that Mr. Deuss was out of the country, but added that he felt it would be inappropriate "to give you a story about Oman and does send his apologies."

Critchfield saw in this a rather bizarre interpretation by the minister of the concept of Omanization. He wanted the institution to go, but not the advisors.

Critchfield returned to Rosslyn. In early March 1987, he received a letter dated February 27 from Al-Shanfari in which he introduced more insight on his version of Omanization. He also wanted Critchfield to know how he felt about TTI.

> TTI had throughout its presence in the Sultanate of Oman rendered its distinguished services to the Ministry of Petroleum and Minerals and helped the ministry achieve a better understanding and more effective control of many of its activities. Omanis have by now developed their own capabilities and gained the experience necessary to make them stand on their own feet without looking for much external assistance. The drive to be self-dependent is further dictated by the economic circumstances prevailing over all the Gulf states without exception. I would like to notify you of the government's decision to bring to an end our long relationship and not to renew the contract for providing advisory services to the Ministry of Petroleum and Minerals on its expiration date on June 30, 1987. To relieve you of any contractual obligations towards the staff currently seconded to the ministry, we offer to employ such of them as shall accept our terms of employment. It gives me pleasure to preserve your personal relationship with us and for that purpose request that you make your services available for us when needed in the field of technical studies on terms to be agreed at the relevant time. We also wish that circumstances would improve in the near future to the extent that would allow us renew our strong relationship with Tetra Tech. We are very grateful to Tetra Tech and very proud of what we have achieved together.
>
> Best regards, Said Al-Shanfari[13]

[13] James H. Critchfield, *Oman Papers, 1968-1991*, letter from Minister Al-Shanfari to Tetra Tech International, Inc., MOO 3/9/85, February 29, 1987.
[14] Ibid., letter from Minister Al-Shanfari to Critchfield, MOO 3/9/84, February 28, 1987.

In a separate letter on ministry letterhead, also dated February 28:

> The government of the Sultanate of Oman wish to bestow on Mr. Critchfield the role of an advisor to the government assigned the task of providing or helping to procure the technical services needed in the field of petroleum and minerals as identified by and agreed with the Ministry of Petroleum and Minerals. The government is confident that Mr. Critchfield shall accept the assignment and shall remain, as he always was one of the trusted friends of Oman.[14]

In a separate meeting with Al-Shanfari, John Sasser was advised that the minister had a package-deal offer to hire the remaining TTI advisors and asked Sasser to solicit their interest. The offer was somewhat less than they were realizing with TTI, and none of the advisors accepted. On March 30, Sasser informed the minister of this. He also asked him why he did not address the staffing issue by renewing the TTI agreement, especially because the difference in cost was minimal. Al-Shanfari responded that the termination of the TTI contract was not a matter of money, but an issue of principle. He maintained that, as a matter of policy, the ministry should consist of its own staff rather than those provided by a company. This was the first necessary step to get the ministry to stand on its own feet and to "Omanize" itself. He had attempted to make a reasonable offer to TTI advisors in order to help people who had been with him so long, but if they were not ready to accept, then the ministry would just have to find replacements. Finding replacements was not a problem. All he had to do was pick up the phone and call Shell.[15]

Subsequent efforts at direct hire of the TTI technical staff failed, and all the advisors departed prior to July 1. The technical work reverted to PDO.

Minister Said Al-Shanfari and James Critchfield had been closely associated since 1975, when Sultan Qaboos appointed Al-Shanfari Minister of Petroleum and hired Tetra Tech as advisors. When he took over the ministry, Al-Shanfari actually did not know he was getting TTI as part of the package. Back in those days, however, one took all the help one could get. Everyone pulled together like a band of brothers.

[15] Ibid., interoffice memo from Sasser to Critchfield, March 30, 1987.

That included families. The Bodines, for example, embraced the Al-Shanfari family and throughout the years helped the children in many ways, particularly when they got to be college age. Said and Jim were on a first-name basis. They had a very warm relationship, so when disagreements arose, they could talk with each other frankly. He liked Al-Shanfari.

Critchfield thought the minister was extremely shrewd and an increasingly successful oil trader, but wished that he would insist on more transparency in his dealings with PDO. There is no question that in the later years, Said Al-Shanfari became a bit prickly in response to Critchfield's constant hammering to "cut production, increase exploration, and seek independent reservoir studies." Al-Shanfari had a good relationship with PDO and he wanted it kept that way. As he told Tom Barger back in 1977, it is better to deal with the devil you know.

When his decision was made and there would be no going back, Minister Al-Shanfari closed the door on TTI, albeit with words of praise. Critchfield wanted any new contract, even a personal one, to carry on the TTI name. It was important for him to keep the door open. As 1987 ended, the two old friends were talking past one another, and a personal contract disappeared into the ether of the Oman bureaucracy.

In a letter to John Sasser dated June 30, 1987, marked Personal and Confidential, Critchfield noted that the ending of the contract with the Ministry of Petroleum that day was obviously an event of some significance in the history of TTI in Oman. Things had changed.

> We could speculate endlessly what brought it about. Tim's departure, the Ashland affair in which we were totally innocent of any involvement, the emergence of John Deuss as the magician who kept Oman sales expanding while everyone else was losing market share, a lingering resentment of the Al-Zawawi's that I remained independent of them for so many years and was reluctant to sell the company to them. Who knows how these influences were weighed? I would agree with you that our stock with Salem Al-Ghazali, Al-Mutasim, Yousuf bin Alawi, Sayyid Badr and many others remains high, but

[16] Ibid., letter from Critchfield to Sasser, June 30, 1987.

not high enough for any of them to successfully intervene to reverse the trend. My own view is that John Deuss's role and our unusual insight into the affairs of the ministry led to a decision to phase us out. The loss of rapport on my part with His Majesty, Qais, and the Palace Office has convinced me that I have little ability to influence our position. But the fact is that I have passed my 70th birthday and must admit to you that the drive, energy and enthusiasm to try and turn things around in Muscat are significantly diminished. I have no idea what has really transpired in the way of an effort to arrange an audience with His Majesty but my remaining sense of dignity rules out any further initiative on our part in this matter. In spite of Muhammad Musa's overtures to Arthur (he tried to hire him permanently), we have no expectation that Qais will basically do a turn around and involve us in his affairs.[16]

On July 17, 1987, Critchfield wrote to General Ali Majid in the Palace Office and asked that the special agreement with TTI be terminated effective December 31, 1987.[17] This would free the company from its commitment to have no financial relationships with any Omani or foreign firm in Oman. Critchfield visited Oman from October 22 to November 2, 1987. He had a meeting with Ali Majid in his Palace Office. It was a warm and personal session followed by a dinner hosted by him at the officers club, with John and Josee Sasser attending. During that trip he also saw Al-Mutasim and Sayyid Badr regarding MDC and RDC matters, but he did not see either Qais Al-Zawawi or Said Al-Shanfari. In December 1987, Critchfield was informed of the Oman government's decision to terminate TTI's role in Oman by March 1988.

End of an Era

Sitting back in his office in Rosslyn in early 1988, Jim Critchfield began to think through next steps for his company, his employees and himself. At 71 years of age, he had had a full career, actually three careers – military, intelligence and business – all separate and extremely rewarding experiences. Personally, he could step down and retire to his small farm in northern Virginia and tend to his horses. In fact, the prospect was

[17] Ibid., letter from Critchfield to General Ali Majid, July 17, 1987.

extremely attractive. What nagged him was what he considered unfinished business in Oman, a country he had come to love and admire, and its leader, who had done an amazing job of bringing his nation out of the dark into a truly enlightened period. Critchfield was proud of TTI and the work it had done in the sultanate for the past thirteen years. He could not think of any other non-Arab consulting company with that kind of longevity anywhere in the Middle East. TTI had indeed become woven into the fabric of the Oman community. Critchfield was not an emotional man, but he could not help but feel strongly about his company's coming under scrutiny in the way it had.

As he frequently did when he was trying to reach important decisions, Critchfield closed the door to his office, pulled out a yellow pad and began writing. He started out at the beginning.

> The history of Tetra Tech International in Oman was an evolving special relationship with His Majesty Sultan Qaboos and the country to which we gave advice – at times unsolicited. We were given tasks to perform, were excused from regulations regarding local partners, were permitted to have no financial relationships with any Omani or foreign firm and sat always and only on the government's side of the tale. The tasks given us were related to resource and regional development. They resulted in a gradual expansion and a decade or more of being a company that concentrated on its work, was loyal and dedicated to the interests of the sultanate and gave considerable attention to quality control. The image sometimes portrayed in the press is that we are an important part of the U.S. presence.[18] The reality is that we have been a dedicated engineering company that has made a considerable contribution to Oman's development.

[18] Here Critchfield is referring to the periodic press reports about his former intelligence career. One such article in the March 24, 1986, *Washington Post* reported extensively on TTI's role in the Musandam Peninsula and that the project was headed by an ex-CIA man. That very newspaper's ombudsman took the *Post* correspondent to task for using language and innuendo unjustly. He noted that Mr. Critchfield had been phoned at his Arlington office and had confirmed his previous association with the CIA, which, the ombudsman added, was already known to the *Post* and practically everybody else. Yet, "the correspondent referred to him in a way that made it seem as though he'd unearthed the dark side of his life, the implication being that there was something sinister about an

Our influence was significant in turning around Oman's oil future of decline in 1976 to one of promise for quite a long time. Looking back, TTI's main contributions were:

A program in the mid-1970s to ensure that the sultanate maximized its revenues by obtaining fair prices for its crude oil in the world oil market.

Expansion in the mid-1970s of the scope of oil exploration with particular emphasis on accelerating exploration in south Oman.

The increase of Oman's ultimate recovery of oil reserves by improved methods of production using advance reservoir engineering techniques and technology.

Emphasis in oil field practices designed to make available more efficient use of associated and non-associated gas.

Conservation and utilization of natural gas, including the initiation of a national gas system and the substitute of gas for oil in the electric power system.

We have given Oman one of the best foundations for water resources management in the region. Our performance in this field is not well understood.

We originated a blueprint for the Musandam Peninsula in early 1975 and have quietly and efficiently gone about the development of this small but important province.

Our performance in Musandam led to the unsolicited appointment by His Majesty to accelerate the development of the politically sensitive Buraimi region. The work we did there is, in my opinion, at least on a par with Musandam.

A few years ago we were brought into the Ministry of Electricity and Water when its minister discovered he was faced with major problems in short term water supply for the Greater Capital Area. There is a well-documented record on this.

ex-CIA employee running a business in Oman." See *Washington Post*, Joe Laitin, "The CIA: Something Sinister?" April 1, 1986. On the lighter side, Critchfield was amused about being thought of as a James Bond – a 70-year-old James Bond. But with each press article, he made sure the clients understood there was no basis to these allegations. He was proud of his service to the CIA and in fact was named one of the CIA's fifty "trailblazers" at a ceremony in 1998, the fiftieth anniversary of the founding of the CIA. Those awards were given to the fifty men and women who contributed the most to the development of the Agency from its inception. It was a great honor.

I have witnessed Oman's emergence from being an undeveloped country with almost total diplomatic and political isolation to an established world-wide international position as a modern nation state and have played the role of a quiet advisor and supporter the entire way.

Our efforts to get the Ministry of Petroleum and Minerals involved in an independent long term planning function failed. In the years 1983-85, the minister clearly had other priorities. The high demand for revenues in 1984 and 1985 and the accompanying decline of demand and prices in the oil market were among the factors working against us. But it is probably now time to take another look at planning what oil will mean to Oman in the 1990s and the early 21st century. I will work on this, with or without a contract.

I must admit that I have found the experience of phasing TTI out of Oman more difficult and demoralizing than I had anticipated. I am psychologically not well suited for the experience of running down a company that was, in its own way, quite remarkable. Casting associates and old friends out into the rigors of the real world causes me more pain than I would have thought.[19]

These notes went into the file without further distribution.

In a letter to Tim Landon dated February 12, 1988, Critchfield wrote:

The hand over of operations to the ministries is in process. By the first week of April we will have closed out and departed. I believe Khalfan Nasser may temporarily retain one or two of our engineers most involved in the Buraimi water situation. We are within months of having a permanent municipal water system in operation there with water brought in by pipeline from a carefully tested well into the mountains. I know we have transformed the quality of life in Buraimi and Musandam regions with net gains in water and electricity probably exceeding that in any other region remote from the capital area.

[19] Ibid., handwritten notes from the Critchfield personal files.

I wish to express my most genuine admiration to you for the role you played in advising His Majesty through his early years of responsibility. It simply would not have happened without you. You left a gap that has never been filled and probably cannot be, given the character of the government. I have not the slightest doubt that the net impact of our presence in petroleum affairs brought about the change that will result in substantial additional oil revenues. Also, I think our basic decision to go and find water instead of doing endless studies paid off. That Khasab and Buraimi will have well-established water systems is a tangible gain of political and security significance.

There is in the Omani makeup a capacity to act suddenly without full consideration of consequences to Oman's interests. I think the destruction of the PAWR was wrong. And I anticipate that there will be adverse consequences from the hasty total close out of the staff familiar in great detail with development affairs in the Dharirah and Musandam provinces. Omanization, with some residual continuity in a small group of advisors, would have been preferable. With regard to oil and gas, I thought the need for independent government assessment of long-term plans was apparent. But I failed almost totally to stimulate such an effort any place within the government. The Ministry of Petroleum wants to conclude a personal services contract with me for 1 July 1987 to 1 July 1988. I doubt very much I would be able to do more than give my view of the world oil market et al. I suspect the initiative was on the instructions of His Majesty.[20]

John Sasser, in a very professional manner, supervised the closeout of TTI's offices in Muscat. All employees were terminated by March 31, 1988. Per instructions from Qais Al-Zawawi, the files were segregated and returned to the appropriate ministries. These were to include final reports to be written by Sasser on the MDC and RDC. Some files were also sent to the new Sultan Qaboos University.

In April 1988 in Salalah, His Majesty Qaboos bin Said decorated James Critchfield with the Order of the Star of Oman and John Sasser

[20] Ibid., letter from Critchfield to Brigadier Landon, February 12, 1988.

with the Order of Oman. Sultan Qaboos expressed appreciation for their past efforts and, in response, Critchfield said with all sincerity that it had been an honor and he deeply appreciated the recognition in the form of the decoration. He then went directly to Seeb airport and departed for London.

Postscript

Jim Critchfield did not retire to his farm. Gulf Futures Inc. partnered with Middle East Consultants (MEC) Ltd., a British firm, and together they produced a newsletter called Perspective on Development. MEC also did business in Oman, and Critchfield had known Geoffrey Hancock, its president, for many years.

The newsletter provided the views from Washington and London on current Middle East political and economic affairs and on world energy. The client list included companies on both sides of the Atlantic. Critchfield also sent copies to the Palace Office and to the ministers as part of his still unsigned agreement to continue as a personal advisor to the government.

Critchfield, using the same methodology that was used in the LTEP, produced for his clients a long-range survey, called "Perspective on World Energy, 1985-2025." He continued his role as energy advisor to the chief of naval operations and oversaw a similar effort for the U.S. Navy. Arthur Rypinski stayed on with the reduced Gulf Futures staff in Rosslyn until 1991 when he joined the U.S. Department of Energy. Kirk and Nga Agon joined EDS Systems and spent the next several years in Malaysia before returning to the northern Virginia area, where Kirk joined SAIC and Nga remained with EDS. John and Josee Sasser returned to the Middle East almost immediately with the company Intergraph, and John became president of an Intergraph subsidiary. He and Josee reside in Dubai, and he continues to do business in the Gulf region.

EPILOGUE

Fast-forward twenty years from the time this story ended. It is 2009 and the Sultanate of Oman is preparing for a future that will be less dependent on oil.

Vision 2020, as it is known, is a long-term planning strategy initiated by Sultan Qaboos in 1995 during the 25ᵗʰ National Day celebrations. It was the dividing line between two stages of the sultanate's economic and social development, the one begun in 1970 and the one from 1995 to 2020, in which diversification and Omanization would be the key words.

Changing of the Guard

There is no question that the untimely death of Qais Al-Zawawi in an automobile accident in Muscat in 1995 marked the beginning of a new hierarchy in Oman. Sultan Qaboos and Qais's brother, Dr. Omar Al-Zawawi were also in the vehicle but escaped unharmed. Qais Al-Zawawi's role as Deputy Prime Minister for Economic and Financial Affairs (Sultan Qaboos was still prime minister) was only a microcosm of the major role he had played from the very beginning of Sultan Qaboos's assumption of power in 1970. Next to the sultan himself, he had been the most powerful voice in Oman.

Sultan Qaboos appointed Ahmed bin Abdul Nabi Makki to take over. Ahmed Makki, who had been the ambassador to the United Nations back in the 1970s, accompanied Sultan Qaboos when he was establishing diplomatic relations with his neighboring Arab states.[1] He continued to be a key figure in government from those early days. In 1997, shortly after the sultan named him to replace Qais Al-Zawawi, he was appointed

[1] See Chapter Four.

Minister of Economics and Finance (the ministry is now known as the Ministry of National Economy) and, in 2001, became deputy chairman of the Financial Affairs and Energy Resources Committee. He was now wearing all the important hats.

In 1997, Minister of Petroleum Said Al-Shanfari retired, ending a twenty-two-year career as the first and only oil minister; he was replaced by Muhammad bin Hamad bin Seif Al-Rumhi. The ministry was then renamed the Ministry of Oil and Gas. Al-Rumhi, a petroleum engineer, had been a professor of petroleum engineering at the Sultan Qaboos University. In April 2003, Sultan Qaboos made Al-Rumhi chairman of the PDO board of directors, succeeding Salem Shabaan, who retired after more than twenty-five years of service in the ministry.

Prior to this appointment, Al-Rumhi had been a critic of PDO; he blamed PDO in particular for having lacked proper planning in enhanced oil recovery operations. In late 2002, he was quoted in PDO's internal newsletter *Al Fahal* as saying: "We have been too preoccupied with trying to get that extra barrel rather than formulating a plan for the long term."[2]

World oil prices in the 1990s were on a rollercoaster. The Iraqi invasion of Kuwait in 1990 saw the price level rise from $18 to $34 a barrel. Efforts by OPEC to influence prices through production agreements, sometimes but not always successful, and the United Nations program of Iraqi oil for food in the mid to late 1990s resulted in oil prices ranging from $12 to $24 a barrel.

In Oman, while prices fluctuated in the $15–20 range, production rose steadily – from 660,000 bpd to a peak of 972,000 bpd in the year 2000. Oman's total production fell sharply thereafter to 780,000 bpd in 2004. That production level has been maintained largely because of the introduction of additional enhanced oil recovery measures and an increase of the production of natural gas liquids.

In 2009, crude production was expected to reach 830,000 bpd, with the average for the year at 800,000 bpd.[3] Oman's proven recoverable oil reserves are 5.5 billion barrels, the bulk of which are located in the country's northern and central regions.[4] These fields, which include Yibal,

[2] "Shell in the Middle East," *Al Fahal,* Issue 20, January 2003.

[3] Statement by Minister Muhammad Al Rumhyi at an industry event in India. Reuters, May 30, 2009.

[4] U.S. Department of Energy, International Energy Agency, Oman Country Analysis, March 2006.

Fahud and al-Huwaisah, are now mature and face future declines in production. If output continues at the present pace and no major new reserves are discovered, the U.S. Department of Energy's Energy Information Administration estimates that Oman has less than twenty years left as a significant oil-exporting nation.[5]

To delay the inevitable, the Ministry of Oil and Gas's top priority was to find ways to increase oil recovery. Financially, 2006 turned out to be a very good year for Oman. With the advent of rising world oil prices, it once again was given a reprieve from budget cuts. Oman crude went from $44.75 in 2005 to $61.02 in May 2006, increasing government revenues by 41.6 percent to $7.46 billion. Further price increases since then have resulted in a doubling of oil revenues, estimated to be $14 billion as of January 2008.[6] This provides a substantial boost to Oman's efforts to diversify and become less dependent on oil. But it is not abandoning oil. As part of its attempts to expand its reserves, Oman contracted with a British firm, Spectrum Energy and Information Technology, to have old seismic studies reprocessed.[7]

There has also been increased activity in oil exploration. At the present time, Oman is drilling at full capacity. This brings to mind the Dallas oilman who back in 1973 wrote to Stribling Snodgrass, the sultan's advisor at the time, seeking a small concession, saying that Shell had had them long enough. His theory was that if you split the offshore and onshore blocks into 50,000-200,000 acre tracts and invited several dozen companies to come in, it would not be unreasonable to have over a million barrels per day within ten years. In his view, competition was the key to success in finding oil in quantities.[8] That is now happening.

Since 1996, no less than nineteen companies have been awarded exploration and production sharing agreements. They include oil companies from the United States, United Kingdom Japan, Canada, Australia, Denmark, Saudi Arabia, Thailand, India, Indonesia and China. The areas being explored largely come from acreage released by PDO.

[5] Ibid.

[6] Ministry of National Economy, *Gulfnews.com*, January 1, 2008.

[7] USGS, Oman Minerals Yearbook, 2003.

[8] See Chapter Five.

[9] "Oman Producers Pursue Active Drilling at Fields, New Prospects," *International Oil Daily*, June 20, 2005.

Omani officials stated that the introduction of competition in PDO's acreage should help spur a targeted revival of oil production.[9] Déjà vu and hats off to the Dallas oilman.

In line with this, Royal Dutch Shell announced on September 28, 2006, that the company was applying enhanced oil recovery techniques to reservoirs around the world to extend oil production. That included two major fields in Oman: Qanr Alam and Marmul. Shell vice president John Barry said that PDO had dusted off a chemical and water flooding project a couple of years ago that had been shelved for a number of years during a period of low prices. PDO was planning development of twenty-seven wells, which could result in a 10 percent increase in oil recovery.[10]

This new aura of competition has "energized" the oil industry. This may have been brought on by a deal made by the Omani government with a consortium led by the U.S. Occidental Corporation in June 2005 in which PDO transferred the Mukhaizna field to them. As the operator at Mukhaizna, which had been producing about 10,000 bpd, Occidental aims to achieve production of 150,000 bpd by 2012. In 2009 it was producing 60,000 bpd, accounting for the anticipated increase in total production by year's end. Oman officials acknowledge the desire to test ways of operating other than the Shell model that had dominated for decades. The objective is to raise oil production to over 1 million bpd.[11]

In 2006 alone, Minister Al-Rumhi signed seven agreements with multiple companies granting oil and gas exploration rights for fields throughout Oman. He indicated that Oman would be signing a number of other exploration and production sharing agreements in the future.[12]

When Will Oman Run Out of Oil?

This question is, of course, rhetorical. There is no magic date on which oil from the Oman fields will stop flowing. The Energy Information Agency estimates that Oman will stop being a significant exporter of oil by 2026. At the same time, the question of when Oman

[10] Deborah Kelly, "Shell Pins Hopes on EOR to Boost Recovery," *International Oil Daily*, London, September 29, 2006.

[11] *Petroleum Intelligence Weekly* quoting Ali Battashi, director general of planning at the Ministry of Oil and Gas, June 27, 2005.

[12] "Oman's Oil and Gas Minister Signs Concession Agreements," *Asia Pulse*, Asia Pulse Limited, June 29, 2006.

will run out of oil is one that continues to be analyzed. One such study began this work back in the early 1980s.[13]

Tetra Tech International's Long Term Energy Plan (LTEP), produced in 1984, projected that oil production in 2022 would be 300,000 bpd, two-thirds of which would come from enhanced oil recovery technology. But that was based on the premise of an average annual production of 300,000 bpd plus expanded exploration efforts. In the real world, this did not happen.

Nevertheless, the 1984 LTEP production forecasts for Oman, and for the Yibal field in particular, were remarkably accurate given the actual production that has occurred up to the present time. The LTEP predicted that production for the entire country would peak in 1998 and then decline at about 12 percent a year. Production actually peaked in 2002. Furthermore, the total production history of Oman as posted by the Energy Information Administration provides evidence that production from the discovery of new reserves in Oman proceeded along the lines forecast in the LTEP. Interestingly, the focus on exploring for natural gas fields in the past five to ten years in Oman is most likely responsible for the boost in oil production in early 2000 by the addition of lease condensate (liquids recovered from the natural gas stream before it is retailed). If you separate out the lease condensate from the oil production, the forecast and actual decline curves would match more closely.

The LTEP's production forecast for the Yibal field was based on the PDO program of 1983. The decline of oil production using conventional recovery methods began in 1990, as predicted in the report. Enhanced oil recovery practices (water flooding and horizontal drilling) increased the production rate. Since that time, production at the Yibal field has dramatically increased its water/oil ratio, with some petroleum engineers estimating the amount of water to be as much as 90 percent of the total volume of oil extracted.[14] This in turn has led to greatly increased production costs.

While the LTEP's estimates of the potential reserves garnered from enhanced oil recovery were conservative, it did in the end reflect a more

[13] James H. Critchfield, *Oman Papers, 1968-1991, Long Term Energy Plan for the Sultanate of Oman 1983-2022,* dated July 1, 1984, prepared by Tetra Tech International, Rosslyn, Virginia.

[14] Jeff Gerth and Stephen Labaton, "Oman's Oil Yield Long in Decline, Shell Data Show," *New York Times,* April 8, 2004.

realistic conceptual model to develop the Yibal field. Had Oman produced its fields at a lower rate, as suggested by the LTEP, it might have alleviated the current situation. In a letter to Critchfield dated January 24, 1996, Ken Bodine, then retired in Colorado, mused that he would like one last time to get on a plane with Critchfield and "try to convince His Majesty to follow the Tetra Tech recommendation on reservoir management, instead of caving in to Shell, over pulling the reservoirs and leaving millions of barrels of oil behind, never to be recovered with secondary or even tertiary enhanced oil recovery."

The practice at Yibal in the early years of this century, which was effective in accelerating production, did not result in the huge increased reserves predicted by Shell. In March 2004, the company became embroiled in a controversy over its exaggeration of oil and gas reserves, not only in Oman, but worldwide. On April 8, 2004, the *New York Times* made public information based on internal Shell documents that suggested that the figure for proven oil reserves in Oman was mistakenly increased in 2000, resulting in a 40 percent overstatement.[15] Two engineering reports written by PDO officials in 2003 showed that production in Yibal had fallen at an annual rate of 12 percent for six years. Moreover, Shell overstated its proven oil reserves in Oman primarily because the company had failed to trim the figures back in light of recent downturns in oil production rates. This internal analysis differed from the optimistic public statements by Shell that continued even after news of the production difficulties began to circulate outside the company.[16] This, plus reserve issues in other parts of the Shell empire, led to a corporate overhaul in late October 2004 and a downward revision of Shell reserves worldwide.[17]

The Tetra Tech advisors – Strib Snodgrass, Brad Dismukes, Stan Thurber, not to speak of Jim Critchfield and Ken Bodine – would certainly have felt vindicated had they been in Oman when this news broke. From the mid 1970s to the late 1980s, they had been a burr in the side of PDO Shell, particularly on the subject of reservoir

---

[15] Ibid.

[16] Ibid.

[17] "How Shell's Move to Revamp Culture Ended in Scandal," *Wall Street Journal*, November 2, 2004.

[18] See, for example, Chapter 17.

engineering.[18] From the arrival of Snodgrass in 1972 through the years when TTI served as petroleum advisors sitting on the Oman side of the table, PDO deeply resented what it considered interference in its technical operations. Up to the time TTI's contract ended, these men never gave up their call for independent oil studies of Oman's oil and gas reserves.

From Oil to Gas?

Is it possible to replace oil revenues with gas revenues? This is another rhetorical question. Oil in 2006 brought in an estimated $7.4 billion. What will it take for gas to earn something even close to this? Gas revenues in 2006 totaled $1.4 billion. The Oman government is investing heavily in its gas industry, both in exploration and in the production of LNG (liquefied natural gas) for export. World consumers are snapping up LNG as quickly as modern tankers and ports can be built to handle it.

In February 1994, Oman established Oman LNG LLC, a company participated in by the government, Shell, Total and several Japanese companies. Liquefaction facilities to handle the gas, which comes from fields in central Oman operated by PDO, were built in Qalhat near Sur. The complex was completed in 2000 at a cost of $2 billion. Clients for Oman LNG are mainly in Asia, in Korea, India and Japan, who supplied the tankers for transport. In 2003, Oman formed the Oman Maritime Transport Company (OMTC), which has been buying into tankers being built in Japan and Korea and is now in the transport business itself. The OMTC currently has a fleet of six LNG tankers.[19]

But unless Oman can add significantly to its gas reserves in the coming years, this heavy capital investment in the gas industry and in gas-fired industries could backfire. Rather than exporting gas either by pipeline to the UAE or by LNG in Omani tankers, the government could find itself importing gas from neighboring countries, such as Qatar and Iran. So the answer to the question, "Can gas revenues replace oil revenues?" is no. But of even greater concern to Omani planning officials is where the gas will come from to supply the increasing numbers of industries that are currently on the drawing boards or under construction.

[19]"Gas Waits in the Wings," June 30, 2003, and "World Gas Intelligence, Oman Pushes Hard For Faster Gas Development," June 29, 2005, *Oman Oil Company News*; "Nizwa LNG Carrier Joins Services," *Times of Oman*, December 9, 2005.

So in one sense, natural gas in the twenty-first century replaces oil as the key to the future.

The Omani Population

As of 2009, the population of Oman was estimated at 2.8 million, with 43 percent being under the age of fifteen. Twenty-five percent of the Omani population is currently in school.[20]

Despite continuous efforts by the government to push its Omanization program, there are still 625,000 expatriate workers making their livelihood in Oman. There are 425,000 Omanis in the workforce, which is only 17 percent of the population as a whole. Omanis are employed principally in civil service, defense, education and wholesale and retail trade. The expatriate workforce is found principally in construction, household services, wholesale and retail trade, manufacturing and agriculture.

These are stark statistics. There is a real need to engage more Omanis in the workforce and prepare the younger generation to move into the workplace in a broader field of jobs, particularly in the private sector. As of January 2008, there were 62,415 Omanis employed in the private sector. Only 42 percent of those were graduates of secondary schools or higher.[21]

From the very beginning of his reign, Sultan Qaboos has pushed for Omanization, a program to engage more Omani citizens in productive work. It has been an uphill battle. It is not surprising that Sultan Qaboos' 36th National Day address to the Council of Oman on November 24, 2006, focused on this issue. Much of his speech was taken up with the subject of jobs and education. He emphasized that success in the future can only come with a more effective use of human resources, the politically correct term for the workforce. In his usual gentle manner, he laid down what can only be described as a mandate, something just short of a Royal Decree:

> Dear Citizens
> You are aware of the extent of the attention we accord to
> the development of human resources in order to provide our

[20] *The Arab World*, 2009. IMF Estimates, Economist Intelligence Unit, *The Economist*, July 25, 2009, and the Oman Ministry of National Economy, Muscat, 2005.
[21] Oman Manpower Ministry, *Times of Oman*, January 12, 2008.

young sons and daughters with wider and better opportunities of education, training and employment. This is almost a fixed item in each of our speeches addressed through you to all the people of Oman. There can be no doubt that the human being is the basic component and the cornerstone of any viable civilization. We, therefore, once again reaffirm the importance of this element in the development and modernization of society. Therefore, we are glad to express our satisfaction over the serious steps taken in recent years by the government and the private sector in the fields of Omanization and training of the emerging generations.

We are also delighted to see a growing tendency to take jobs in various fields. We hope that this is an indication of an increasing awareness among individuals in the society of the importance of work, regardless of its type. In this regard, we would like to reiterate that expertise and skills can only be gained by remaining in jobs. From this platform, we salute all those who work diligently with persistence and dedication in any field of work that will benefit the individual and society.[22]

Jobs need to be found for the many thousands of Omanis who will be entering the workforce after completing their education. The very point of Omanization was that these young, educated Omanis would replace expatriates. But even under the best of circumstances, there will not be enough job openings to satisfy the numbers of job seekers. Public statements by Sultan Qaboos show that he is concerned and understands the importance of a productive and engaged population.[22]

Vision 2020

With Vision 2020, Sultan Qaboos has charged his people to accept that the nation is moving toward an era without oil. There will be shifts in planning to maintain a viable national economy without it. Several basic changes in Oman's practices are taking place.

1. Oman has relaxed restrictions on foreign investments.
2. Oman is working towards expanding trade with its neighbours in the region and the Indian Ocean rim.

[22] Ministry of Information, HM Speech to the Council of Oman, November 24, 2006.

3. Oman is building modern ports and free trade zones to enhance export-import trade.

4. Oman is investing heavily in tourism.

5. Oman has joined the global information-technology revolution.

The government has been working hard to attract large-scale international investment. One plan is to build an industrial complex in Sohar that will bring together many industries to support a large export-import facility at the port of Sohar. But a massive project such as this has to be fueled by natural gas.

As a result of the improving foreign investment climate in Oman, there has been a major increase in private investments in industries such as aluminum, petrochemicals, chemicals, cement, electronics and a dozen other projects. Trade missions from the United Kingdom, Germany, Holland and Italy have been promoting joint ventures. India and Oman exchanged state visits in 1997-98 and a number of joint ventures with Indian water, power and engineering companies have resulted.

On September 27, 2006, President George W. Bush signed the U.S.–Oman Free Trade Agreement, making Oman the fifth Middle Eastern country to enter into such an agreement with the United States. Hunaina Sultan Ahmed Al-Mughairy, Oman's ambassador to Washington, sees this as an important step in Oman's efforts to lessen its dependence on oil. "The agreement could have profound implications on Oman's economy. It's going to open doors for investment and that's something we need very badly."[23]

Oman has committed itself to the development of a tourism industry. The Omanis hope tourism will add a new dimension to the revenue stream without damaging Oman's conservative culture. The sultanate is increasingly becoming a vacation spot for citizens of the Gulf and Europe.

Ambassador Al-Mughairy, in a September 2006 interview in Washington, noted that Oman was working to establish itself as a premier Middle Eastern tourist destination. On the drawing boards since 2005 is the $15-20 billion development called Al Madina Al Zarka, or the Blue City. It will be an entirely new city with residential and commercial properties. Phase one of the seaside development project,

[23]Michael Coleman, "First Arab Woman Ambassador to U.S. Promotes Oman as International Player," *The Washington Diplomat*, September 2006.

[24] Ibid. Also see the Blue City website.

located just thirty minutes from Seeb International Airport, will include four hotels, two championship golf courses, villas and apartments, a heritage museum and a waterfront amphitheater.[24]

Sultan Qaboos has stated that he wants each region in Oman to have a major industry and to increase the number of Omanis engaged in these activities. That is slowly happening. In the Dhofar region, the port in Salalah has been turned into a major world-class container port and free trade zone. In the Sharqiya region, there is the LNG facility at Qalhat. In the Batinah, the oil refinery at Sohar is now operating and expansion of the Sohar industrial port is under way. In Musandam, there is the joint development with Iran of the Henjam gas field discovered back in 1976. There is the beginning of a tourist industry in the Musandam province, focusing on scuba diving and snorkeling off the rugged fjord-like coast of the peninsula. A high-speed ferry service between Muscat and Musandam began operations in mid 2008, cutting travel time and opening up new business and employment opportunities. Tourism is being developed in Buraimi as well. Both Buraimi and Khasab are now easily accessible from the UAE, making day or weekend visits possible.

This diversification is now driving Oman's future. Oman is truly an outward-looking nation, reminiscent of the days of its forebears doing their business by the sea, and, in turn, extending their traditional Omani hospitality to those visiting Oman's shores. One can only wish the Omanis the very best in their quest for a prosperous life with a bright future.

كـان ولـم يكـن

الله أنصـــــر الســـلطان

There was, There was not

Allah send victory to the Sultan

APPENDIX ONE
PROFILE OF JAMES CRITCHFIELD

By the time James Critchfield met Sultan Qaboos in 1971, he had already completed two careers: nine years with the U.S. Army, and twenty-six years with the Central Intelligence Agency. North Dakota-born and bred, upon graduation from North Dakota State University in 1939 he accepted an ROTC commission in the regular U.S. Army In World War II he served in the Seventh Army's Sixth Corps under the command of General Lucien Truscott. He commanded a battalion of the 36th (Texas) Division in the landing in southern France in August 1944. The battalion fought continuously through France into Germany and was in Bavaria when the European fighting ended in 1945. When the war ended he held the rank of colonel.

After the war, Critchfield remained in Germany for two years serving as a staff intelligence officer in the U.S. Occupation Army in Heidelberg and Vienna. He was on the Pentagon's fast track, and in 1948 was one of six officers selected to attend a doctoral program at Princeton University.

It was at that point the Central Intelligence Agency was created. Critchfield's decision to join the CIA was not easy. His career in the U.S. Army was prospering, and few doubted that eventually he would become a general officer and perhaps even rise to the level of chief of staff.

No one can ever say with certainty why one decides to walk down one road instead of another, but this was 1948, and the U.S. Army in 1948 was very different from the service Critchfield had joined in 1939. The single most important event to change this, in his view, was the dropping of the first atomic bomb on Hiroshima in 1945. This had a revolutionary impact on the science of war, for even if belligerents refrained from using atomic weapons again, which in his view was unlikely, another global war would be infinitely more destructive to civilization than World War II. He believed that no nation could possibly win such a war.

In his view, military solutions were no longer the answer to the economic and social problems that beset the world. The new CIA, he believed, could become vital to the establishment of a secure, politically mature and internationally minded United States capable of assuming the overwhelming responsibility that had been abruptly thrust upon it by the emergence of a strong Soviet Union, whose backing of world communism would provide many challenges in the coming decades.

It was with these thoughts in mind that Critchfield joined the CIA and began his second career. In June 1948, after a short training program, he returned to Germany. That initial assignment lasted eight years, during which he oversaw the creation of the German national intelligence service.[1]

James Critchfield went on to enjoy a long and productive career in the CIA's clandestine service, serving in 1956 as chief of the Eastern European Division and, beginning in 1960, as chief of the Near East Division. In the early 1970s, he became one of the agency's top experts on international energy affairs and was the first person to hold the position of national intelligence officer for energy.

After retiring from the CIA in June 1974, he met Nicholas Boratynski, president of Tetra Tech Inc. The two men formed a close bond that eventually sent Critchfield in yet another interesting direction. And, as Bogey said to the police inspector at the end of *Casablanca*, "Inspector, I think this is the beginning of a beautiful friendship."

It was not long before Critchfield saw an opportunity to play the role of matchmaker and bring American engineering technology to Oman to assist in the nation's ambitious development plans. This would be his third career.

---

[1]See James H. Critchfield, *Partners at the Creation,* Naval Institute Press, Annapolis, 2003.

APPENDIX TWO
TETRA TECH INTERNATIONAL EMPLOYEES
1975–1988

Agon, Kirk
Agon, Nga
Agon, Ted
Ali, Abdullah
Ali, Hassan
Almaldas, Anthony
Al-Mendhry, Said
Anderson, C.
Archer, Steve
Aubel, Jim
Awad, Widad
Azim, Abdel
Babikir
Babkar, Hassan
Bachman
Badr El Din
Balint, James
Bannigan, John
Barger, Tom (consultant)
Berentsen, Carl
Bigham, Gary (consultant)
Black, Charles (consultant)
Bodine, Ken
Bostick, Dean
Boulos, Adib
Bourassa, Gerald
Bowtell, Don
Bray, Geoff

Bray, Pamela
Briley, Martin
Buchanan, Robert
Burger, Martha
Callahan, Joe
Campbell, Alister
Carlson, Warren
Chapman, Meg
Cochran, Kenneth
Creighton, Bill
Critchfield, James
Critchfield, Lois
D'Lugosz, Joe
D'Silva, Peter
D'Souza, Merlyn
Dale, Dr. Robert
Dalton, Russ
Dana, David
Dance, Howard
Davison, Don
Deal
DeJong, Dr. Remy
Dewitt
Dingman, Bob
Dismukes, Brad (consultant)
Donohue, William
Doyel, Dr. William
Duff, L.

Dunn
Dymond, Janice
Dymond, John
Edmonds, Bruce
Elrod
Fatah, Fathiah
Fauzy, Khalil
Fennella
Fernandez, R.
Firfiray, Ahmed
Fitz, Tom
Foley, Mike
Foster, James
Gaddis, Bobbie
Geck, Meta
Ghalil, Mohammed A.
Gibb, N.
Gill, Manjit
Ginther, James
Gleason, Bob
Grace, Scott
Graf, Charles
Griffin, Joan
Habib, Ali
Haggag, Ahmen
Hales, Alan
Hamdi, Fatin
Hanley, Delinda
Hanley, Steve
Haris, N. K.
Harvey, Harry
Hassan, Salah Y.
Heilig, Kay
Her, Tom
Hershey, Lloyd
Hiltner, Don
Hudson, Ben
Hughes, David

Husnain, Mohammed
Hussein, Ahmed
Hussein, Mohammed
Ibrahim, Abdullah
Ishar, Mohammed
Jameson, Don
Johnson, Mel
Jones, Davy
Jones, Digger
Kader, Salah A.
Kellett, Dick
Kennedy
Khaleelullah Khan
Khan, Saeed
Kim, C.
Koya, Ahmed
Kutty, Usman
Le Mehaute, Dr. Bernard
    (Tetra Tech Pasadena)
Leidholdt, Ralph
Lessnau, Ronald
Little, John
Luxton, Steve
Lysonski, Joe
Macleod, Robert
Madgziuk, Kenneth
Magda
Maley, D. Patrick
    (consultant)
Malik, Said
Mani, V.
Manley
Maskery, Rahma
Masood, Abdullah
Mathew, K. T.
McClaflin, Roger
McCullough, Pat
McLaughlin, Dr. Thad

Mehdi, Yousef
Menry, S.
Mergani
Miller, Lee
Mohanan
Mohsen, Abdel
Mohsin, Salah
Moosa, E.
Moran, Bob
Mount, R.
Murany, Dr. Ernest
Nadim
Nair, Chandran
Nasser
Parker, Don
Patterson, Sam (Tetra Tech
   Houston)
Picardo, Vincoy
Pickett, Mark
Polley, Christopher
Pourian, Soli
Preman
Prutton, Peter
Quinlan, Peter
Ramakrishnan, V. N.
Ramarrishnan, C.
Ramdas
Rao, D. S. R.
Rapp, John
Rashid
Redford, Ralph
Reed, Charles
Reiber, Frank (consultant)
Reichenbaugh, R.
Remedios, G.
Rockey, Bill
Roland, Peter
Rotert, J.

Rotert, John
Rouhban, J.
Roussean, Joe
Rousseau, Joe
Rowland, Peter
Rozvi, Syed
Ruel, Judy
Rypinski, Arthur
Sadek, Mohammed
Saidu, M.
Saines, Nick
Salam, Abdul
Saleh, Salim
Samuel, George
Sasser, John
Sasser. Josee
Saunders, Jerry
Schonewald, George
   (consultant)
Seijo, Michael
Sekher
Shaver
Shute, John
Sichel, Peter
Singh, Raghbir
Smerdon, Glenn
Smith, Rex
Sonu, Dr. Choule (Tetra
   Tech Pasadena)
Sorour, M.
Spong, W.
Sreeivasnano
Stach, Robert
Stewart, N,
Storms, Robert
Suseelan
Sweetnam
Tawfiq, Mohammed

Thomas, A.
Thomas, R.
Thompson, Melvin
Thurber, Stan
Tibbits, Gordon
Trunz, Joe
Tunstall, Alan
Turner, Fred
Unnikrishnan
Usman, Kutty
Varghese, B. N.
Vasudevan
Verghese, M.
Viegas, Raphael
Vijayan
Vincent, Robert (Chip)
Vorhis, B.
Waziri, Hassan
Weir, Robert
Wenzel, Roger
White, Craig
Wilkerson, Ted
Williams, C.
Winter, Alex
Wood, Norman
Yaqoob. Juma
Yost, Coyd
Zahir, Malak
Zunzer, Bob

* From personnel records. In some cases the full name was not available.

BIBLIOGRAPHY

Agwani, M. S. *Politics in the Gulf.* New Delhi: Vikas Publishing House, 1978.

Akehurst, John. *We Won A War: The Campaign in Oman 1965-1975.* Great Britain: Michael Russell Publishing, 1982.

Al Maamiry, Ahmed H. *Whither Oman.* New Delhi: Lancer Publishers, 1981.

—————. *Oman and East Africa.* New Delhi: Lancer Publishers, 1980.

Allen, Calvin and W. Lynn Rigsbee. *Oman Under Qaboos: From Coup to Constitution, 1970-1996.* London and Portland: Frank Cass Publishers, 2002.

Anthony, John Duke. *Arab States of the Lower Gulf: People, Politics, Petroleum.* Washington, D.C.: The Middle East Institute, 1975.

Clapp, Nicholas, *The Road to Ubar: Finding the Atlantis of the Sands.* New York: Mariner Books, 1999.

Clements, F. A. *Oman: The Reborn Land.* London and New York: Longman Group, 1980.

Duchess of St. Albans. *Where Time Stood Still.* London: Quartet Books, 1980.

Eilts, Hermann Frederick. *A Friendship Two Centuries Old: The United States and The Sultanate of Oman.* Washington, D.C.: The Middle East Institute, 1990.

Graz, Liesl. *The Omanis: Sentinels of the Gulf.* London and New York: Longman Group, 1982.

Halliday, Fred. *Arabia without Sultans.* New York: Vintage Books, 1975.

Hawley, Donald. *The Trucial States.* London: George Allen & Unwin, 1970.

Jeapes, Tony. *SAS: Operation Oman*. London: William Kimber & Co., 1980.

Kechician, Joseph A. *Oman and the World: The Emergence of an Independent Foreign Policy*. Santa Monica, CA: Rand, 1995.

Landen, Robert Geran. *Oman Since 1856*. Princeton: Princeton University Press, 1967.

Morris, James. *Sultan in Oman*. New York: Pantheon Books, 1957.

Peterson, J. E. *Oman in the Twentieth Century*. London: Croom Helm, 1978.

Phillips, Wendell. *Uknown Oman*. New York: David McKay Company, 1966.

Searle, Pauline. *Dawn over Oman*. Beirut: Khayat Book and Publishing, 1975.

Sindelar III, H. Richard and J.E. Peterson. *Cross Currents in the Gulf*. London: Rutledge,
1988.

Skeet, Ian. *Oman Before 1970: The End of an Era*. London: Faber and Faber, 1985.

————. *Oman: Politics and Development*. Hampshire: Macmillan, 1992.

Smiley, David. *Arabian Assignment*. London: Leo Cooper, 1973.

Townsend, John. *Oman: The Making of a Modern State*. London: Croom Helm, 1977.

Wilkinson, J. C., *Water and Tribal Settlement in South-East Arabia: A Study of the Aflaj of Oman*. Oxford: Oxford University Press, 1997.

Yergin, Daniel. *The Prize: The Epic Quest for Oil, Money and Power*. New York: Simon and Schuster, 1991.

INDEX